10
KEYS TO
HAPPIER
LIVING

A Practical Handbook
for Happiness

VANESSA KING

headline

Dedication

Past
In memory of my parents, with much love and gratitude

Present and future
For John, Alex and Ben
With love. May you be happy

First published in 2016 by HEADLINE PUBLISHING GROUP

6

Cataloguing in Publication Data is available from the British Library

Trade Paperback ISBN 978 1 4722 3342 4

Produced by Bookworx
Editor Jo Godfrey Wood
Designer Peggy Sadler

Printed and bound in Great Britain by
Clays Ltd, St Ives plc

Headline's policy is to use papers that are natural, renewable and recyclable
products and made from wood grown in sustainable forests. The logging
and manufacturing processes are expected to conform to the environmental
regulations of the country of origin.

HEADLINE PUBLISHING GROUP
An Hachette UK Company
Carmelite House
50 Victoria Embankment
London EC4 0DZ

www.headline.co.uk
www.hachette.co.uk

Contents

Foreword
Professor Lord Richard Layard, London School of Economics

It is my great dream that together we will make the world a happier place. I hope it's one that you share too and that you will join me in doing what we can to make this dream come true.

In 2011, Geoff Mulgan, Anthony Seldon and I started the movement, Action for Happiness, following the publication of *Happiness: Lessons from a New Science*. In it I argued the case for happiness, and people kept asking me 'How can we take action?' Our vision in Action for Happiness is to create a society where there is more happiness and less misery. We aim to support people to make positive changes in their lives, but also to create more happiness for those around them – where they work, learn, live and play. We know from scientific research that doing things that increase other people's happiness makes us happier too. This is central to what we are trying to do.

This handbook has been written to help you join us in making a difference. We hope it captures the 'head' and 'heart' of happiness, appealing to both your rational mind and your emotions, and providing food for thought to help you reflect on where happiness comes from (for you), why it matters and, most importantly, what you can do to increase it – for yourself and for others. It's based on an increasing body of research evidence that is helping us to see what is most effective, adding the weight of scientific rigour to principles and teachings enshrined in more ancient sources of wisdom.

I am in no doubt that there is a great need. Despite greater affluence, our lives are increasingly stressful. Many of us have more materially, yet we are no happier and there are rising rates of mental ill health among the young. As an economist, I am very aware that for too long we have equated the well-being of our societies with gross domestic product, and individual happiness with purchasing power. This must change. Change is needed at policy level and also in our communities, schools, workplaces, families and in us as individuals, if our societies are to improve.

I have no doubt that we can create a happier world. You, me and those around us – we can all make a difference. I hope this book inspires you to take action.

A Message from Action for Happiness

Dr Mark Williamson, Director of Action for Happiness

Action for Happiness is a movement of people taking action for a happier and kinder world. The central idea is simple but profound: people commit to creating more happiness – for themselves and for others too. We are secular, science-based and open to everyone. Our patron is His Holiness the Dalai Lama, whose universal messages about happiness and compassion resonate with people of all backgrounds.

Since we launched in 2011, millions of people in 170 countries have engaged with our ideas, and hundreds of thousands have joined our global community. Members of the movement take action in lots of different ways: teachers have brought our resources into their classrooms; business leaders have used them to create happier workplaces; and wonderful volunteers have held events, run our eight-week course and set up Happy Cafés in their local communities. Most importantly of all, individuals have made meaningful changes in their lives. These include practising mindfulness and gratitude, improving their relationships, coping better with difficulties and doing more acts of kindness. These may be small steps, but they make a real difference.

The Ten Keys to Happier Living in this book are the guiding force behind Action for Happiness. They show us that the best things in life aren't things. And they remind us that while there are always factors outside our control, we have a conscious choice over our attitude, our actions and the way we treat others.

Happiness is not about denying negative feelings or being joyful all the time. It's about making the most of good times and learning to cope effectively with bad times too. Matthieu Ricard, scientist turned Buddhist monk, describes happiness as 'a deep sense of flourishing, not a mere pleasurable feeling or fleeting emotion but an optimal state of being'. We hope this book will help you live in ways which create more of this happiness – for yourself, your loved ones, your community and the wider world too.

Introduction: Unpacking Happiness

Your happiness matters. People who are happy not only enjoy life more and are more resilient, they also tend to have more and better relationships, be physically healthier, and be more engaged and do better at work. These are just a few of the benefits recent research has revealed.

The aim of this book is to unpack happiness so you understand what science shows are its active ingredients – the Ten Keys to Happier Living – and why these make a difference. You'll learn practical actions you can take, all backed by the latest research.

The Ten Keys are a menu, NOT a prescription. Different things work for different people at different times and personal choice is important. Some actions are things you'll want to make a regular habit of; others might inspire you to change your thinking or shift where you focus your attention and energy. Some of the Keys will be especially helpful when times are hard or you're feeling low. Many of these approaches don't need money or even take much precious time.

You can make a difference – we all can. Even small actions really can help lead to a happier you, and that contributes to a happier world around you.

In practical terms what does happiness mean?

When we ask people what makes them happy, they usually start by listing things that bring them pleasure – a nice meal, a glass of wine or an indulgent chocolate cake, seeing an exciting film, buying a new pair of shoes or downloading a fun new game or app. And these aren't necessarily bad things, but for happiness they're not enough. And when we're busy or unhappy it's easy to focus on them too much.

If we probe further, people generally start to list things that are perhaps more fulfilling and longer-lasting, such as spending time with friends and family, caring for people, learning something new, work or hobbies or a sense of contentment and being at peace with themselves. So, we often do have a sense of what really makes us happy, but it isn't necessarily reflected in our actions day to day.

That's where the science comes in – it can help us understand why happiness is important and know what's likely to have the most impact in our lives. It suggests, too, that caring about our own happiness isn't merely selfish or indulgent, it seems to be contagious. If we're happy, those around us are more likely to be happy, and we'll tend to help others more. And here's the thing, it's no coincidence that giving and relating are the first two of the Keys – we're more likely to be happy if we care about other people too. So it's circular. I believe this means we have a responsibility to do the best we can to manage how we feel.

Being happier is not about trying to experience pleasure all the time or avoiding unpleasant emotions, like sadness or anger. It's about being realistic about what life brings and making the most of its good times and finding ways to bounce back when things get hard*.

Among psychologists, economists and social scientists there has been a lot of debate over what 'happiness' is and how it is similar or different to 'well-being' or 'flourishing'. They usually define happiness as feeling good in a fleeting sense as well as about life in general, and there's a lot that can affect that. But as our natural wisdom suggests, there's more to a fulfilling life than just our passing moods and judgements. The term 'well-being' variously includes: a sense of self-acceptance and worth; good relationships with others; feeling our life has meaning and purpose; being interested and engaged in much of what we do; using our potential and/ or experiencing a sense of achievement. We're said to be flourishing when our well-being is high – and we can languish when it's low.

Most of us want to be happy and what we usually mean in practical terms is all of the above! That's what these Keys capture. They can help you feel happier and more able to flourish. They've made a difference in my life: I hope they'll do the same for yours too.

The story behind the Ten Keys to Happier Living

It's funny how life happens sometimes. I worked as a consultant helping to develop leaders and help organisations change, but was feeling dissatisfied and unhappy, worried that my work wasn't making enough of a real difference. In 2008, I happened across the newly emerging field of

*There may also be times where you might want or need to seek some professional support – see the Resources section for good places to start. If you have a diagnosed psychological illness such as depression or anxiety, these actions can help alongside clinical treatment – but do seek the advice of your doctor or therapist first.

positive psychology (the psychology of 'optimal functioning' – happiness, well-being and flourishing to you and me). I knew instantly that I wanted to find out more. I felt it had to be part of the future, certainly my future. I applied to study for a Masters degree with Martin Seligman at the University of Pennsylvania. He'd been the catalyst for the broadening of psychological research from a focus on what's wrong with us to also include what's right. To my amazement I got in and found myself in Philadelphia. It was fantastic and I felt more alive than I had for ages... and I needed to find something useful to do with this new knowledge. Back then, positive psychology wasn't widely known and nowhere near mainstream.

So a year or so later I was on a plane. I'd just finished my studies and I'd been offered the opportunity to deliver a seminar at the first positive psychology conference in China. I found myself sitting near someone I recognised but didn't know, Anthony Seldon – the headmaster who had introduced happiness lessons into his school in the UK. I knew he knew Marty Seligman, whom I'd been studying with. So when the plane landed I said hello. Anthony kindly offered to drop me off at the university where I was staying. During that journey, I mentioned that I was coming back to the UK having immersed myself in positive psychology in the US and was hoping I could find a way to put what I'd learned into practice.

'Ah!' said Anthony. 'Richard Layard, Geoff Mulgan and I have just established a new social movement and charity, Action for Happiness. We've found an excellent director, who has just started, Mark Williamson. You must meet with him and get involved.' And that was that. A month or so later I found myself having coffee with Mark and bouncing around lots of ideas together. My positive psychology knowledge was just what was needed to help identify actions people could take to make themselves and others happier in preparation for the official launch in April 2011. I set about going through everything I'd learned as well as the research then available, and with the help of a small army of other volunteers, spent many months synthesising and summarising it all for our website.

Mark, Richard and I discussed long and hard which actions were the most important and how we could hang them together. We wanted to build on the 'Five Ways to Wellbeing' that the New Economics Foundation had developed in 2008 as part of a big government-backed research project. Five areas of activity (Connect, Be Active, Take Notice, Keep Learning and Give) shown to increase happiness and well-being were increasingly being used in health, education and other settings across the UK and beyond. We came up with an acronym for these – 'GREAT'. From our research it was also clear some 'inner' factors were important too, ones that we could influence for ourselves. Also boiling these down to five, we needed to find a further acronym. An idea suddenly came to me – I'd thought of a word that seemed fitting. It was the founders' dream that Action for Happiness would create a happier, more caring, society and even world, so our acronym for the Ten Keys to Happier Living became: 'GREAT DREAM' (Giving, Relating, etc.). The ten areas in which we can take action – from the inside out as well as the outside in – to increase and maintain our happiness. There's a chapter on each in this book.

Since the launch of Action for Happiness, via our website, talks, courses and workshops, the Ten Keys have already reached far and wide across the globe. They've been used in schools, communities and workplaces, and we've been told so many stories of how they have inspired people to take action that has made them and others happier. I hope they'll help you to be happier too.

How to use this book

Most of all, this book is about taking action. It's full of tried-and-tested practical activities and ideas, as well as why and how each Key contributes to happiness.

It's up to you how you approach this book – you can read it from start to finish or pick and choose chapters: perhaps an area that catches your eye or that you know you want to learn more about. You can go straight to the activities and get started. And if you're curious about it, you can get into the science behind them.

This book is based on many, many experimental studies – and I hope you'll approach it in the same way. Give the ideas a try – even if they seem odd or new or not quite 'you'. It's only by doing this that you'll discover the actions that work best for you and it's at the boundaries of our comfort zone that we most readily learn and grow. Like any researcher, you may want to have a notebook – whether paper or electronic – where you can capture your thoughts and reflections and refer back to over time.

It's been said that 'happiness is a journey, not a destination' – I hope this book will help you enjoy the ride.

GIVING
Do things for others

Curious isn't it? The first Key to Happier Living
is about other people's happiness, not our own. This
idea may seem strange at first glance, but giving, being
kind and helping others can be powerful ways to
increase the happiness of those around us –
and become happier ourselves. But it's not always
easy, so in this chapter we'll also look at evidence-
based ideas to make giving to others sustaining
rather than draining.

Giving: introduction

> 'The best way to cheer yourself up is to try to cheer somebody else up.'
>
> Mark Twain, *Mark Twain's Notebook*

Old wisdom, new science

It's sometimes said that happiness is best achieved 'sideways on'. In other words, if we want to be happy we shouldn't focus on our own happiness, we should concentrate our attention and actions on something, or someone, else. A growing number of scientific studies back this up, showing that caring about other people's happiness is an important ingredient for our own. People who give to, or help, others have been shown to: be more satisfied with their lives; have a greater sense of meaning and feel more competent. It can also improve our mood, reduce stress and distract us from our own troubles. And it seems that being compassionate and kind to others is hard-wired into what it means to be human.

While the science is new, the wisdom it represents is ancient. 'Do unto others as you would want them to do unto you,' known as the 'golden rule', is found in many philosophical and religious traditions. Since most of us would like to think that, when we need it, others would be there to give us a helping hand (whether from friends, family members or even complete strangers), the golden rule prompts us to think about how we help others too, and in doing so contribute to creating the sorts of communities, workplaces, cities and societies that we want to be part of.

In this chapter we'll explore some highlights of the scientific research into the connections between giving and happiness, and ways of helping that maximise the benefits for others and at the same time the happiness boost for ourselves. I hope that it will inspire you to give more, more often and in new ways... and encourage you to ask for help when you need it too.

Think about it A windfall for happiness

Imagine you put on a jacket you haven't worn for ages. Reaching into your pocket you find a crumpled £10 note you'd forgotten you had. What would you be most likely to do with this windfall?

Ⓐ Put it in your purse/wallet thinking 'this will cover my lunch today'.

Ⓑ Use it to buy a treat for yourself – luxury chocolates, a delicious cheese, a new bestseller – whatever you'd most enjoy.

Ⓒ Treat a friend, acquaintance or colleague to a coffee or a drink.

Ⓓ Give it to a person collecting for charity or to a homeless person you regularly pass in the street.

Find out which of these is likely to have the biggest happiness-boosting effect at the end of the chapter (see page 35).

What does 'giving' mean?

We may think giving is about money or things, but there are many ways to give that don't involve either, such as helping or being kind. In essence, giving is an act of thoughtfulness for another person, a moment of attention, caring and connection. Here are some examples of different ways we can give that don't involve money:

* **Be kind,** whether you know them or not: strangers, family, friends, colleagues, neighbours, whether old or young, or those in need, both close to home or far away.
* **Give time,** such as offering your skills, sharing your knowledge or resources or loyalty, or just being there to listen.
* **Help others in good times as well as in bad.** This might mean helping someone to learn and grow, to develop ideas or to make and build relationships.
* **Cut people some slack.** When someone (for example a colleague or family member) is having a hard time and is causing difficulties for others, be generous and 'give' by backing off and letting them have the benefit of the doubt.
* **As part of your routine,** such as making a habit of calling in on an elderly neighbour or mentoring a new junior colleague.

★ **Small or simple acts.** Giving doesn't always take huge amounts of effort. It can be as easy and quick as voicing a kind or encouraging thought, giving your attention for a moment, gracing someone else with your smile or a thoughtful gesture.

★ **Acts we plan in advance,** such as doing something special for a friend or neighbour, training for a sponsored run, organising a charity event, or helping a friend move house or clear their overgrown garden.

★ **Spur-of-the-moment acts,** whenever you notice a need. This might be just picking up someone's dropped glove, or an unprompted act of generosity such as letting another driver take a parking space ahead of you. It can be making someone laugh or simply listening to them.

As Winston Churchill once said, 'We make a living by what we get. We make a life by what we give.'

 Pause point...

> ★ In what ways, small or large, have you helped or given to other people in the last few weeks?
>
> ★ What triggered you to help or give?
>
> ★ What impact or reaction did your generosity have on the recipient(s)?
>
> ★ What impact did helping have on you?

The science of giving

> 'Do unto others 20% better than you would expect them to do unto you, to correct for subjective error.'
>
> Attributed to Linus Pauling, lecture at Monterey Peninsula College (c.1961)

A virtuous circle

It seems there is a two-way relationship between happiness and helping others:
★ Helping others can make us happier
★ Happier people tend to help others more

Whatever age we are, giving has been shown to increase happiness. For example, pre-school children who displayed empathy towards others were more likely to display happy moods themselves. People who gave a proportion of their monthly income to charitable causes or spent it on others were found to be happier than people who did not spend on others, and this was regardless of income level. Volunteering is related to increased happiness, irrespective of the social and financial circumstances of the volunteer.

And if we are happy, we are more likely to be interested in, or be inclined towards, helping others. We are more likely to have recently performed acts of kindness or spent a greater percentage of our time or money helping others. At work, if we're happier, we are more likely to go beyond the call of duty to help colleagues and customers.

This scientific evidence suggests that there's a 'virtuous circle' – happiness makes us likely to give more and giving can help us to be happier, which leads to a greater tendency to give – and so on.

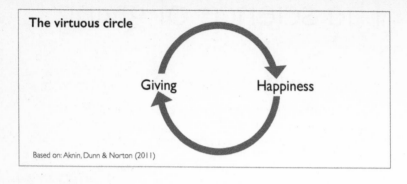

The virtuous circle

Giving

Happiness

Based on: Aknin, Dunn & Norton (2011)

Giving FEELS good

Psychologist Elizabeth Dunn and her colleagues have conducted a number of experiments on spending money and happiness. They've found that our predictions about what would bring us the greatest happiness are often wrong. For example, in one study, participants were given $5 or $20 to either spend on others, donate to charity or to spend on themselves. The impact on how they felt was measured at the end of the day. Participants who spent money on others or donated it experienced greater happiness than people who were given the same amount to spend on themselves. The amount of money did not affect the level of happiness generated – the smaller amounts had a similar personal impact as the larger amounts. Yet when people were asked to predict what would have the greatest impact on their personal happiness they thought that this would result from having the larger amount to spend on themselves.

Studies of the brain suggest that giving money to a good cause can literally feel as good as receiving it oneself, especially if the donations are voluntary. Experiments from the field of neuroscience show that when we give money to good causes, it activates our 'reward centre' (the orbital frontal cortex and ventral striatum) – the same parts of the brain that are activated if we receive money or a gift for ourselves.

It's not just giving money that feels good. Experimental studies have shown that other types of giving can lead to greater happiness. For example, when participants performed five new acts of kindness on one day per week over a six-week period (even if each act was small), they

ANNA'S STORY: BIKE-RIDER TO THE RESCUE

'I'd just picked up my daughters from their weekly after-school dance class. Driving home, traffic was heavy and the girls were tired, hungry and bickering. We'd just reached a busy intersection when the car just stopped dead. The engine cut out and wouldn't start again. We were in the middle of traffic so I couldn't safely get the girls out of the car and I couldn't leave them while I got help. My first reaction was to pick up my phone, but its battery was dead. Not only that, I realised that the engine cut-out had been my fault. I'd forgotten to fill up the car with fuel.

Other drivers were sounding their horns. I felt myself panicking, but I couldn't let the girls see that: they were already starting to get frightened. Just then a motorbike drew up beside us and the rider knocked on the window. "Are you okay?" he asked. "We're stuck," I said. "We need to get you to the side of the road" he replied. The rider jumped off his bike and flagged down a couple of other drivers. Between them, they pushed us to safety. Before I could properly thank them, the rider was back on his bike and the other drivers were back in their cars, driving off. They'd been like angels! The girls and I were able to walk to a garage to get petrol and 30 minutes later we were on our way again. I was so appreciative, too, that the girls had seen how kind other people could be. I'm figuring out a way I can return the favour, if not to those kind people then to another person who is in need of help.'

experienced an increase in feelings of well-being, compared to control groups. (See the box on pages 20 and 21 to try this out for yourself.)

In another study of over 1,700 female volunteers, scientists discovered that many of the women experienced a 'helpers' high'. This was a euphoric feeling after the act of helping another, resulting from the release of endorphins, followed by a longer period of feeling calm.

There is evidence that the 'warm glow' felt as a result of giving is found across all cultures and economic circumstances. For example, researchers have found a positive relationship between pro-social giving, such as making charitable donations, and happiness in 120 different countries, both rich and poor, regardless of the level of income of the people giving.

Giving DOES US good

As well as feeling good, helping others literally seems to do us good. For example, in the study of female volunteers we've looked at on page 17, in addition to feeling happier and calmer after giving, the women also experienced a longer-lasting period of improved emotional well-being and an enhanced sense of self-worth. In turn, this reduced their stress levels and improved their health.

Other studies have also found that adults who volunteer have higher psychological well-being and feel better about themselves. Teenager volunteering has been associated with improved self-esteem, reduction in anti-social/problem behaviours and school truancy, improved attitudes to school and increased educational achievement. Giving can distract us from dwelling on our own problems and it helps us to be grateful for what we have. Certainly, volunteers have been shown to feel more hopeful and have fewer symptoms of depression and anxiety than non-volunteers.

Giving, whether taking the form of financial, emotional support or in other ways, has been shown to be associated with greater overall health and may even influence how long we live. Studies of older people show that those who give support to others live longer than those who don't. This included support to friends, relatives and neighbours, and emotional support to their spouses.

Volunteering may even help to keep our brains functioning well in our old age. Unpicking the benefits of volunteering from other factors can be tricky. Benefits might exist because volunteers are healthier in the first place, and so are more able to volunteer. However, evidence does suggest that there is a relationship between doing things for others and physical and psychological well-being. It seems that helping others is an activity that people can engage in as a strategy to increase well-being and maintain optimal health and cognitive functioning throughout life, up to, and including, old age.

A THANK YOU TO TONY FROM ME

I'd flown to Philadelphia to attend the World Congress of Positive Psychology. It was a big investment of time and money for me, but it's important for my work to keep up to date with the latest research. It had been an intense, inspiring and tiring four days, packed with workshops, talks and lectures. My notebook was full of great ideas and new learning. Except that I'd lost it. The whole point of the trip was in it and I'd left it in the back of a taxi. Not only that, it was in a beautiful bag that my partner had bought for me for Christmas – it would be difficult to replace.

As soon as I realised what had happened I thought I'd ring the central number for lost property, but I soon discovered that there wasn't one. Each cab company in Philly operates separately and there are a lot of cab companies in the city. I hadn't asked for a receipt for the journey, so had no idea which company I had used. I just had to ring round them all, which took the whole night. No one had found my bag. I was emotional, seriously annoyed with myself for my lost notes and sad about losing a thoughtful present I'd been given. There was nothing else I could do. I packed up my luggage, ready to fly home to London the next day.

At 7.30am the next morning, my phone rang. 'Hello', said the voice on the other end. 'Did you take a cab last night to the Pine Street area?' 'Yes,' I said, 'I did.' 'I'm Tony, the cab driver, and I think I've found a bag belonging to you. Did you lose one?' I couldn't believe my ears. 'I'm round the corner,' he said. 'I'll drop it off to you shortly.' Within ten minutes he was there. I had been his last passenger the day before and his kids had found my bag and its precious contents as he'd taken them to school. Of no monetary value, of course, just a notebook and a few pens, but important to me, and luckily I'd written my phone number in the front, so he knew who to contact. He wouldn't take any money to cover his costs or time. 'It looked like there was a lot of work in that book,' he said.

That was four years ago and I still remember this act of kindness.

Try this! Acts of kindness

In an experimental study, psychologist Sonja Lyubomirsky and her colleagues asked participants to carry out five acts of kindness per week over a six-week period, in addition to what they would normally do. These acts were spread out across the week or carried out on a single day. The acts could be anything, small or large, spontaneous or planned. For example, holding open a door for someone loaded with bags, letting another car go in front, donating blood, paying for the coffee of the stranger next in line, washing up for a friend, visiting an old people's home or taking a neighbour a home-made cake. Participants kept note of the acts of kindness they'd carried out. Their happiness levels were measured before the experiment and after six weeks.

Participants who carried out all their acts on a single day each week increased their happiness levels, whereas those who spread out their acts didn't. So timing seems to be important.

The variety of the acts also seemed to make a difference. In another study, one group of participants was asked to repeat the same three acts of kindness per week for ten weeks. In contrast, a second group was also asked to carry out three acts of kindness per week, but they could vary what they did. The first group actually reduced their happiness levels in the middle of the study (though they returned to their pre-study levels at the end), while the second group experienced a boost in happiness levels. So choice and variety seem to be important.

Based on: Lyubomirsky, Sheldon & Schkade (2005). Lyubomirsky (2008)

Try your own kindness experiment

★ Each week aim to do five different acts of kindness in addition to what you would normally do. Be sure to vary what you do. (You might want to start by making a list of all the acts you can think of.)

★ Try to do all your new acts of kindness on one day (or as close together as possible).

★ Keep a note of what you try and what you notice in yourself and in others.

See opposite for some ideas for acts of kindness you could try.

- ★ Tell someone they're doing a good job

- ★ Give up your seat for someone

- ★ Pick up litter in the park or street

- ★ Give a (sincere) compliment

- ★ Make someone laugh

- ★ Take time to really listen to someone

- ★ If you drive, let at least one car in on every journey

- ★ Offer directions to someone who seems lost

- ★ Let someone go in front of you in the supermarket queue

- ★ Tell someone they mean a lot to you

- ★ Offer change to someone who is struggling to find the right amount

- ★ Offer to help carry someone's heavy bags

- ★ Visit someone who seems lonely

- ★ Forgive someone for what they've done

- ★ Visit or send a card to a sick friend, neighbour or relative

- ★ Offer to look after a friend's children, to give them a break

- ★ Offer to mow your neighbour's lawn or help them in their garden

- ★ Give food to a homeless person and take time to talk with them

- ★ Cook/bake something special for others as a surprise

Reflection

- ★ How did you feel after intentionally carrying out new acts of kindness over the six weeks (or however long you did the experiment for)?

- ★ What do you notice about the reactions of the people you helped?

- ★ What acts could you continue to do? Are you starting to notice more opportunities to be kind?

The London Underground network is one of the largest metro systems in the world, carrying 1.265 billion people each year. Its passengers are a true cross-section of London life, mixed with many visitors from all around the world. At peak times the Tube, as it's known, can be really crowded with people in a rush to get from A to B. Like many big cities, London has a reputation for unfriendliness. But I don't think that's really the case.

In 2011, Art on the Underground commissioned artist Michael Landy to realise 'Acts of Kindness', a project inviting and inspiring people to share stories of the kindnesses they'd experienced or witnessed during their journeys on the Tube. Uplifting stories were submitted to art.tfl.gov.uk – from someone's mum's life being saved by a stranger administering CPR when she collapsed with a heart attack, to frequent stories of strangers offering a helping hand with carrying heavy bags up stairways or people giving up their seats to another passenger in greater need.

Michael Landy, Acts of Kindness (2011). Commissioned by Art on the Underground © the artist

This story inspired me to experiment with my own acts of kindness on my frequent Tube journeys. At first I felt hesitant – nervous that people might think I was strange, or be annoyed or even aggressive. Would this result in an embarrassing scene, I wondered? But that has never been the case. I've found people to be appreciative and gracious of my offers of help – even if they don't need it! It's made me tune in more and notice other passengers' needs and so be able to help in many different and small ways, for example:

- ★ Noticing when tourists are looking lost or confused, unsure of where to go and asking if they'd like help with directions (no one has told me to get lost yet!).

- ★ Moving seats so two friends can sit together and continue their conversation.

- ★ Noticing a young woman crying and offering her a tissue to dry her tears.

- ★ Seeing that someone is feeling unwell and passing them a bottle of water.

- ★ Noticing a wallet someone has dropped. When I picked it up I found it was stuffed with what looked like a week's wages. I wanted to make sure it was safe so, despite being late, I went back up to the ticket hall to hand it in, even though it meant I missed my train.

My acts aren't pre-meditated, they're often instinctive and just feel like the right thing to do. When I help, I experience a momentary sense of human connection with that person. And perhaps a feeling that I've made a small, positive impact on their day.

I wonder if it's made me more approachable. For example, a nice young guy sitting next to me asked for a squeeze of the hand cream I'd taken out to use, as his hands were really dry too. I offered him some and we then had a fun conversation for the rest of the journey – much better than the usual stony silence! I've become more conscious of, and grateful for, people helping me. Frequently, other passengers have noticed I've dropped my scarf or left my umbrella, helped me with heavy bags or given me a seat when I was loaded down with parcels and looked tired. Sometimes we exchange a few words, sometimes we don't, but I sense it makes both of our days a little bit better. And perhaps even our view of the world – believing that people out there are good and willing to help another stranger. These are small acts that I hope make our transport system, and indeed our city, a good place to be.

To read the stories, visit art.tfl.gov.uk and search 'Acts of Kindness'.

Kindness is part of human nature

If you think about it, perhaps it makes perfect sense that helping others contributes to our own happiness and well-being. Human beings are a highly social species and we've evolved to live in large groups. Scientists used to believe that humans only did things when they could get something back in return. But if that was the case, how could we explain people doing kind acts or donating money anonymously?

If people are altruistic, they are more likely to build social connections and stronger, more supportive, social networks, which also leads to increased feelings of happiness and well-being. Our social connections with others are a core need for psychological and physical well-being (to be explored more in the next chapter). In many ways we could argue that giving and helping each other are a sort of 'social glue' that keeps our communities together and which helped them, and the human race, to survive.

In his book, *Altruism*, writer and Buddhist monk, Matthieu Ricard, shares the idea of 'psychological economics'. Acts of giving may cost us externally in terms of money, time, energy or effort, but if we have an internal psychological gain from it, whether through a boost to positive emotions, greater personal connection or a sense of meaning, then we win, as well as the person who is the recipient of what we have given.

We start to exhibit giving behaviours from an early age. Children as young as two can be observed sharing, helping and looking after others and, as we have seen, the benefits continue throughout life. Participating in shared tasks, such as community service and other social activities, predicts how satisfied people are with their lives, even after other factors are taken into account.

Kindness seems to be catching. When we see someone do something genuinely kind or thoughtful or we are on the receiving end of kindness, it inspires us to be kinder to others ourselves. In this way, giving can spread from one person to the next, even influencing the behaviour of people who never witnessed the original act and so help to create happier, more trusting, communities. Indeed, kindness towards others may be the glue between individual happiness, community and societal well-being.

Scientists are now exploring the evolution of altruism, cooperation, empathy, compassion and kindness, and are challenging the idea of the purely 'selfish gene' – that we only do something if it benefits us directly. We can also do things because they're for the benefit or survival of the group, even if they are not good for ourselves. From an evolutionary perspective, it makes sense, then, that there are happiness benefits for us from doing so, since it helps the survival of our species.

Try this! A kinder world – one act at a time

The Pay-it-Forward idea is a simple one. Someone does a good deed or kind act for you and you then do something kind or helpful for someone else and ask them to pass it on in the same way. It's not a new idea, but it's come to prominence in recent years through being the centre of Catherine Ryan Hyde's best-selling novel, *Pay it Forward*.

In this book, a teacher sets his students an assignment to 'Think of an idea for world change, and put it into action'. One twelve-year-old, Trevor, decides to do a good deed for three people and in exchange asks them to 'pay it forward' to three more people, and so on. So one kind act leads to nine, then to twenty-seven, then to eighty-one and so on. Trevor's vision is that it ripples out to really change the world, achieving more than one person could do alone.

The book has been made into a film and the idea was adapted for teachers to use in their real-life classrooms. Pay it Forward Foundation has been established, and there's even an annual Pay it Forward Day.

Can you start a pay-it-forward ripple effect? You don't need to wait until someone needs help – here are some ideas to get you thinking:

★ Pay for someone's coffee in the queue behind you.

★ On a rainy day, give away a spare umbrella and ask that person to pass it on when they have finished with it.

★ Put some extra coins into a vending machine with a sticky note to say you are treating the next person and suggest they might find a way to treat someone else.

How to keep giving

> 'Be kind whenever possible. It is always possible.'
>
> H. H. Dalai Lama

Okay, so giving is a good thing to do and it's good for us, but it's not always easy. What can help us to sustain helping others over the long-term, in ways that also take care of ourselves too?

 Pause point...

★ What motivates you to help others? Check back to any notes or thoughts you had at the previous pause point (see page 14).

★ Dig deeper. What really motivates you to help?

It turns out that our underlying motivation to help is important – for the quality of our helping, its impact on the recipient and for our well-being.

Motivation maintenance

Adam Grant is the youngest tenured professor at Wharton Business School. As well as being an extraordinary teacher, thinker and a prolific writer he's also an extraordinary giver. He's an expert in the science of giving too. His research shows that helping others isn't just a good thing to do but can also boost personal and career success... or the opposite.

The difference between 'successful' and 'unsuccessful' givers is that the former not only care for others, they know what matters for their own well-being too. An in-depth study of the motivations of 'super-givers', in this case recipients of the Caring Canadian Award (that country's highest recognition of people who have sustained extraordinary giving efforts), showed that winners of the prize scored three times higher on concern for the interests of others than a comparison group (people of similar age, gender, education and ethnicity), but who did not maintain the same level of giving over a sustained period of time. So these super-givers care more about others – not unsurprising, you might think.

What was surprising, however, was that the winners also scored higher on self-interest – knowing what was important for them in the act of giving. They'd aligned what mattered to them with what would make a difference to those they were giving to. This might seem the opposite to our notion of super-givers, who we often think of as subjugating their own needs in the service of others. We might also feel that it is somehow wrong to think about ourselves in the context of giving, but it seems not. Grant argues that being other-focused or self-focused aren't at the opposite ends of the same spectrum; they're different, separate, motivations. In fact, it seems that being high on motivation to help others and high on drive to achieve our personal goals is what enables these super-givers to give extraordinarily over a sustained period of time.

Grant describes two different types of giver: 'selfless-givers' and 'other-ish givers'. Selfless givers are high on other-interest and low on self-interest. In the longer term they can pay a price for giving their time and energy without regard for their own needs. Other-ish givers are high on both concern for others and on self-interest, meaning they can successfully maintain giving over time. Clearly neither is selfish.

Take Sam, one of the Canadian super-givers in the study we discussed above. He had co-founded a charity, Big Brothers, to help fatherless boys. He talked about a high point in his life, which was achieving recognition for his charity's work. At a big event they'd organised, his co-founder said: 'The motto of Big Brothers is: "No man stands so straight as when he bends to help a fatherless boy". And the man that stands straightest is Sam...' Sam, delighting in this recognition, had interwoven his organisational acumen and achievement drive with his passion for helping disadvantaged children.

Meeting your needs

Let's not kid ourselves, not all acts of giving boost our happiness. For one-off acts that's not necessarily an issue, but if we want to sustain our giving, it's an important consideration, especially given that there is a virtuous circle between the happiness of givers and the extent to which we help others. If regular giving makes us happier, we are more likely to continue giving and help more.

Three simple factors, or core psychological needs, make a critical difference to the boost we get from doing kind things for others. These ingredients are common to all of us:

★ **Connection** Does your act of giving help you to feel a sense of connection with other people?
★ **Control** Have you chosen to carry out your act of kindness freely and is it aligned with who you are, what you're interested in and your personal values?
★ **Competence and impact** Are you effective in your actions? Are your actions useful and do you make a difference?

If our acts of giving aren't increasing our happiness, it's likely that these needs aren't being met. So, rather than just stopping giving, we should see if we can tweak our actions to match these needs. It's good for us and it will have a greater benefit for those we are helping too.

Choosing to give matters

Our sense of control or choice over giving seems to be especially important. Our motives can be externally driven – for example, helping others primarily for reward or recognition, or because we want to be thought of as a good person, or would feel ashamed or guilty if we didn't. Or we can help because we simply want to, because it aligns with our values or what we are genuinely interested in. This is called 'autonomous motivation' and arises from within rather than from, or in reaction to, an external factor.

Studies have shown that when we are autonomously motivated to help, not only does that mean we are much more likely to experience a positive impact on our well-being, but the helping is likely to have a greater benefit for the recipient too. We are likely to put in more effort, what we do will likely be more effective, and the recipient will experience us as being warmer and more attuned to their needs. By contrast, when the helper motivation is externally motivated, for example being told to help, the helping could even have a negative impact on the recipient.

Now situations and ways we help vary. The spontaneous act of helping when someone has dropped something, needs a quick helping hand or is in danger tends to be instinctive and so likely to be internally driven. However, when we think of helping regularly at home, in work, college, school or in our community, finding something we like doing matters.

 Pause point…

Think about a time when you helped someone and it increased your happiness. In what ways did it satisfy the following basic psychological ingredients?

★ Feeling a connection to others?

★ Feeling a sense of competence and impact?

★ Feeling a sense of choice or control over what you did and an alignment with who you are?

Be specific

How we frame our goals for giving matters. In a number of experiments researchers found that when we set a specific goal to help (for example, make someone smile) this has a greater impact on how happy we feel as a result of helping than if we set a more abstract goal (for example, help the homeless). When we set more specific goals we are more likely to be accurate in our expectations of the impact of that act. In contrast, when we set an abstract goal, we tend to overestimate its likely impact and therefore become disappointed that it doesn't achieve what we'd hoped. We'll be looking at goals and happiness in a lot more detail in Chapter 6.

Giving when we're already busy

Many of us feel we already have more to do than we can fit into the time available. Work, daily chores, exercise or staying connected to friends can give us a sense of what psychologists call 'time famine'. This can mean we feel we just don't have time to help people more. It can also mean we are less likely to notice or take action when others need our help. In one well-known study, students in a hurry to attend a seminar on the Good Samaritan rushed past a person slumped at the side of the road. Those not in a rush were more likely to stop and offer help. In cities, this phenomenon can be exacerbated, with a correlation between pro-social acts, of which there were fewer. Surprisingly, though, recent experiments have shown that the quick actions we carry out to help others can actually increase our sense of having time, rather than adding to a feeling of overload. In comparison to wasting time, spending time on ourselves or being given unexpected spare time to help others increased participants' sense of time affluence. Of course there would likely be an upper limit on this effect – the point at which giving time could be detrimental to our well-being. However, it seems helping others, even in quick acts lasting as little as five minutes, can increase our sense of self-efficacy and as a consequence how much time we feel we have.

Let's go back to Adam Grant (see page 26). Remember he was also an extraordinary giver, he's also unimaginably busy. He's a dedicated teacher, so helping his students has top priority, as well as colleagues and

organisations he works with, but Adam still helps a lot of other people, including many former students and readers of his book or popular blogs. How does he do this? He's developed some simple strategies for ways he can help as many people as he can in the most efficient/achievable way. If you are super-busy but want to help others, these ideas might help you:

★ Do a five-minute favour – what can you do to help the person in five minutes or less?

★ What is the highest value you could contribute at the lowest personal 'cost' to you?

★ Are you uniquely qualified to help or can you introduce the person to someone who'd be more suitable?

★ Can you connect the person to others who are working on similar things – so that they can help each other?

★ How, and what, is your preferred way of helping? What's easy for you? What are your strengths? How could you use these to help? (See Chapter 9 for more on strengths.)

Try this! Kind but quick

What are the three quickest ways you could help the people you know? Give them a try over the next day or so.

Sustaining yourself if you're a full-time giver

But what if our daily lives are all about giving, for example as a parent, as a carer of an ill or elderly person, as a teacher, as a professional in one of the 'caring professions' – or perhaps even a mix of these?

Long-term carers of sick or frail loved ones can experience burnout (cumulative emotional and/or physical exhaustion) and those in caring professions can experience 'compassion fatigue' too.

When we are busy caring for others, taking care of our own well-being is often at the bottom of our to-do list (if it's on there at all), and we rarely get to it. But it's important. Not only does it help prevent burnout, meaning we can sustain our caring role in the long term, but our well-being has a ripple effect on those around us. So, looking after your well-being isn't just for you, it will help those you are caring for and others around you too. It's like the advice we get on planes before take off: 'Put on your own oxygen mask before helping others.' Taking care of your own well-being is important.

Throughout this book you'll find many small, quick actions you can take that can make a big difference to well-being over time, be it a ten-minute walk in the park, a few minutes of mindfulness, a quick dance to a favourite song or a five-minute call to a friend.

We looked at the importance of controlling how we give above. We might not have had a choice about becoming a long-term carer, so making sure we take care of our own well-being is perhaps even more important. Not only will this help us directly, but indirectly too, since even small actions that we choose to take will help us feel a greater sense of control, which is important for well-being too.

Asking for help

> 'A little boy was trying but failing to lift a heavy stone. His father came along just then. Noticing the boy's difficulty, he asked, "Are you using all your strength?" "Yes, I am, father," the little boy replied irritably. "No, you are not," his father answered. "I am right here just waiting, and you haven't yet asked me to help you." '
>
> Author unknown

How easy do you find it to ask for help?

Everyone needs help from time to time – when we are facing a challenge or difficulty, or perhaps learning a new skill, researching something, looking for, or testing, new ideas or simply when an extra pair of hands would be useful. Yet many of us are reluctant to ask for help, putting it off or not asking at all because we are fearful that we might be imposing on someone, or be thought of as stupid or weak.

But think about it. If giving helps make people happier, then asking for help is an opportunity to help them as well as you. When we ask others for help, it can make them feel valued and it can help build our relationship with them too. By showing some vulnerability yourself, it means others are likely to be vulnerable with you too and feel able to ask for help when they need it.

You can do a lot to help the person you are asking feel good – through helping, by thinking about how their core psychological needs can be met (see page 28), for example, by:
★ Being warm and open and showing you appreciate what they are doing.
★ Ensuring they don't feel obliged and have choice over how they help.
★ Letting them know the difference they've made.

Pause point...

★ Who has helped you in the last two weeks or so, and in what ways? What did you most appreciate about their help?

★ What can stop you asking for help?

★ Is there something that you'd appreciate help with right now? Who might be able to help?

TURNING AROUND A LIFE OF PAIN

Jasmine had been in chronic pain for over a decade. Degenerative spine disease, carpal tunnel syndrome and fibromyalgia created a toxic mix that had brought her life to a standstill. After a career of thirty-five years, due to a serious accident, Jasmine was unable to work. She spent her days in despair. A pain-management course brought no relief, plunging her into depression. 'I felt I had no hope,' she said. 'This is my life: no life.' Her pain also meant she felt isolated. 'I didn't want to be around other people and thought that no one really cared about me.'

By chance she stumbled on the Action for Happiness website and its Ten Keys to Happier Living made her realise that there were practical steps she could take to help herself become happier. Then, feeling a bit better about herself and her life, she realised that she could change her relationship to her pain: accept it rather than fight against it. This internal shift lessened her emotional distress, even though the sensations of pain remained.

She resolved to work with other people also suffering from chronic pain to see how she might help them too. 'I was still fairly depressed, but I started to do more things,' Jasmine said.

'Thinking about how to improve support for other sufferers, I realised we needed a new approach – one that is more hopeful and uses some of the ideas that I had learnt from Action for Happiness.'

Jasmine now counsels others with chronic pain about ways they might be helped and how they can find hope. She's in the process of becoming a mindfulness teacher. 'I still have bad days and life certainly isn't perfect. But now I'm trying to be the change that I want to see.'

KEY ONE: GIVING

To sum up

Here are five key points to take away from this chapter:

1 There's a virtuous circle between happiness and giving – happier people give more, and giving to others can make us happier. Kindness can be catching too – seeing other people helping makes us more likely to help others too.

2 Giving or helping others can do us good – physically and psychologically.

3 Giving to others doesn't have to take lots of money or time – there are plenty of ways we can give to others that only take moments to carry out.

4 To sustain giving, find ways to make sure that how you are helping increases your own sense of connection to others; that it aligns with your values, strengths and interests, and that you understand its impact for the person or people you are trying to help. This will maximise the benefit for those you are giving to too!

5 Ask for help when you need it. Think of it as an opportunity for the person (or people) you ask to get a happiness boost too! (Make sure you give them a choice about it and tell them what a difference they've made for you.)

Connections to other Keys

Other keys you might like to explore in connection with Giving:

★ **RELATING** (See page 36)
Giving is a way to build connections with other people.

★ **AWARENESS** (See page 108)
Building mindfulness skills can enhance our compassion for others.

★ **ACCEPTANCE** (See page 266)
Building understanding of strengths/how to use these to help others.

★ **MEANING** (See page 298)
Giving/being of service can be a key source of meaning in our lives.

Answers to Think about it Boosting happiness

(See page 13 for the question.)

If you answered C or D you're most likely to be happier. As we saw on page 16, despite what we might think will bring the biggest boost to happiness, spending money on others can have a greater effect than spending it on ourselves.

There is some evidence that spending on close 'others' (good friend/family member), might give a bigger boost of happiness than spending it on looser acquaintances. This is likely because of the importance of our closer social ties for happiness, though of course, by spending time with them, our looser acquaintances may become closer. Donating to charity has also been shown to make us happier. To maximise the happiness boost we receive, having a sense that our donation makes an impact seems to be important. So giving to causes that are clear about where our funds go and the difference our contribution makes is important.

See: Dunn, Aknin & Norton (2014); Aknin, Sandstrom, Dunn & Norton (2011); Aknin, Dunn, Whillans et al (2013)

G
R
E
A
T

35

D
R
E
A
M

RELATING

Connect with people

Feeling connected to other people is at the heart of happiness. And a growing body of research is showing what actions make a real difference when it comes to building new relationships and nurturing our existing ones. Even tiny moments with others matter!

Relating: introduction

'For happiness, remember... other people matter.'

Dr Christopher Peterson, lecture, University of Pennsylvania, 2009

Chris Peterson was one of the professors I studied with. This quote was his mantra and he repeated it often. Frequently in his lectures, he'd prompt us: 'For happiness, remember...' 'Other people matter,' we'd all duly reply.

Chris was a pioneer in positive psychology and at the forefront of the movement. A self-confessed introvert, with depressive tendencies, he was a classic academic. Despite his natural preference for spending time alone, he'd learned the importance of focusing on connecting to others through his work. He worked at it. He consciously made time for people and when he spoke to them they had his full attention. He took an interest in who they were and what interested them. From students, colleagues and friends to waiters, bartenders and taxi drivers, he treated everyone the same: everyone mattered and it made a difference. Chris was a favourite lecturer, nominated by students for numerous teaching awards and he was much loved as a colleague and friend. It made a difference in his own life too: he said it made him happier. What Chris discovered has been shown, time after time, in numerous studies – being and feeling connected to people around us is central to our well-being, our resilience and for our happiness.

Human beings are naturally social as a species – the survival and evolution of the human race has depended on it! Social ties are important through-out our lifespan, from birth through to old age. It seems we are literally wired for relationships. Think of emotions and behaviours that feel good, such as love, compassion, kindness, gratitude, generosity, smiling and laughing or how painful it is when we break important social bonds.

Think about it

Research shows that people with strong social relationships live significantly longer than people with fewer and weaker social relationships (this relates to both the number and quality of those relationships). Thinking about this, what's your first thought?

Is it:

Ⓐ 'Mmm... Do I have enough good friends and family relationships to ensure that I live a long and happy life?' Or

Ⓑ 'Who am I a friend to, or relative of, and how can I ensure our relationship contributes to them living a long and happy life?'

Like many of us – your instant response might have been A. But A isn't possible without attention to B. As Ralph Waldo Emerson said, 'The only way to have a friend is to be a friend.' To that end, I hope you find the ideas in this chapter helpful in nurturing your existing social connections with others and in making new ones.

Based on: Peterson (2013).'Having a friend and being a friend'. *Pursuing the Good Life*, Oxford University Press

Yet life today seems, in many ways, to undermine this: loneliness is increasing, as are divorce rates. Fewer of us live near our extended families, the nature of our working lives means that we may have less involvement in our local communities and more of us are living alone. Despite technology giving us more ways to stay in touch or reconnect with old friends, it can also get in the way of face-to-face connection, which brings greater benefits for our health and happiness.

In this chapter we'll explore why and how relationships are important for happiness, and there are lots of ideas for small actions to take that can make a big difference to the quality of our connections with others.

KEY TWO: RELATING

Relationships & happiness

'Relationships are themselves a crucial part of psychological wealth, without which you cannot be truly rich.'

Ed Diener & Robert Biswas-Diener,
Happiness: Unlocking the Mysteries of Psychological Wealth

We're happier together

Apparently we are thirty times more likely to laugh when we are with other people than when we are alone. While this might seem like a fun fact, it's just one way in which research is showing that relationships are central to happiness for each one of us. Indeed, our need to feel connected to other people is regarded as a fundamental nutrient for psychological well-being.

We may have differing needs in terms of how much time we spend with others and how much we want to be alone, but we tend to feel better when we are with others than when we're not. Yes, of course that depends on who we're with and what we're doing, but when psychologists buzzed people at various points of the day and asked them what they were doing, with whom and how happy they were feeling at that time, on average happiness was higher for times people were with others than when they were on their own. This even applied to the introverts. Even though they tended to spend less time in social situations than the extroverts, when they did so they actually got a bigger mood boost from being with others.

It seems that on average we need at least six hours a day in which we have social contact with others, including time at home, at work, interacting via the phone, email or online social networking.

There are many ways relationships and connections with others contribute to how happy we are, for example:

★ **Loving and being loved** Some leading psychologists regard love as the supreme emotion and the greatest human capacity. Our deepest bonds with others are a key source of meaning in our lives: feeling connected to, and caring for, them, sharing our journeys in life, having someone who values us and is proud of our achievements, and we of them, are all important in our well-being.

★ **Belonging and identity** The various social groups we are part of help to shape and define who we are and connect us into something larger than ourselves. These may be families, schools, workplaces, neighbourhoods, countries, regions, community groups, religions, political parties, or interest or activity groups.

★ **Learning, growing and developing** as infants, children and adults. From our parents and family, teachers, colleagues, coaches and mentors through to being part of loving, romantic or other close adult relationships, our connections with others help us to grow. Other people, with their infinite variety of perspectives, talents and skills, can educate and inspire us, expand our horizons, help us to develop wisdom and emotional maturity, and fuel our own creativity.

★ **Being resilient** Support from others helps us deal with life's ups and downs, whether through literally lending us a helping hand to get things done or being there to give us emotional support in tough times or encouraging us when we take on new challenges.

★ **Meaning** In addition to the meaning we get from loving and caring for those closest to us, we can get a sense of meaning from knowing that what we do makes a difference to others. That doesn't just apply to the caring, health or teaching professions, or the emergency-service workers who keep us safe. We can derive meaning from any job by knowing how it makes a difference to others. For example, a designer developing products that make people's lives easier; service agents, restaurant staff and shop workers helping customers; accountants ensuring that our money is secure and spent wisely; architects and builders developing homes for us to live in; cleaners making sure our workplaces, public buildings and streets are free from dirt and litter, and so reducing disease and accidents; even tax inspectors making sure there is enough money to deliver public services... the list goes on. And as we saw in the previous chapter, helping others can be a source of meaning too. (We'll explore meaning in Chapter 10.)

★ **Enjoyment** Apart from anything else, doing things with other people is often more fun. Sharing the experience with others increases our enjoyment of most activities, whether that's cooking together, exercising, going to the cinema, going for a walk, seeing a play or a band, travelling to other places and countries. Even our daily chores can be more fun if we do them with others.

Relationships are essential for flourishing

There is a strong base of scientific evidence showing that our social relationships are a vital ingredient for happiness and flourishing. For example, a major study of the general population in the US found that of the various factors in life that impact happiness, family relationships come out as the most important, more so than our financial situations and work (which came in second and third). And community and friends were in fourth place.

How satisfied we are with our family and friends is strongly connected with how happy we are. Feeling that we have supportive relationships is associated with higher self-esteem, better coping strategies and lower risk of psychological ill health, such as depression. Feeling you have supportive relationships at work is associated with being engaged in what you do.

The human species survived and thrived by living in social groups, so perhaps it makes sense that happiness is a direct benefit from loving, caring about and being with others. As we evolved, living in larger and larger social groups enabled us to work together and master our environment to hunt and compete with other species for resources; it protected us and helped us nurture and raise our young. In fact, it's argued that we have developed large fore-brains to help us co-exist with others. We need lots of brain power to co-operate, co-ordinate and live harmoniously with others. The big pre-frontal cortex of our brains means that we can deal with complex social problems such as balancing different people's needs, perspectives and capabilities with our own, from moment to moment. These are social puzzles that we have to solve many times each day.

Relationships are important for our physical health too. If you're asked what lifestyle factors are good for your body, what would you answer? Chances are, like most of us, you'll list: not smoking, getting enough exercise, watching your weight and drinking alcohol in moderation. But what about your social relationships? Would these feature on your list?

We might not immediately think of our relationships as important for physical health, but they are. They play a key role – as big, if not bigger, than the factors we commonly think of as important for living long and healthy lives. Studies suggest that if our social relationships are adequate in terms of quality and quantity, we can have as much as a fifty per cent greater chance of living longer – that's comparable to quitting smoking and a bigger impact than not being obese or being physically active!

Our social relationships influence our physical and psychological well-being in three key ways:

★ Having a direct positive impact on us: cognitively, emotionally, behaviourally or biologically (we'll look at these reactions in a little more detail later in this chapter, see page 67).
★ Being a source of support and a resource we can draw on when we have difficulties. In this way our social relationships can have a 'buffer' effect in tough times, reducing our stress levels, which in turn has physical benefits such as lowering cortisol, reducing blood pressure and inflammation, all of which can precede serious physical illness. Feeling that we have social support also makes it less likely we'll engage in risky behaviours such as excessive drinking.
★ Through the 'contagion' of happiness and health behaviours via our social networks. When our friends feel happy it tends to spread. We expand on this in the following pages.

The ripple effect of happy people

Our happiness is influenced not only by what we do but who is around us and how happy they are.

Scientists at Harvard University found that if someone you are in direct contact with was happy, you are fifteen per cent more likely to be happy yourself. But it doesn't stop there. If they are also in contact with someone who was happy, this has a ripple effect out to us, meaning we are ten per cent more likely to be happy. And if that person was also in contact with a happy friend, that could increase our own happiness by six per cent. So, in other words, your friend's friend's friends can impact your happiness even if you never meet them. And while these percentages might not seem especially high, compare them to the estimate that an increase of income of $10,000 equates on average to a two-per-cent potential increase in happiness. Unhappiness also spreads through our social networks, but curiously (and thankfully) its ripple effect is lower.

It's not just happiness that spreads through our social connections. If our friends and family, and people they are connected to, eat well and manage their weight, exercise regularly and don't smoke we are more likely to do so as well (and vice versa). These ripple effects work in reverse, meaning that our happiness and health behaviours are potentially impacting people we're in direct contact with and others we have never met!

Interestingly, people who are happier have also been shown to have greater interest in social activities, leading to more and higher-quality interactions and better relationships. If we are in a good mood we're more likely to expect social interactions to feel more rewarding and that we have more energy to put into them. We're also more likely to be open and share more information about ourselves, which helps build the connection. Typically we'll be perceived as more likeable by others too.

Quality versus quantity of social relationships

How many social relationships do we need to support our happiness and well-being? Well, there's no simple answer. It depends on quality as well as quantity (and, of course, personal preferences and circumstances play a part too).

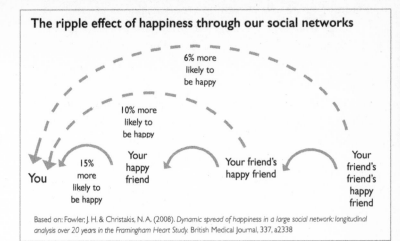

The ripple effect of happiness through our social networks

6% more likely to be happy

10% more likely to be happy

15% more likely to be happy

You

Your happy friend

Your friend's happy friend

Your friend's friend's happy friend

Based on: Fowler, J. H. & Christakis, N. A. (2008). *Dynamic spread of happiness in a large social network: longitudinal analysis over 20 years in the Framingham Heart Study.* British Medical Journal, 337, a2338

One research study found that people with three or fewer close relationships (relatives or good friends) were more likely to develop common mental illnesses such as depression. This was especially true for men. Other studies have shown that people who have at least three or four very close relationships are healthier and have increased well-being. But quality matters as well as quantity. Indeed, poor quality and problems in our close relationships can contribute to physical illness, lower immunity as well as unhappiness, depression and anxiety. So it could be argued that fewer high-quality close relationships may be better than more relationships that cause us stress, too much conflict, damage our confidence and let us down too often.

So what makes a quality relationship?

Quality relationships are those that help us feel valued, loved and cared for, where we can be ourselves, where we feel trust and the other person can be relied on. They also provide support and encouragement, companionship and intimacy, and we enjoy being part of them. As a consequence, feeling that we have quality relationships is strongly associated with better well-being, health, greater life satisfaction and relationship functioning. Having a good-quality marriage can even mean we recover from illness quicker. Feeling that we have good support available when we need it may be even better for our well-being than actually receiving it!

The nature of our interactions within a relationship has an important impact on its quality and therefore well-being. Positive exchanges with partners and children – feeling you're understood, can rely on the other person and can open up with them – are associated with a lower likelihood of depression. In contrast, negative exchanges, such as feeling criticised, being let down or annoyed by someone can increase the likelihood of depression. Negative exchanges between friends and other types of family member can also increase the likelihood of depression.

In the context of marriage, relationship expert John Gottman suggests that for relationship well-being and happiness, we should aim for five positive interactions with our significant other to every negative one. He suggests consciously aiming to achieve this balance by showing affection, saying thank you and thinking about what we value in our partners. Gottman watches five-minute clips of couples' normal behaviour and can predict with ninety-one per cent accuracy which marriages will survive and which will not, based on the quality and nature of their interactions. He says criticism, defensiveness, contempt and stonewalling are the most highly corrosive threats to the quality of relationships.

The quality of our relationships at work is also important. For example, not getting on with your boss and/or colleagues can be a significant cause of long-term absence due to stress. And feeling that you have a best friend at work can make you seven times more likely to be engaged in what you do! Later on (see page 57) we'll look at what to do to increase the quality of your relationships, small things that make a difference with your partner, as well as with friends, workmates and other connections.

Feeling lonely

Feeling lonely can be worse for us than actually being socially isolated. Although having a bigger social network is associated with higher well-being, we all vary in terms of the level of social contact we prefer. For example, we may only have one or two people in our close social circle but feel quite happy with that. Or we may have quite a lot of social contact with people but still feel lonely.

If we are lonely we are not only unhappy, but we can also feel unsafe and we are more likely to experience depression. It can be a risk factor in physical health and even dying earlier. John Cacioppo, who is a leading researcher into the effects of loneliness says, 'It doesn't just feel sad, it can be dangerous.'

As humans are a highly social species, feeling lonely is a natural response to lack of time spent with people we like and who understand us. A bit like being hungry compels us to focus attention and energy on finding food to eat, feeling lonely is a signal we've evolved to motivate us to seek more social contact. Lonely people tend to move towards the edges of their social groups. This can exacerbate the situation – being on the social perimeter it can make us more wary of others and feel less like being sociable – a vicious circle.

From an evolutionary perspective, if we didn't have safety in numbers we needed to take extra care in looking after ourselves. This protected us in the short term, but it can be detrimental to our well-being in the long term. So if we feel lonely we may not realise that we are naturally acting in more defensive and self-protective ways, which can, in turn, undermine our need to be more socially connected.

What can you do if you feel lonely? The ideas for action included in this chapter (see page 57) are examples of small things that any of us, lonely or not, can do to build our social connections and nurture close relationships over time. And the ideas put forward throughout this book can help us to be happier, which, in turn, makes it easier for us to connect with others too.

Small moments of connection have the potential to give hope that there are things we can do, even small steps that have a positive impact, triggering upward spirals in ourselves that increase our openness to, and concern for, others. So while we may not have a special person or significant other in our lives, or enough people we feel close to, we can find ways to interact more and better with other people in our day-to-day lives.

Personal communities

'Good friends are like stars. You don't always see them, but you know they're always there.'

Source unknown

Our close, secure and supportive relationships are generally the most important for our happiness and well-being, whether these are with a husband, wife or partner and/or other relatives and close friends. As well as these we are likely to have numerous connections with people across the different circles in our lives, such as at work, school or college, where we live or through our social activities, all of which can also contribute to happiness. Researchers Pahl and Spencer use the term 'personal community' to describe the set of personal relationships that we each consider important in our lives at any given time. These may include family, friends, workmates and neighbours and, of course, some people may fulfil more than one role for us – a sister might also be a best friend.

We can think of our relationships as being either 'given', such as family, or 'chosen', such as friendships that are voluntary. While tradition or culture suggests that we give highest commitment to our given relationships, this doesn't reflect the realities of modern life or, indeed, the complexities of modern families. Indeed, as the saying goes, 'You can choose your friends, but not your family', we may have relatives to whom we aren't close and where a high degree of mutual commitment does not exist. At a time when more of us live alone than ever before, this itself does not mean we are socially isolated and that we'll miss out on the positive benefits from close friends and other social connections. Indeed, it is possible to live alone and have a personal community of close connections within a large social network.

✎ Pause point…

Who are the people who are important in your life? They could be family, friends, colleagues or neighbours in your local community. Write their names on the 'map' below, placing the people who are most important for you nearer to you and those who are less close or important further away.

Your personal community

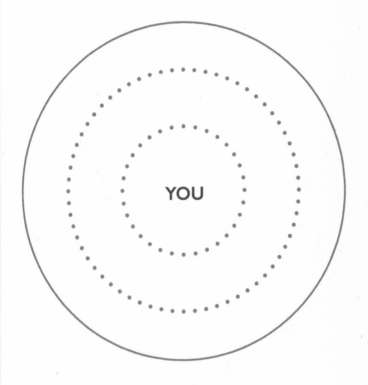

YOU

Who are the people you spend most, and least, time with?

Who do you currently give most, and least, attention and energy to?

Circle any people you'd like to more actively build, or nurture, your relationship with.

Based on: Pahl, R. & Spencer, L. (2010). Family, Friends, and Personal Communities: Changing Models-in-the-Mind. Journal of Family Theory & Review, 2(3), 197-210.

G
R
E
A
T
D
R
E
A
M

KEY TWO: RELATING

We all need friends

'Of all the things that wisdom provides to help one live one's entire life in happiness, the greatest by far is friendship.'

Epicurus

I was running a workshop on well-being and resilience in a large organisation. We were about to start an activity and I asked participants to think of two examples of recent interactions they'd had with another person: one from work and one from home. We duly completed the activity and then stopped for a break. Over a cup of coffee one of my most attentive students, a sparky thirty-something woman, pulled me aside and said, 'You really need to change "home" to "outside work",' she said. 'Not all of us are lucky enough (or not) to have a partner or spouse.' She was right. Certainly the number of single households is growing. And while much psychological research is focused on marriages or parent–child relationships, having close friends is important to us all. Having good friends is consistently and robustly associated with life satisfaction, and certainly friendships can be as important as blood ties.

Even within romantic partnerships or marriages, friendship is important. According to John Gottman, one of the world's leading experts on relationships, friendship is the biggest factor in whether both women and men are satisfied with the sex, romance and passion in their relationship. So your 'best friend' could be your 'significant other' as well.

Friendships are important throughout life. The word 'friend' enters the vocabulary as early as three or four years of age, focused on shared activities, helping us learn and develop through play. As we grow, our friendships help us feel accepted and navigate transitions (such as to middle school and to high school). Teenagers usually distinguish between 'best' friends and 'good' friends, and as well as sharing activities, these friendships also provide emotional support and intimate disclosure: 'We tell each other everything' is a description commonly heard. As adults, time is often increasingly spent with a romantic partner, but even so friendships remain important, helping to reassure us of our worth, providing companionship and practical, as well as emotional, support, with the latter characteristics being especially important into old age.

✎ **Pause point...**

What makes a lasting friendship? Think of your best friend (someone you've been close to for some time).

★ What factors contributed to you becoming friends initially?

★ What do you value most about your friend?

★ What helps you to stay close?

If you have a romantic partner, husband or wife, you may want to reflect on the above questions with them in mind too.

What makes a best friend/what helps that relationship last?

We can form our close friendships early in life, such as at school or college, or they may be people who we've met more recently and 'clicked' with or have built up a bond with over time. In terms of what makes our friendships enduring, one study asked adults about their best friendships: relationships that had endured from five years to as long as forty-nine years. Commonly, people said:

★ Sharing interests and values
★ Sharing experiences together
★ Having fun together, sharing laughs
★ Being able to relax with each other
★ Getting on well, finding each other good company
★ Being able to talk openly, sharing trust and loyalty
★ Acceptance of each other
★ Reciprocity – feeling as though the relationship was balanced overall in terms of give and take
★ Making time for each other

Interestingly, proximity didn't seem to be essential – forty-four per cent of respondents said that their best friend did not live close by.

The top personal characteristics people describe in their very best friends often include being dependable, honest, loyal, committed, kind, loving, playful and/or being fun. Their status, skills, attractiveness and accomplishments aren't seen as important.

While our best friends enhance our well-being, bad friends can compromise it. These may be people to whom we have an emotional attachment, but who aren't supportive, drain our energy or who undermine us. Potentially, bad friends can reduce our well-being more than our good friends add to the relationship. In psychologist Chris Peterson's words: 'Bad friends aren't friends at all.'

Sustaining our friendships

Our close relationships are dynamic, changing over time in response to what's going on in each of our lives, the different situations we are in, stresses and complexities, changing interests and priorities and how we're growing personally. So how do we maintain our friendships?

Relationships expert John Gottman says that being familiar with the details of our close friends' lives and their inner worlds is important for being, and staying, emotionally connected and really helps to ensure that our relationship with them lasts and is happy. Gottman refers to our 'love map' of the other person: the detailed map we have in our head of the other person and their world. This means knowing their likes, dislikes, good and bad life experiences, personality quirks and foibles, what they're enjoying or what is making them stressed and what their goals and dreams are.

We tend to naturally invest a lot of time building our map of the other person in the early stages of our relationship with them, but this can wane longer-term. We need to make sure we regularly update these mental maps by taking an active interest in what is happening for the other person. This can help them feel valued and understood too.

SUE'S SIXTY BIRTHDAY PICNICS

Sue enjoys a fulfilling life, balancing a wide range of interests with running a business. She lives alone and has never had children. In all the time I've known her, she's not been romantically involved. This isn't because she hasn't wanted to have a partner, but it just hasn't happened. However, it's not something she's let hold back her happiness. She occasionally misses having a special someone, but I have never known her to get stuck on this. She has a wide network of friends locally of all ages, around the country and in other parts of the world. She puts effort into meeting her friends and, importantly, sharing activities and experiences with them, and is always open to making new ones. She and her closest friends help and support each other when needed.

A couple of years ago Sue celebrated her sixtieth birthday. Toying with the idea of getting all her friends together for a big party she thought: 'While this would be lovely and a lot of fun, it wouldn't give me any individual time with my guests and I'm inviting them because I like them – many I haven't seen for quite some time!'

Instead she decided to have picnics with sixty people over the year. She loved picnics and so this would spread the fun out. She'd also get to spend time with friends and loved ones individually or in small groups, meaning there was time to catch up and connect properly. Given that some of the picnics would have to be in winter and in cities, Sue defined 'picnic' as sharing food and conversation in an untypical setting – so not over the dinner table or in a café or restaurant. This made it quirky and fun. Swedish friends in Paris created a Moroccan feast on the floor of their front room, one couple arranged a picnic in the foyer of a theatre, another on top of Hadrian's Wall – meaning the view was shared as well as the food. The coldest was sharing a big cake in sub-zero temperatures, in a cemetery in Berlin – creativity was required to eat the food as no one had brought a knife!

Sue achieved her goal of sixty picnics in the year and truly valued the time to share, reconnect and laugh with friends, both old and new.

Try this! Do you know your friend?

Bring to mind a close friend or a romantic partner. Can you answer these questions about them? Why not get together with them and work through the questions together?

★ Current favourite food

★ Latest hobby or interest

★ Last place they went on holiday and what they most enjoyed about it

★ What they're currently most enjoying about work/school/college

★ What they are most stressed about at the moment

★ Their happiest life event so far

★ The person who had the biggest impact on them growing up

★ What's their ideal job?

★ The first thing they'd do if they had a large surprise inheritance

★ A secret dream or ambition they hold

★ What they're most proud of about themselves

★ The goals they are currently working towards

★ Their key values

Think back to your personal community map (see page 49). Who are the people you wanted to nurture your relationships with more? Can you answer these questions with them in mind? If not, how can you update your understanding? What other questions would you ask?

Based on: Gottman, J. & DeClaire, J. (2001) *The Relationship Cure: A 5 Step Guide to Strengthening Your Marriage, Family and Friendships*. Three Rivers Press

Connecting into our local communities

While our close ties are really important for happiness, our more casual (or 'looser') connections matter too. Building our connections where we live can positively impact how we feel, increasing our sense of security and well-being. When people know and trust their neighbours they feel safer and have a greater sense of belonging. This doesn't mean you have to be best friends with everyone. Even just recognising neighbours' faces, smiling or saying hello makes a difference and means people are more likely to look out for, and help, each other. And making these small connections can pave the way for closer ones.

Robert Putnam, a professor at Harvard University, talks about the 'social capital' of an area, reflecting its level of neighbourliness, community spirit and strength of local community networks. Investing in building social capital, he says, can have a positive impact on the well-being of the community as a whole.

Bonding and bridging

Putnam describes two types of connections that are important in building social capital: 'bonding' and 'bridging'. Bonding is the network of ties that exists between people with similar social characteristics or identities (for example, income level, ethnicity or educational background). Bonding connections tend to come most easily to us because, to some degree, we share common values or cultural norms. However, connections that 'bridge' are critical to building community well-being.

Bridging connections are those that bring together people with different backgrounds, often through a shared interest. For example, living in the same street or building, being members of a neighbourhood group, having children at a local school, working together to improve the community environment or belonging to a local club or sports team.

Naturally, we are drawn to people who are more 'like us' and we are wary of those who aren't. The greater the perceived (or subconscious) difference between social groups, the more wary we will be and the more effort we may need to put into building bridges between us. But it's likely to be worth it. Bridging is powerful in terms of community cohesion as it facilitates greater trust between different groups and so has benefits for our individual and whole community well-being.

OUR STREET PARTY

Valentina and Laura, friends from Italy, moved together to London. Unlike in their home town, it was hard to get to know people locally. Everyone had busy lives, rushing to and from work, school runs or other commitments and activities.

Spotting an article about the upcoming Big Lunch Day in a free newspaper, they decided they'd take action. That week they wrote a short flyer and posted a copy through all ninety letterboxes up and down the street. It read: 'Anyone interested in helping us organise a street party on Big Lunch Day? If so please join us at 4pm outside Number 72 this coming Sunday to share ideas and make a plan.'

Around ten people turned up – some they'd never seen before, including me, and all enthusiastic and interested in helping. An organising group was formed and over the next six weeks more people got involved, making bunting, planning children's games and music, liaising with the local council about closing the street to traffic and, importantly, to connect with everyone in the street, making sure they were kept up to date with arrangements and could feel part of it.

It all came together on the day – about 150 adults and children joined in, everyone contributing food and something to drink. It was a great success and it made an impact far beyond that day.

It changed the character of the street. The children have new friends to play with, the adults are much friendlier – they smile and say hello when you pass or stop to chat, and they look out for each other and are more willing to ask for help or offer it when needed.

Building & nurturing relationships

> 'People will forget what you said, people will forget what you did, but people will never forget how you made them feel.'
>
> Source unknown, after Carl W. Buehner

Small moments matter

Our connections with other people are made up of tiny moments that can impact how we feel in the moment and add up over time to influence the quality of our relationships and our well-being. These momentary interactions can be positive, negative or neutral. They can be with strangers, acquaintances, neighbours, colleagues and our nearest and dearest. Even a few seconds count.

For example, imagine you're in a shop trying to get some advice about something you want to buy. If the shop assistant comes across as not interested, perhaps ignoring you by continuing to chat to a colleague or grumpily asking: 'What do you want?', you're likely to feel upset or angry, which can carry over to the next thing you do or the next person you meet. In contrast, if the shop assistant is friendly and keen to help, you're more likely to go away in a positive mood.

Or think about a close relationship with a friend or a partner. If your interactions with that person tend to be more positive than negative – you sense they are warm, interested and care about you, they notice what you do well and are appreciative of efforts you make. It's likely that even small moments with the person feel good and boost your well-being, whereas if they constantly criticise and moan at you, or even ignore or dismiss you, that can make you feel upset or bad in some way and, even if you are used to it, could eventually undermine your well-being. Leading researchers agree such 'micro-moments' matter in our connections with other people. They matter in the moment and they add up, little by little, over time, to help us, our relationships and even the organisations we work in, flourish. Award-winning psychologist Barbara Fredrickson even believes that we have the potential to transform lives through the multitude of tiny interactions we have day to day by finding ways to make them more positive. Her research is revealing that micro-moments of positive connection have a unique impact on our biology, boosting both our physical and our psychological well-being (we'll be looking into this science in more detail on page 67). She says it's something that everyone can experience – young, old, single, married, extrovert or introvert. It's not just our closest relationships that can be transformed, but also something we can share with anyone, even strangers.

Excitingly, recent psychological research has identified a number of different ways that we can enhance and increase the moments of positive connection we share with others across all areas of our life. These can make everyday social interactions more enjoyable, help to establish new relationships and nurture existing ones. These actions are small and simple, but they can be powerful. Knowing about them can also make us more aware of our own unconscious behaviours towards others – what's working already and, perhaps, what's not. We'll look at five of these:

1 Stop multi-tasking and start listening
2 Bump up your 'bids and turns'
3 Take your 'thank yous' to another level
4 Ask about the good stuff
5 Focus on what's right with those around you

You might want to start by trying out one and then, when you've mastered that, give another one a go. While there's no guarantee they'll work in every situation, in my experience they do work in many.

It may take us a while to spot opportunities to put these actions into practice and feel at ease when we do so, but each idea really can make a positive difference to our relationships with others and so to our happiness and that of others too.

1 Stop multi-tasking and start listening

Life is busy! There's always a lot to do. We'll cover the impact of this more fully in Chapter 4, but for now let's look at this in the context of having high-quality moments of connection with others.

Think for a moment. What do you do when someone comes to talk to you while you are in the middle of something? Perhaps your partner wants to ask a question or a friend wants to share something with you, or a child asks for your help with something or a neighbour simply wants to say hello and find out how you are. Do you, like many of us, turn your head for a moment while carrying on what you're doing – be that updating something on your smartphone, typing an email or preparing food for supper? Yes, you may glance at the other person, but your attention may dart between what you are doing and them. What message does this send to them? How does it feel when someone does this to you?

Try this! Full attention moments

If you try nothing else, try this. A number of participants in my workshops have found this simple activity has made a big difference. One, a busy manager, became aware that she was always multi-tasking when members of her team came to talk to her. After the workshop, she made herself stop what she was doing and gave them her full attention. She said she couldn't believe the difference it made. Her team members became more engaged and happier, and they got more done too.

Active listening is one of the most effective relationship and communication skills we can develop. It involves listening with our full attention and, importantly, sending non-verbal and verbal signals that we are listening. These signals show the person that we are interested in, care about and respect them.

Non-verbal signals include: eye-contact, smiling (if appropriate), an open-body posture facing towards the other person or nodding. Verbal signals include: sounds that we are listening, like 'uh huh', or 'mm hmm' or saying 'Yes, I agree' or 'I disagree' (again, as appropriate) or reflecting back our understanding of what we've heard or asking questions for clarification.

2 Bump up your 'bids and turns'

We may not realise it, but in our close relationships we make frequent small bids for each other's attention. How you respond to these bids impacts the quality of relationships and how you both feel.

Relationship expert John Gottman and his colleagues first noticed this phenomenon in their observational research on day-to-day interactions between couples. One person will make a small verbal or non-verbal gesture towards the other person (a 'bid') and in turn the other person responds (or 'turns', to use the researchers' term). They found these simple, subtle interactions happen when two people are together, even if they are doing different things. They happen many times a day. Gottman calls these tiny moments the 'micro units of intimacy'.

Imagine you are sitting in the same room as a friend. You are reading the paper and they are catching up on emails on their iPad. They briefly chuckle to themselves and you ask them what's funny. They read out a line in a message and you both laugh for a moment before each going back to what you were doing. In asking your friend what was making them laugh, you made a 'bid' and they 'turned towards' you by sharing it. Little by little, these bids and turns towards each other build and maintain the sense of intimacy between you and the other person, and that's beneficial for you both.

By contrast, you could have just ignored their chuckle or they, when asked what was making them smile, could have responded, 'Oh nothing' and carried on with their emails. These are examples of 'turning away'. In each of these instances the opportunity to connect for a moment would be missed. Or worse, you could have snapped at them to be quiet when they laughed with, 'Shh I'm trying to read, you can't be quiet for even a few minutes!' or they could have said, 'You always want to stick your nose into my business.' Both are examples of 'turning against', which is corrosive to the relationship.

Being playful and having fun and being humorous increases 'turning towards' behaviours, so increasing the sense of intimacy we have with another person, and for couples this leads to more desire, touch and sexual satisfaction.

Gottman and colleagues have found that happy couples 'turn towards' their partner's bids eighty-five per cent of the time. Overall, happy couples make up to twenty (yes twenty!) times more frequent bids and turns than unhappy couples.

Try this! Turn towards

Reflect for a moment. When your partner, husband or wife (or indeed a close friend or family member with whom you spend a lot of time) makes 'bids' towards you, how do you typically respond? Do you 'turn towards' them for a moment or do you ignore their bid?

★ Next time you are with them, notice the bids and turns, or otherwise, between you.

★ How can you increase the number of bids and 'turns towards' you make?

Based on: Gottman, J. & DeClaire, J. (2001)

3 Take your 'thank yous' to another level

Saying 'thank you' matters. Different cultures vary, but in most European and North American cultures it's important. It signals to the other person that you've noticed and appreciated what they've done, and you see and value them as a person.

Think about a recent time when someone thanked you. How did it feel? Contrast that with a time when someone didn't say thank you and you felt they should have.

It turns out that there are different levels of saying thank you and as the levels increase so does the positive impact on the other person.

★ **Level 1 – Thank you** Simply saying 'Thank you'. This shows you've recognised something the other person has done for you.

★ **Level 2 – Thank you plus** Saying 'Thank you', adding the beneficial impact of what the person has done for you. For example: 'Thank you, when you offered to help with the cooking, it took the pressure off me.'

★ **Level 3 – Thank you plus plus** Saying 'Thank you, noting the beneficial impact for you and, in addition, the positive quality or strengths you appreciate in the other person. For example: 'Thank you for offering to help with the cooking, it will really take the pressure off. I really appreciate your thoughtfulness in making time to help'. (We'll look more at strengths in Chapter 9.)

Try this! Say thank you plus

The next few opportunities you get to say thank you – at home, work, college or out and about – try experimenting moving up the levels. It may seem a bit awkward at first, but do give it a try.

What did you notice as a result?

Based on: Fredrickson, B.L. (2013)

4 Ask about the good stuff

'But friendship is precious, not only in the shade, but in the sunshine of life.'
Thomas Jefferson

An important feature of close relationships is sharing our thoughts, feelings and events that happen to us. How others respond is critical to helping us feel understood, validated and cared for.

Consider this question: What do you think is most important in terms of how your friends, family and colleagues rate the quality of your relationship with them?

A How you respond when they share bad news or difficulties with you? Or
B How you respond when they have good news to share?

Like many people, your initial instinct to the above questions is likely to have been A. Surely what's important is being there to support someone at times of difficulty? Of course, that's important, in fact I'd argue that if you aren't there to help those around you in tough times, do you really have a relationship?

In fact, psychological experiments by Shelly Gable and colleagues have found that it's not just listening and being supportive when things have gone wrong that are important for a good relationship, but also how we respond when they share news about good things that have happened to them. How we respond to people sharing good news with us has been shown to have a greater positive impact on how highly the other person rates the quality of the relationship. It also turns out that not all typical ways of responding to good news have a beneficial impact (in fact, some ways can be detrimental). Let's have a look at an example scenario on pages 64–5 in the Responding to good news box.

✎ Pause point...

How do you normally respond to people you interact with regularly? Put their names in the box that represents your most frequent way of responding to them. (Check the 'Think about it – Responding to good news' box on the next page.)

	Constructive	Destructive
Passive	**A** I acknowledge the news and move on	**B** I grab the limelight
Active	**D** I focus on them – show an active interest by asking questions; help the person relive their good news	**C** I immediately identify the downsides, risks and concerns

Often we have typical patterns of responding that we frequently use with particular people. For example, we may find that we most frequently use response A with both those closest to us and other people we interact with, or that we use D with young children, but more frequently use C with teenagers. What do you notice? Is there anyone you want to respond to more actively and constructively?

Based on: Gable, S. L., Gonzaga, G., & Strachman, A. (2006). Will you be there for me when things go right? Supportive responses to positive event disclosures. Journal of Personality and Social Psychology, 91, 904-917.

Think about it Responding to good news

You're out and about and bump into a friend. You're pleased to see each other. They say:

'Good to see you! We haven't caught up in a while. What's been happening?'

You reply:

'Good to see you too. I'm really pleased, I've just heard that I've got a new job. I'm really excited!'

Here are some different ways in which they might respond next. Reflect on the impact that each response might have on you – how might you feel? Their potential responses:

A

That's great. I'm so pleased for you. Where are you on your way to now?

B

That's great. I'm so pleased for you. I've just got a new job too. I'm really looking forward to it. It's a really top organisation and very hard to get into. There were hundreds of applicants for the role.

C

That's great. I'm so pleased for you, but I know you've got a lot going on in your personal life at the moment. Is it really a good time to change jobs? You know what it's like in a new role – you have to give 110 per cent. It could be very stressful for you at this time.

D

That's great. I'm so pleased for you. What's the new role and what are you most looking forward to about it?

Which would most actively build and nurture the relationship for you? Let's look at what the experts suggest.

These different types of responding typically have different impacts on the other person. Not all of them positive!

A **Acknowledges your news and moves on.** This is known as 'passive-constructive' responding and at best has a neutral effect on the other person. It may not hurt the relationship, but it doesn't build it either.

B **Acknowledges your news and shares a similar piece of their news.** This diverts attention from you to them, which can make you feel they aren't interested in you (known as 'passive-destructive' responding). We often respond in this way when we are trying to show the other person that we understand them by sharing a similar experience, but it has the opposite impact! Worse, it can come across as trying to outdo them. Both scenarios can be detrimental to the relationship; obviously the latter more so!

C **Immediately identifies the downsides of your good news.** This is actively destructive for the relationship. It replaces good feelings with concerns/worries. We often use this style of responding for people we care for and worry about. It causes the other person to be defensive or withdraw, meaning it can actually stop them from listening to our concerns. Does this mean we should never raise any concerns? No – especially if there are real dangers. It's about timing. If we respond actively constructively first (as in D), it helps the person feel listened to and understood and so, in turn, more open to listening to our concerns. Also we'll find out more about what aspect of the news the person is most pleased about – so we can moderate our concerns accordingly.

D **Shows an active interest by asking a few questions.** Psychologist Shelly Gable and colleagues' studies show that this is the only way of responding that actively builds the relationship. It is known as 'active-constructive' responding. It is 'active' because you are being asked about the event and 'constructive' because it builds on what went well. It signals interest, listening and it helps us relive a positive event, which is beneficial too. It also encourages us to share more, which can further build the relationship. In contrast, the other ways of responding have either a neutral or negative impact on the other person.

Try this! Responding to good news

Next time someone shares good news with you, try the following responses. Examples could be an opportunity at work, good feedback from a colleague, resolving an issue, getting fit or achieving a personal goal. Respond actively and constructively. Express interest by asking questions. Be curious and enthusiastic to hear more. Here are some examples:

★ 'Well done! When did you find out? What led up to it?'

★ 'Where are you going? What attracted you to that?'

★ 'Great! Tell me all about it. Who was involved? When did it happen? '

★ 'I'm so pleased for you. That's fantastic! I want to hear all about it.'

Reflect on what you notice about the impact your new approach has on the other person. How does that feel for you? Which would most actively build on, and nurture, your relationship?

5 Focus on what's right with those around you

Think of the last two or three interactions you had with someone close to you. What were you focusing on? Perhaps you noticed something you like, appreciate or admire in them; or maybe your attention was on something you find irritating or wished would change.

One of the foundations for a happy relationship is knowing and staying focused on the magic – what we like/love about the other person. In contrast, what can cause relationships to fail is a drip-feed of criticism. Yet it is so easy to fall into this trap, especially in established relationships. After all, as human beings, we naturally tend to focus on what's wrong rather than what's right (see Chapter 8 for more). Familiarity, it seems, really can breed contempt if we're not aware of what we're focusing on.

We need to make an effort to focus on what's right. And it's not just in marriages and close friendships that this technique works. Recent studies, where therapists and coaches spent a few minutes thinking about their client's strengths before meeting with them increased the connection between the therapist/coach and the client, and led to more successful outcomes from their sessions together.

I have tried this in a range of contexts and have found it really helps. It's also helpful if I want to raise a difficult issue, helping me to moderate my approach, rather than launching into a list of the issues as I see them!

Try this! Focus on what's right

Here a few simple things to try. You may want to make these a habit!

★ Before spending time with your partner, a family member, colleague or friend, bring to mind the things you value about them – their strengths. No need to tell them you're doing this. After spending time with someone, take a few moments to reflect on the things you appreciated about them during your interaction.

★ You may find that you want to tell your partner or friends what you value about them. This is great to do, especially if you give them real, specific examples to illustrate what you mean.

What impact does this have on the quantity and quality of the positive moments of connection you have?

The science of connection

Positive moments of connection have an emotional base – they feel good, but like all emotions they are short-lived. They occur and then fade in seconds or minutes, but can be renewed and repeated.

Like all emotions, they're not just feelings, they are accompanied by natural physiological responses that influence what we do next. For most emotions this chain of reactions, from mind and body to behaviour, happens individually. However, uniquely in moments of positive connection with another, this chain of reactions is shared between us.

When two or more people connect over a shared pleasant or positive emotion, whether it is mild or strong, it sets up a series of unconscious physiological reactions within and between them. Our subtle micro-behaviours start to mirror each other (known as 'bio-behavioural synchrony') and this leads to an increased willingness to care for each other's well-being. Psychologist Barbara Fredrickson says it's as if, for a moment, energy reverberates and is amplified back and forth between people (she calls this 'positivity resonance'). Experiencing positive emotion feels good and momentarily opens us up, expanding our awareness so that we literally perceive more, in turn enabling us to be more flexible in our thinking and responses, more creative and more open to others (see also Chapter 8). When we share a positive emotion with others, it momentarily blurs the boundaries between us and amplifies the beneficial impact, and this is potentially powerful.

Two brains become one

It used to be thought that communicating – sharing a story and listening to it – were two processes, happening separately in different brains, but actually it's a single, shared process performed by two brains. 'This isn't a Jedi mind trick,' said Uri Hasson, the scientist who led this discovery, 'This is communication. It's what human beings do best and it's unique and amazing.' Imagine you're waiting for a train and you find yourself chatting to a stranger and they start to share a story. You find yourself listening closely. In your head at that moment, parts of your brain are being activated – in exactly the same areas as in the storyteller's own brain. As his/her brain activity shifts, so does yours. The more closely you listen and understand the story as it progresses, the more closely your brains are activated in parallel, a phenomenon known as 'brain coupling'. You are literally on the same wavelength at that moment! And it's much more extensive than earlier studies on mirror neurons suggested. (Mirror neurons are brain cells that help us feel empathy and connection with others. They fire when we do something and also when we observe another's experience. For example, if we see someone stub their toe, we also wince.)

The brains of the most intent listeners: those with the deepest, most accurate, understanding of the story, weren't just following the brain activation of the person they were listening to, their own brains were anticipating those patterns. When we share positive emotional moments, such as a laughing, common interests, when we have a sense of 'getting' the other person, brain coupling is greater. This opens us up to the other person and our propensity to care about each other is enhanced.

This coupling of our brains with other people enables us to co-ordinate far more complex behaviours than we could do alone, such as playing music together or working as a team. Our brains induce similar brain patterns in response to facial and hand gestures too. And the better we know someone, the tighter our brain coupling is likely to be.

Keep calm and connect

You may have heard of oxytocin, the 'love' or 'cuddle' hormone, as it is sometimes known. Human beings need social interactions not just to survive but to thrive, and oxytocin is central in facilitating this. We produce oxytocin as a result of interactions with others and, in turn, it induces in us behaviours that enable social bonding such as eye contact, social recognition and trust. It surges at pivotal moments such as birth and sexual intercourse, increasing our bonds at those times, but it also ebbs and flows less dramatically, but still importantly, during day-to-day interactions with others.

Social interactions can be scary or threatening, which would naturally cause us to disengage from the situation. Oxytocin calms our fears, making us more willing to connect and display gestures of friendliness, which in turn increases oxytocin in the other person, triggering a spiral of mutual connection, responsiveness, trust and care. This is pronounced between parents and infants, but it also occurs in other interactions, including with strangers, increasing the potential for them to become part of our social network.

Oxytocin is part of our 'calm-and-connect' response (in contrast to our more well-known 'fight-or-flight' response). Our brains are more open to positive social opportunities and less sensitive to threats, helping us deal with social challenges less stressfully.

The increase in our oxytocin levels makes us see others as more attractive and trustworthy. This could leave us gullible, however, it also makes us more attuned to others and so more able to pick up on subtle and non-verbal cues as to whether their motives can be trusted or not. For example, we're hard-wired to pick up on, and respond to, smiles and are acutely sensitive to whether they are genuine or not. Genuine (or 'Duchenne') smiles trigger tiny muscles that aren't under our conscious control to cause creases at the corner of our eyes when we give a heartfelt smile. Genuine smiles are infectious, so if someone smiles at us, it's hard not to return it. In contrast, we subconsciously pick up on smiles that don't involve the eyes, making us instinctively wary of the motives of the other person.

In addition to smiling, experiencing shared positive emotions triggers other non-verbal gestures, which in turn make us seem friendlier and more approachable. These include lifting and expanding the chest, increasing our use of open-hand gestures (such as showing an outstretched palm), subtly leaning towards the other person and increasing the frequency with which we nod our head to show our affirmation and acceptance of them and what they are saying. We also tend to mirror their body language.

Unbeknown to you, these reactions, among others, are being co-ordinated by your vagus nerve. This nerve travels from deep within your brain to your heart, stomach and other internal organs. It helps you to make eye contact, synchronise your facial expressions with those of other people and helps your ears track voices against background noise – all of which help you tune into, and connect with, other people.

Along with oxytocin, the vagus nerve is another key part of our 'calm and connect' response and it helps restore us after we've experienced danger or anxiety. In those states, adrenalin pumps, our heart rate quickens and our bodies prepare to fight or flee. The vagus nerve returns us to normal.

Upward spirals of connection
On a less dramatic level, the vagus nerve also regulates our heart rate with our breath, subtly increasing our heart rate when we breathe in

(to speed the flow of oxygenated blood around the body) and slowing it down when we breathe out. The difference between our heart rate when we breathe in and when we breathe out is called 'vagal tone'. The greater the difference between our heart rate on inhalation and exhalation, the 'higher' our vagal tone is said to be. Higher vagal tone is associated with a range of benefits for physical and emotional health through being better able to respond and adapt. It also has benefits socially. People with higher vagal tone have been shown to be better able to navigate interactions with others and build connection, and hence experience more positivity resonance. In fact, psychologist Fredrickson describes our level of vagal tone as our capacity for micro-moments of positive connection (or, in her words, 'love').

Our vagal tone isn't something we are consciously aware of, but scientists can measure it with specialist equipment. At rest it tends to be stable over time. So does that mean we're either lucky to be born with high vagal tone or not? Well, it was thought that it was more or less fixed, like our height. However, recent research is showing that this is not necessarily the case. It appears that by consciously generating positive emotions we can change our vagal tone, leading to more social connection which, in turn, has physical and psychological health benefits.

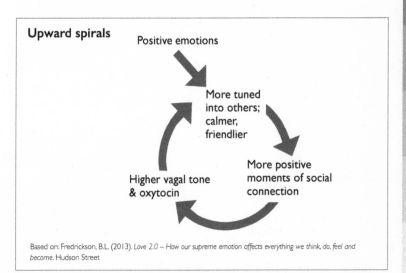

Upward spirals

Positive emotions

More tuned into others; calmer, friendlier

More positive moments of social connection

Higher vagal tone & oxytocin

Based on: Fredrickson, B.L. (2013). *Love 2.0 – How our supreme emotion affects everything we think, do, feel and become.* Hudson Street

KEY TWO: RELATING

In a remarkable experiment by Bethany Kok, Barbara Fredrickson and colleagues, participants were trained in a form of meditation known as 'Loving Kindness' (see Chapter 4), increasing their individual capacity to self-generate positive emotions through focusing on compassion for self and for others. This increased their vagal tone and, in turn, increased the frequency of positive moments they experienced in day-to-day social connections, which created yet higher vagal tone (and oxytocin) leading to a greater likelihood of more positive social connections. In other words, an 'upward spiral' of positive connection. Further, recent scientific research is suggesting that over time this starts to structurally change our brain in ways that facilitate further positive connection, leading to healthy social bonds, not just in infants, but in adults too. As Fredrickson says, 'Simply put, love changes your mind.'

Tips for dealing with difficulties

In any relationship there will be things we disagree on that cause conflict. It's normal and can be healthy, a chance to air views, needs/concerns and understand the other better. Being able to do this is important for our own happiness, as well as for the quality of relationships.

Sooner is better than later

Many of us avoid conflict as we don't want to cause upset. But that means irritations can fester, leading to resentments and contempt – toxic for the relationship and sometimes causing us to explode over something small. This leaves the other person wondering where that came from, unaware we had been quietly seething inside! Sharing niggles before they grow helps the other person understand us better and means they can do the same. Over time this can help you get closer or at least be clear about how you differ! Relationship expert Gottman suggests that about two-thirds of conflicts in both happy and unhappy relationships are unsolveable, often persisting for years – so it is key to recognise this, accept these differences and find ways to defuse issues when they arise.

The first three minutes

The way we approach and deal with conflicts is important for the quality of the relationship. Gottman says that the first three minutes of any conflict is particularly vital. These minutes set the tone and determine whether the conversation is constructive or escalates. A gentle opening (what Gottman calls a 'softened start-up') is most likely to lead to a successful outcome. Softened start-ups help us avoid some of the ways we can trigger a defensive, hurt or angry response. It's important to avoid the other person feeling overly criticised or diminished such as blaming their character rather than focusing on the incident.

Tips for a 'softened start-up'

Be clear about the specific issue and why it's important for you. Generalising, as in: 'You *always* leave the door open', can trigger defensiveness in the other person and mean they are less likely to take on board the issue you're raising. They'll focus on the time they didn't do what you are complaining about! So keep focused on specific situation(s). You might also find it effective to highlight a positive example of when they actually did what you're asking of them: 'When I came back from that work trip and you'd tidied the bathroom. It was a nice surprise.' This isn't always easy. Staying calm, focused on the issue (rather than bringing up a back catalogue of irritations) and being clear on why it matters to you requires management of our own emotional state. We'll look at tips for this in Chapters 4 and 7. It's vital to keep it focused – staying on track with one issue rather than spinning out to several; simply stating the facts and how you feel rather than going on and on.

One approach I've found helps I learned from Dr Marshall Rosenberg. It's a core building block of what he calls 'Nonviolent Communication' (NVC) – based on compassionate communication. It has been used to build relationships and resolve conflicts across the world. The starting point for NVC is that we all share the same basic human needs and that each of our actions/behaviours is a strategy to meet one or more of these. Many of the difficulties in relationships come from us not being clear and/or not communicating what our needs are, or from someone feeling that their needs are not being met. When our needs are not met an emotional response can be triggered. Just being more aware that needs underlie emotional reactions in others and ourselves can help us to navigate conflict better. Other people can trigger our feelings, but the choice is ours about how we respond. We'll explore this idea more in Chapter 7.

NVC provides a simple framework to enable us to identify/communicate what our needs are in different situations, look beneath the surface of our own (and others') feelings and help us understand our values better. There are five steps to help you prepare for, and have, your conversation:

1 **Notice your judgements** We often jump to conclusions about what's behind another's behaviours, why someone is doing something or what they should do. If we act on these judgements without expressing them or asking about the person's needs it can lead to miscommunication at best, and at worst disagreements, without either understanding what was important to the other.

2 **Be a neutral observer** Identify the facts, taking a neutral perspective. What would someone uninvolved in the situation observe?

3 **Name your feelings** What did you feel when it happened?

4 **State your needs** What are your needs behind your feelings?

5 **What's your request** What specific thing would you like to ask the other person to do in order to meet your needs?

For example: 'When you don't answer (observation), I feel hurt (feelings) because I need to know you've listened (needs). I'd really like it if you'd respond when I'm telling you something (request).

Although the steps of NVC are simple, they take practice and patience. Try to stay in the conversation until you feel you have been understood and have understood the other person, which may take a few turns of each of you expressing feelings/needs. By truly understanding each other's needs we can find a way that works for both. It will help to eliminate ongoing irritation that can lead to frustration/criticism.

Listen for the other person's attempts at repair and build on these as they de-escalate the situation and help you both move towards resolution. For example, if you are raising an issue about tidying up the kitchen and a family member says, 'I didn't think about how things got tidied away,' don't respond with a sarcastic: 'Well, things don't get put away by magic.' Rather respond with: 'Food left out bothers me as it can go off and it's unhygienic. It would make a real difference for me if you could put things back in the fridge after you've finished and wipe up any crumbs.'

To sum up

Here are five key points to take away from this chapter:

1 Our relationships are an essential ingredient to happiness – so nurturing them is good for us and for others too.
2 Quantity/quality of relationships both matter – quality matters more.
3 Seconds count – we build/nurture relationships a few moments at a time, so it's important to be aware of momentary interactions with others, which means there are evidence-based actions we can take to increase positive interactions and so strengthen connections.
4 Giving attention, being an active listener and responding constructively to good news are core skills for building/nurturing relationships.
5 Close ties are the most important for happiness, but bridging to others in our community makes a difference too.

Connections to other Keys

Other keys you might like to explore in connection with Relating:

★ **AWARENESS** (See page 108)
Loving kindness is a form of meditation that fosters compassion and connection.

★ **RESILIENCE** (See page 198)
• Understanding the thoughts that underlie our feelings can help us manage our reactions and enable more constructive communication and connection.

• Our connections with others are a source of resilience.

★ **EMOTIONS** (See page 238)
A more detailed look at the science of positive emotions.

★ **ACCEPTANCE** (See page 266)
• Being clear on our strengths and values can help us understand what's important to us in our relationships and what we bring to them.

• Seeing the strengths of others helps us value and appreciate them for who they are. It's a foundation for great relationships.

★ **MEANING** (See page 298)
Our relationships can be a key source of meaning in our lives.

3

EXERCISING

Take care of your body

Looking after your body looks after your mind, and new research into the brain is showing just how important this can be. It's a great route towards feeling happier and functioning better – fast.

Exercising: introduction

> 'Our bodies are our gardens — our wills are our gardeners.'
>
> William Shakespeare, *Othello*

Moving for our minds

A growing body of compelling evidence is now showing us that physical activity is just as important for our minds as it is for our bodies. In fact, leading Harvard psychiatrist, John Ratey, argues that, in his view, the primary purpose of moving is not for our bodies, it's to maintain the functioning and condition of our brains.

It seems that exercise really can be medicine. The idea of the 'runner's high' – the feel-good factor that most people get during or following exercise – is widely known about. In fact, physical activity has been shown to help us cope with stress and so increase our resilience, protect us from psychological ill health and keep our brains working well as we get older. It can be an effective treatment for depression and anxiety, among other conditions. And it even goes beyond this – to actually changing the structure, size and functioning of our brains. Any movement that results in expending more energy than we do when we are in resting mode can be beneficial, whether it's a structured exercise regime or woven into other activities in our daily lives.

As nature intended

We've evolved over hundreds of thousands of years to be precisely suited to the natural environment. However, in recent times our way of life has dramatically changed and how we use our bodies today is significantly different from how we have behaved for millennia before.

In many ways the way we live our lives now is quite astonishing. We can do a full day's work or connect with colleagues or customers around the world from the comfort of our own desks – whether we are at home or in an office. We can easily travel significant distances. We have an abundance of food from around the globe readily available in our local shops and boundless opportunities for entertainment or connection at the click of a mouse or a swipe of our screen. As fantastic as all this is, it's contributing to ill health now and raising the potential for it in the future. Our bodies are simply not designed for the life we lead today. Indeed, it has been suggested that for the first time in history the younger generation may live less-healthy lives than their parents. Importantly, this isn't just impacting on our bodies, it's also affecting how we feel, making us more likely to be unhappy.

A magic bullet?

If you were offered something that would help you feel happy, healthy and stay that way, with virtually no side effects – would you go for it? Well, it seems that there is something like this available to us already. Dr Ray Fowler, clinical psychologist and former American Psychological Association President, emphasised this very point in a lecture I once attended, 'Exercise is the closest thing we have to a magic bullet for health – physical and mental.'

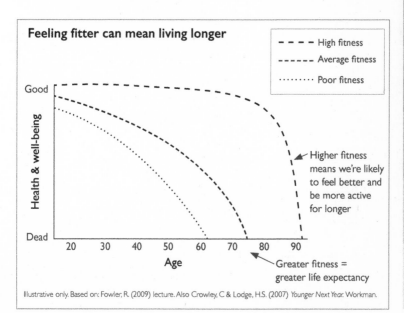

Feeling fitter can mean living longer

- – – – High fitness
- – – – – Average fitness
- ·········· Poor fitness

Health & well-being (Good to Dead)

Higher fitness means we're likely to feel better and be more active for longer

Greater fitness = greater life expectancy

Age — 20 30 40 50 60 70 80 90

Illustrative only. Based on: Fowler, R. (2009) lecture. Also Crowley, C & Lodge, H.S. (2007) *Younger Next Year*. Workman.

We are all born to be physically active. It doesn't matter if you are naturally athletic or not. Our bodies need to move, whether through structured, deliberate exercise or physical activity that is a natural part of other things we do, such as getting from A to B, doing the housework or our paid work.

Not being active reduces the quality and length of our life. It's now well established that lack of physical activity increases the likelihood of us having at least thirty-five different chronic diseases, making our bodies less comfortable and our lives less enjoyable as we get older – and it increases our risk of dying early.

If you aren't very physically active at the moment, you're not alone. In the UK and US many of us don't reach the recommended levels of activity. But there's hope. The good news is that you can make a significant improvement to your happiness and your health by moving about more and weaving activity into your everyday life... you don't even need to join a gym!

 Pause point...

1 What ways of being physically active and exercising have you most enjoyed in your life – as a child, teenager or earlier in your adult life? What was it about these activities that you most enjoyed?

2 What ways of being physically active and exercising do you mostly do now?
Of these, which do you most enjoy? What is it, specifically, that you enjoy?

3 What new ways of being active do you think you'd enjoy trying?

Reflecting on your answers to the first question – is there anything you can learn from your younger self to help you enjoy moving more now?

Mark was a successful management consultant working for one of the best consultancies in the world and heading up big, high-profile projects. He also suffered from constant back pain.

He'd seen top doctors and orthopaedic surgeons and their diagnoses were the same – a herniated disk and misaligned spine caused by a hereditary spinal disorder. The pain would continue, he was advised, and it was likely to get worse. Mark had stopped exercising and some days he couldn't even get out of bed or walk. He was angry, frightened and depressed.

Mark's wife, Kate, was training to be an osteopath and had come across a book called *Back Sense*. She thought it might helpful so she asked Mark to take a look at it. The book explained that often back pain comes about as a result of muscle tension caused by underlying stress and anxiety. If these fail to be acknowledged and managed, they often manifest as physical pain instead.

At first Mark wasn't convinced. He'd been told his back problems were structural and not a single expert he'd seen had mentioned emotions. Yet, as he thought about it, he realised that not only was he finding his high-pressure job stressful, it was making him miserable too. He decided to try out some of the book's advice. He started mindfulness meditation to help him relax and within weeks his pain had subsided, so much that he was able to play sport again.

Being able to think more clearly, Mark realised his back pain was most likely due to stress, so he decided he needed to change his career to do something that made a bigger social difference. Now, twelve years on and pain-free, Mark's career has moved in that direction and he now leads 'Action for Happiness'.

Walking the talk, he is aware of how looking after his body helped his mind function at its best. He is fitter than ever and he also knows that his back serves as an early-warning signal if he becomes stressed.

Recently he's taken up cycling and discovered that it's his passion. 'It's definitely helped to find something physical I love to do. I used to run but I didn't enjoy it that much – cycling is the answer for me.'

KEY THREE: EXERCISING

Moving makes us happy

'All people in a bad mood should go for a walk, and if it does not improve, walk again.'

Hippocrates

The benefits of being active

If the positive impact of being active on our physical health isn't enough to boost our happiness alone, the potential effects on our psychological well-being should be! Science is showing that physical activity gets your heart beating faster than when it is at rest (such as brisk walking, jogging, running, cycling or swimming). It can:

1 **Increase our happiness,** both shorter and longer-term
2 **Boost our resilience,** helping us to manage stress and anxiety
3 **Keep our brain in shape,** maintaining how well it functions now and as we get older
4 **Reduce unhappiness,** preventing and treating depression

Let's look at each of these areas in a bit more detail.

1 Being physically active increases happiness

★ **It boosts our mood** It turns out that many studies suggest that Hippocrates was right about moving being good for our mood. People generally feel more positive, less negative, more energised and less fatigued after being physically active. As little as twenty minutes' moderate-intensity exercise can have a beneficial effect on our mood that lasts from between two and twelve hours after we've exercised. That's not a bad return on investment for a few minutes a day!

★ **It helps us feel good about ourselves** Our body image (how we see, feel, think and act towards our bodies) can be enhanced by participation in exercise. Exercise can both reduce dissatisfaction with our bodies and increase our positive feelings towards our physical selves. Regular exercisers are more likely to experience these positive

Top tips Feeling good from exercise

★ **Don't be put off at the start!** So if you haven't exercised for some time, your first session might be tough until you are familiar with what you are doing and with your environment. The mood-boosting benefits from exercising seem to be greatest for regular exercisers.

★ **Focus on enjoyment rather than on your weight or appearance**
Our reasons for exercising make a difference. Curiously, focusing on the health benefits and on enjoyment seems to have a greater positive benefit for how we feel about our bodies than focusing on improving our appearance and weight loss. Perhaps this is because visible changes to our bodies take time and can overshadow the more immediate benefits from a positive emotional boost.

★ **Our self-esteem increases as our fitness does** Regardless of how fit we are or what our level of self-esteem is before we start to exercise, the greatest boost seems to come as our fitness levels improve. For example, in one study participants were randomly assigned either to an exercise programme in which they did three aerobic sessions per week for ten weeks, or to a control group that received no assigned exercise. Those in the exercise group showed increased self-esteem during and at the end of the programme compared to the no-exercise group.

See: Buckworth et al (2007); Homan & Tylka (2014); Biddle & Mutrie (2007)

benefits. This is important since poor body image and low self-esteem, experienced by both men and women, is linked with depression, anxiety and with the likelihood of detrimental health behaviours such as smoking, excessive alcohol consumption and extreme dieting.

2 Being physically active boosts our resilience
★ **It helps us manage stress** Stress is a part of everyday life for many of us, and exercise can help us deal with it. For example:
  • A single exercise session can help reduce immediate emotional distress and feelings of anxiousness. People who are more physically active report fewer incidences of these symptoms.
  • It buffers us from emotional effects of stress, making us less likely to react strongly when things go wrong and recover quickly if they do.

Top tip Remember to exercise if you're stressed

People who have an exercise habit are more likely to recognise that it helps and so use it as a coping mechanism during tough times. Those who don't exercise regularly might not think of turning to it when they are stressed, despite its potential to help. So if that's the case for you, why not add in some exercise alongside the other things you do to help you manage your stress?

See: Homan & Tylka (2014); Faulkner, Hefferon & Mutrie (2015)

- Exercise can serve as a distraction from our worries and it can help us get to sleep quicker, sleep better for longer and more deeply.
★ **Exercise can help reduce, manage or even prevent anxiety.**
  - Regular exercise can help to reduce our general predisposition towards anxiety.
  - Studies show that those of us who are more anxious and less fit tend to experience the most benefit from exercising more.
  - Exercise can help people with clinical anxiety to manage the condition and it can be effective as a treatment.

3 Being physically active keeps our brain in shape

★ **It can make the brain function better** Growing evidence is showing that physical activity can help children and teenagers learn and do well at school. Kids who do more regular aerobic exercise have been shown to improve in maths, literacy, problem-solving and creativity. And time spent on exercise during the school day (so less time in the classroom) doesn't impair academic performance.

As adults, it can help us to perform too. In the view of psychiatrist John Ratey, 'Aerobic activity – it's an indispensible tool for anyone who wants to reach his or her full potential.' He once advised after a lecture – if you've a tough meeting or exam coming up, get out and do some exercise before it, you'll do better. Or as Nelson Mandela remarked, 'I found that I worked better and thought more clearly when I was in good physical condition.'

★ **It benefits us as we age.** We may think cognitive decline is inevitable, but it seems that it doesn't always have to be that way.

Top tips Exercising as we get older

★ **It's not too late** Don't worry if you've not been very active in your life so far – it may not be too late. A review of eighteen early studies (published between 1966 and 2001) looked at how fitness training impacted the cognitive functioning of previously sedentary fifty-five-year-olds. It found unequivocally that exercise had positive benefits for a range of cognitive functions. The biggest effects were for 'executive functioning' (scheduling, planning, working memory, multi-tasking and coping with ambiguity, etc). This has also been shown in later reviews.

★ **Mix it up** Combining aerobic activity with resistance training may have the greatest benefits for older adults. In the above study, aerobic training was effective but the best impact was found in:

- Sessions of between thirty-one and forty-five minutes that persisted for six months or more.
- Programmes which combine aerobic and resistance training.

Recently it's emerged that tai chi may be one of the most beneficial forms of exercise for maintaining cognitive functioning in older adults. It typically combines aerobic, resistance and flexibility training. Perhaps science is catching up with ancient wisdom and the millions of Chinese older people who practise tai chi each day!

See: Hillman et al (2008); Smith et al (2010); Colcombe & Kramer (2003), Kelly et al (2014)

When scientists have followed large populations over a period they have consistently found that physically active adults tend to have better cognitive functioning later in life and are less likely to experience cognitive decline, dementia or Alzheimer's. One review of sixteen studies showed that people who were highly active had a twenty-eight per cent lower risk of dementia and a forty-five per cent lower risk of Alzheimer's than people with low levels of physical activity.

Exercise keeps our brains healthier. Studies looking at the brain images of older adults found that those with higher aerobic fitness have significantly less age-related tissue wastage, greater grey- and white-matter density and greater volume in certain key brain areas (they have healthier brains than the less fit or sedentary).

4 Being physically active can decrease unhappiness

★ **Exercise can help prevent depression** There is strong evidence that regular physical activity sustained over time helps prevent depression. For example, a recent study of over 26,000 working women found that physical activity (taking into account both duration and intensity of activity) reduced the risk of mental ill health four years later, regardless of social–economic status, lifestyle, physical health and body mass index.

- The UK National Health Service suggests that we are thirty per cent less likely to experience illness if we meet recommended activity levels (see page 91).
- Research shows that something is better than nothing – even as little as ten minutes per day walking at normal pace can make a difference.
- More activity is better. The more active we are, both in terms of the intensity and amount of time we exercise, the greater the protective benefits are. Conversely, reducing activity levels increases the risk of being depressed.

★ **Exercise can help treat depression** Doctors increasingly prescribe exercise as a first-line treatment for mild to moderate depression as it can be effective for this. They may also suggest that physical activity is combined with other treatments. Medication can relieve symptoms faster. However, longer-term, exercising more can mean we're less likely to be depressed and it may also enhance our sense of self-efficacy in managing the illness. While there is no single proven way to treat depression, exercise can certainly be part of a holistic approach. As it's low-cost or free it can help some sufferers manage their condition themselves and sustain greater well-being in the long term.

Top tip Every little helps

If you are feeling low or lacking in energy, getting started with exercise is often the biggest challenge. This is because we can get stuck in a vicious cycle: having no energy stops us being physically active and not being active means we have low, or no, energy. The best advice is to start soon with at least a small amount of activity. If you don't usually do any physical activity, then walking around the block for five minutes each day at a pace that feels a little brisk for you is an achievement and you can build up from there (see Julie's story for inspiration, page 95).

Try this! Planning ahead

Think of an event or occasion coming up at work, home or school for which you want your brain to be performing at its best.

★ Can you schedule thirty minutes just before it to do some exercise? If you are used to running, swimming or cycling, try that. If you aren't a regular exerciser yet, use that time to go for a brisk walk.

★ What did you notice? Did your mind feel clearer? Were you more energised or less nervous? Did you perform better than you might have done otherwise?

Most people find that they work better and think more clearly when they are in good physical condition.

Sitting less may make us happier too!

It looks as if taking the weight off our feet might not always be good for happiness. It seems that moving more isn't just about being physically active, we need to take care not to sit still for too long either. Given that being sedentary is known not to be good for our cardiovascular and metabolic health, it's reasonable to hypothesise that it may affect psychological well-being too. And evidence for this is emerging.

Sitting and happiness

In 2015, the first study of the relationship between sedentary behaviour and positive emotions found that the two were inversely related. The longer we sit per day, the less frequently we experience positive emotions and this leads to lower psychosocial resources (as we'll see in Chapter 8). In contrast, sitting less had the opposite effect. This was over and above the mood boost we get from being active, showing that being sedentary could be a separate issue for happiness, as it is for physical health.

Sitting and unhappiness

There is also a growing body of research showing an association between sitting and depression. For example, a study of 3,645 women between eighteen and forty-five years of age found that higher overall sitting time was linked to a greater likelihood of being depressed. Of course, people who are depressed may well be more inclined to be sedentary. However it looks as if sitting increases the likelihood of being depressed. There also seems to be a link between sitting and anxiety. The first review of studies looking at this was published in 2015. It suggests that the more time we spend being sedentary, the more likely we are to suffer anxiety, and the longer the sitting time the greater the risk of it. So how much, or how little, sitting should we aim for? Well, it's too early to be definitive, but I'd say err on the side of caution and don't sit down for too long at a time (aim for no more than thirty minutes in one go, before getting up) or in total. As Australian researchers put it, 'Stand up, sit less, move more, more often.'

Try this! Your own time & motion study

★ During the hours you are awake, when are you the most, and least, physically active? What are you doing at those times?

★ How long, in total, do you sit or recline per day (not including when you are asleep)? Is it seven, or more, hours?

★ Thinking about the time you are sitting or reclining – how frequently is that broken up by standing up or moving at work and at home?

★ How can you break up your sedentary time every thirty minutes or so, and how could you stand more?

★ Thinking about your typical week overall. Do you meet the guidelines for moderate-to-vigorous physical activity (see page 92)? If not, how could you start being more active?

Brains & movement

> 'To keep the body in good health is a duty...
> otherwise we shall not be able to keep our minds
> strong and clear.'
>
> The Buddha

Miracle-Gro for the brain

Why does moving more have such a positive impact on our brains? Well, it seems that our brains and movement are inextricably linked. Exciting new research shows that aerobic activity, such as brisk walking, trotting and running leads to growth of new brain cells and greater protection for existing ones.

When we exercise we produce more of a family of specific proteins called 'neurotrophins', which play a major role in the development of new brain cells, maintenance of existing ones and regulation of brain activity. Of these, one known as 'brain-derived neurotrophic factor', or BDNF for short, is one of the most important. In his book *Spark*, psychiatrist John Ratey describes it as Miracle-Gro for the brain. It literally causes us to produce more new brain cells. And it's thought that its effect may be the by-product of our bodies' adapting to a hunter-gather lifestyle.

Human beings have disproportionately large brains: perhaps three times bigger than might be expected relative to our body size. However, it wasn't always so. It's thought our growth in brain size happened about two million years ago, when we became hunter-gatherers (as well as starting to live in larger social groups). We started to compete with carnivores for food and needed to out-manoeuvre them and our animal prey. Since both were capable of much higher speeds than us, we evolved an ability to outlast them. Our ancestors' bodies became uniquely adapted to covering long distances at a gentle trotting pace. We'd track our prey, say an early antelope-type creature, and since these were capable

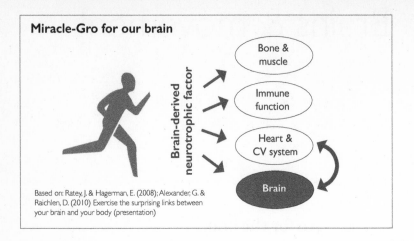

Miracle-Gro for our brain

Brain-derived neurotrophic factor

- Bone & muscle
- Immune function
- Heart & CV system
- Brain

Based on: Ratey, J. & Hagerman, E. (2008); Alexander, G. & Raichlen, D. (2010) Exercise the surprising links between your brain and your body (presentation)

of short sprints but not running long distances, we'd pursue them until they were exhausted. Known as 'persistence hunting', this technique is still practised to this day by some African bushmen.

In contrast with other primates, such as chimps, with whom we share common ancestors, our limbs, muscles, cardiovascular system and metabolism became well suited to this type of activity. In fact, human capabilities are unique – no other primate species is able to endure long-distance running as well as we can. Some researchers say we are designed to be the best endurance runners on the planet. And BDNF is what facilitates this.

When we exercise, BDNF (and other factors produced during exercise) plays a key role in helping to ensure that more oxygen is delivered to our muscles, resulting in better aerobic performance. BDNF and its counterparts stimulate tissue and vascular system growth and repair. So as our bodies adapted to running over long distances it caused our brains to grow and develop.

The evidence for the link between movement and brains extends across species – the structure and size of the brain in different animals being adapted to their typical form of movement. There is also evidence that this relationship can work in reverse. Take koala bears. They once consumed a varied diet and needed to move around to maintain this.

However, over time, they started to eat only eucalyptus leaves. Given that there is a plentiful supply of such trees in their native habitat, Australia, it meant that koalas no longer needed to move very much. They just had to sit in eucalyptus trees munching leaves all day. As a consequence their brains shrank and today are much smaller than the capacity of koala skulls, which haven't quite caught up yet. A cautionary tale for our increasingly sedentary lifestyle, perhaps.

Physical activity and the mind

As we have already explored, there are many ways in which being physically active helps us to be happier, more resilient and to keep our brains functioning well, but how much is enough? Guidelines for the amount of exercise we need to keep us physically healthy are well established, based on scientific evidence accrued over decades.

We don't yet have recommended amounts for our psychological well-being as this body of research is much more recent. But we don't need to wait for formal recommendations. What's most important for both our bodies and our minds is that we do something rather than nothing. As Professor John Ratey suggests, 'A little is good, but more is better.'

Aiming for the recommended amounts of activity for physical health is a good bet. The World Health Organisation guidelines current at time of writing (UK and US guidelines are in line with these):

★ A minimum of 150 minutes of moderate-intensity aerobic physical activity per week, or 75 minutes' vigorous-intensity aerobic physical activity, or an equivalent combination of moderate and vigorous intensities. (See page 92 for what counts as 'moderate' or 'vigorous'.)
★ Aerobic activity should be performed in bouts of ten minutes or more.
★ Strengthening activity should be incorporated at least twice per week.
★ For additional health benefits, increase moderate-intensity aerobic physical activity to 300 minutes per week or vigorous-intensity aerobic physical activity to 150 minutes per week.

Recommendations for children and teens up to the age of seventeen are a minimum of sixty minutes of moderate-to-vigorous activity per day plus strengthening activity at least three times per week.

A quick guide to activity levels

	Moderate Become warmer, heart beats faster, breathe harder but can still carry on a conversation	Vigorous Get warm, heart beats much faster, breathe much harder. Difficult to carry on a conversation	Strengthening and/or balancing Involve using body weight, with weights or working against resistance
Adults (18–64 years)	Brisk walking, cycling, dancing	Running, swimming, sports such as football	Exercising with weights, Pilates, carrying heavy loads such as groceries
Older adults (65+ years)	Brisk walking, cycling, dancing	Running, swimming, climbing stairs	**Strengthening:** Carrying heavy loads such as groceries, activities such as dancing or chair aerobics **Balancing:** Tai chi or yoga
Children (5–17 years)	Playground games and activities, walking or cycling, dancing, skipping	Fast running, swimming, sports like football, rugby, netball or hockey (if already active in the game)	Swinging on playground or park equipment, skipping, hopping, gymnastics, tennis

Based on: UK Physical Activity Guidelines (2011) www.gov.uk/government/publications/uk-physical-activity-guidelines

Note: If you are new to exercise or returning to it after some time or cannot do the recommended amounts of activity due to age or a health condition, you should be as active as your abilities and/or condition allow. Seek advice from a doctor or health professional as to what is most appropriate for you.

92

Quick quiz

If sitting watching TV or playing on your computer has an energy expenditure of 1, how much more energy (as a measure of physical activity involved) do you think you'd be expending doing the activities listed below? (For example, half as much again, twice as much, etc.)

- Standing while working at your desk
- Ironing
- Cleaning and dusting
- Strolling (2 miles per hour)
- Painting and decorating

- Vacuuming
- Brisk walking (4 miles per hour)
- Mowing the lawn
- Running a 10-minute mile (6 miles per hour)

See if you were right below.

Quiz answers

A Sitting watching TV or playing on the computer = 1
B Standing while working at your desk = 2.0 times
C Ironing = 2.3 times
D Cleaning and dusting = 2.5 times
E Strolling (2 miles per hour) = 2.5 times

F Painting and decorating = 3.0 times
G Vacuuming = 3.5 times
H Brisk walking (4 miles per hour) = 5.0 times
I Mowing the lawn = 5.5 times
J Running a 10-minute mile (6 miles per hour) = 10 times

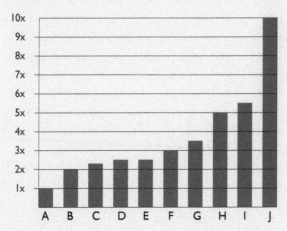

Based on: Start Active, Stay Active (2011). A report on physical activity for health from the four home countries' Chief Medical Officers. UK Government

Ideas for moving more

'Try to limit your sitting and sleeping to just twenty-three and a half hours a day.'

Dr Mike Evans, *23½ hours*, video, 2011

Ten ideas for starters

Want to get started, do more, keep going? Here are ideas to help you:

1 Start slow and small

One of the easiest places to start being active is by walking more. People who walk are three times more likely to meet the recommended activity levels (see page 91) than people who don't. Apart from some comfortable shoes, you don't need any special clothes or equipment and walking is easy to incorporate into your daily life. So why not take the stairs instead of the lift or get off the bus or train a stop early?

2 Keep the end (and middle) in mind

How much we expect to enjoy something impacts on how likely it is we'll do it. When it comes to exercise, psychologists have found that we often think we'll enjoy it less than we actually do because we tend to focus on the first part of the activity or workout, getting started and warmed up, which is often the hardest part. They found that simply by asking people before exercising to think about how they'd feel in the middle of the workout, when they were in their stride, and at the end of it, their intentions to exercise in the future were strengthened.

3 Break it up

Don't have the time for exercise? You don't have to find thirty or sixty minutes in one chunk. Exercising in pockets of ten minutes also counts.

4 Walk, think, talk

Use time getting physical to do something else as well. Trying to work

JULIE'S STORY: JUST A MINUTE

Julie was an overweight, busy single parent with diabetes. She needed to get fitter, but felt she didn't have time to exercise. A psychologist working with her, Dr Robert Maurer, sensed that telling her to do the recommended thirty minutes' exercise a day wouldn't work. She just wouldn't do it and it would likely make her feel she'd failed, causing her to feel worse than she already did.

Instead he asked if she regularly watched TV. 'Of course,' she replied. 'Well,' he asked, 'Could you walk on the spot for one minute each night as you are watching TV? Could you do that for the next two weeks?' 'Okay' she agreed 'That sounds easy. I think I can do it.'

While these minutes might not reduce Julie's weight significantly, they might build her confidence and help her feel more able to be active. Two weeks later Julie came back to her doctor. 'I kept up my one-minute TV-walking. What else can I do for one minute a day?' Julie's fear of exercising and resistance to it had started to melt away. Slowly, over the next three months, Julie was able to find pockets of time to be more active and was able to take on regular aerobics classes.

Used with permission of the author. A full version of this story can be found in: *One Small Step Can Change Your Life: The Kaizen Way* by Dr Robert Maurer (2004), Workman Publishing Company

through a problem or generate ideas? Do it on the move – go out for a walk or a run. If you're at work, why not suggest that meetings are held on the move? Some people say it enhances the quality of conversation and may even make meetings more efficient and shorter.

5 Prepare to avoid excuses

I once heard of a guy who wanted to exercise before work. Realising that any excuse, such as not being able to find his running shorts, could get in his way, he came up with an ingenious solution – he wore his kit to bed. The moment his alarm went off, he was ready. I'm not suggesting you go that far, but what do you need to do in order to be prepared and avoid your usual excuses? For example, if you are working from home, try wearing exercise gear during the day so that you can just get up and go for a walk or a jog around the local park. You are also prepared if you want to

KEY THREE: EXERCISING

Common excuses for not moving more and evidence-based ideas to counter them

'I'm too tired!'
Often we feel tired because we're not physically active. It may seem counter-intuitive, but being physically active can actually give us more energy. Being outside can help too.

'I hate sports, it's just not me!'
It's not all about sports. You can walk briskly, run, dance, do yoga or martial arts, such as tai chi or tae kwon do... the list is endless!

'I'm too busy!'
Can you try to fit in five or ten minutes at a time, inside or out? What about doubling up? For example: walking while having a meeting or seeing a friend or taking the children to the park, walking or cycling to work; using exercise as time to think and plan.

'I'm feeling too down!'
Try focusing on how you'll feel afterwards. Physical activity generates feel-good chemicals in most of us and after the first few minutes we start to feel these. Doing exercise can also help us feel more in control too.

get to a class. For classes, try setting your alarm fifteen minutes before you need to leave – so you can finish off what you're doing before you go.

6 Be social

It can be easier to commit to exercise and more enjoyable if we do it with others. It can also help if we're not confident about it – getting someone we trust to come with us for moral support, or to nudge and encourage us, or to help keep track of our progress. For example, Susie, a retired nurse, has a group of friends she walks with each morning. They meet at the gates of the park at nine and walk and talk for about thirty minutes each day. Knowing that the others will be there encourages everyone to keep at it. They laugh a lot too.

7 Enjoy yourself

Exercise psychologist Guy Faulkner and his colleagues, Kate Hefferon and Nanette Mutrie, advise us to find exercise that we enjoy, can do regularly and will be able to sustain over time. So if you hate the gym but love dancing, do that instead or watch TV or TED talks on the treadmill – if that's your thing. One parent we worked with decided to jog to music as she pushed her child's buggy along each morning.

Deliberately finding enjoyable distractions while we exercise can increase our enjoyment. Jogging around the local park could easily become boring as you literally run round in a circle, the same one every time. So mix things up by trying to notice things around you that change – the birds and wildlife, children playing, enthusiastic dogs chasing squirrels. This is a form of mindfulness, which we'll look at in Chapter 4.

8 Do it outside
There's a growing body of research showing the benefits of 'green exercise' – physical activity we do outside and in nature, be that in the countryside, a city park or in our local streets. It can have extra-positive effects on our psychological well-being and mood, and be vitalising and restorative too.

9 Keeping tabs can keep you going
There are now loads of gadgets and smartphone apps available to help track progress, from counting your steps to monitoring your heart rate or measuring the distance you've run. Many people find that they really help with their motivation.

10 Sit less
It's easy to remain sitting down for long hours, especially if you are busy working or just relaxing, so how about trying:
★ Setting a timer on your phone for every thirty minutes and get up and move or stretch when it buzzes (it's a good excuse to make a cup of tea).
★ Putting your phone or TV remote control on the other side of the room – you'll have to move to get them.
★ Standing during phone calls or while playing computer games.
★ Arranging standing meetings at work and using a standing desk.

Other ways to care for your body & mind

> 'The doctor of the future will give no medicine, but will interest his patients in the care of the human frame, in diet, and in the cause and prevention of disease.'
>
> Thomas Edison

Moving more matters for our minds. Other ways of taking care of the body matter too. Combining these with being active will help you maximise how happy you feel.

Eating and happiness

Each mouthful we eat slowly adds up to how well our body functions. It also has an impact on our mind. Research to date shows that what and how we eat can affect our mood and its fluctuations, our cognitive functioning and link to our likelihood of depression and cognitive degeneration as we age.

Food is more than just fuel for our bodies, it can be a source of pleasure, connection, creativity and meaning, which contribute to happiness. It can also have a lasting impact, longer-term, on the structure and functioning of our brain.

So which foods are best for happiness?

A 2006 report from the Mental Health Foundation reviewed over 500 studies on how what we eat impacts our psychological well-being and found that the most important are:

★**Omega-3 oils** Higher levels are associated with lower risk of depression, impulsiveness and they boost our mood, as well as being protective against Alzheimer's and dementia. It doesn't seem to take too much. For example, one large study found that women who ate fish once a week, or more, were thirty per cent less likely to develop depression. Fats are essential for our brain (the brain is sixty per cent fat), but we need a balance between omega-3 and omega-6 (found in animal fats) of around 2:1. However, our diets today have shifted that balance so that we have too much omega-6 and not enough omega-3 (as well as more transfats from fast/processed foods, which aren't good for us). Omega-3 oils are found in fish and seeds (like flax and linseed), nuts (especially walnuts and almonds), olive oil and sunflower oil, and avocados and eggs.

★ **Vitamins and minerals** – especially:
  • Zinc – from wholegrains, legumes, meat and milk.
  • Magnesium – from green leafy vegetables, nuts and wholegrains.
  • Iron – from red meat, green leafy vegetables, eggs and some fruit.
  • Folate – from green leafy vegetables and fortified cereals .
  • A range of B vitamins – from wholegrain products, yeast and dairy.
  • Antioxidant vitamins such as C and E – from a wide range of fruit and vegetables.

So if our diet is varied, comprising mostly natural foods including lots of green and other vegetables, fresh fruits, nuts and seeds, wholegrains and those with sources of omega-3, it is likely that we are getting the nutrients we need for optimal mental functioning and well-being. Some experts say we should aim for a rainbow on our plates each day. Having a variety of different-coloured veg, fruit and other foods helps to ensure we get all the different nutrients we need.

Are any foods linked to unhappiness?

Modern diets aren't always good for happiness. Processed foods and/or sugar, especially, have been shown to have a negative effect, messing with our moods and being linked to depression.

Sugar and refined carbohydrates (for example, anything white and made of refined wheat such as bread, pasta, many breakfast cereals, cakes) can affect our brain's ability to regulate our moods in the shorter and longer-term. And some people are more sensitive than others.

KEY THREE: EXERCISING

Sugars and refined carbohydrates in our diets break down into glucose, and our brain needs it in a steady supply. However, too much, too fast and we can get a sugar rush or 'high', often followed by a crash, resulting in mood swings. Too little, from going too long without food, and we can experience fatigue, lower concentration, irritability, anxiousness and/or forgetfulness.

The thing is, many of us now consume much more sugar in our diets and so have more glucose in our bodies than we were designed for. Five hundred years ago we would have been unlikely to come across the stuff, while in the year 2000 we were eating 152lb/69kg per year. As well as eating it in sweets and adding it to tea or coffee, sugar is often hidden in foods and drinks (e.g. fizzy drinks, ready meals, alcohol and fruit juices).

For happiness, we need our sugar in a form that takes us longer to digest and we don't need too much of it. So cut down on the white stuff and eat more fruit and wholegrains.

Sleep and happiness

'Sleep is the golden chain that ties health and our bodies together.'
Thomas Dekker, *The Guls Horn-Booke*

How often do you wake in the morning feeling rested and refreshed, energised to take on the day? On those days, you spring out of bed without hitting the snooze button. As the morning progresses, you're thinking clearly and able to tackle a tricky issue that's been around for a while and when something goes wrong, you take it in your stride without getting upset or frustrated. And if an idea or opportunity comes your way, you're open to it, interested and curious.

This happened to me recently – I'd got back from a break where I'd been going to bed an hour or so earlier than my usual time and decided to try out the same routine back at home. I was amazed at the difference that extra time asleep made in how I felt and how I functioned: it improved my outlook, my interactions with others, my ability to deal with what the day had in store. And I realised that I had spent most of my adult life being sleep-deprived. I simply didn't know what it felt like to regularly get enough rest. And it turns out, I'm not alone. Sixty-three per cent of Americans say they don't get the amount of sleep they need during the week. A 2013 study of Britain's bedtime habits found that a whopping seventy per cent of people sleep for seven hours or less, with a third of the population getting by on only five to six hours, with that figure up from the previous survey three years earlier.

But sleep isn't just a nice bonus, an idle luxury, it's a health and well-being essential. When we sleep, it is primarily for the brain, enabling it to process the day, recover and regenerate. Good-quality sleep is essential for learning and for proper brain functioning too.

Sleep and psychological well-being

Many of the functions of sleep have been a mystery, but gradually it's becoming clearer. It's widely accepted that sleep and psychological well-being are intrinsically linked. A good night's sleep fosters our resilience, while persistent lack of it can lead to negative thinking and emotional vulnerability, setting up a downward cycle, which can lead to depression and anxiety if we're not careful.

How we process emotional information plays a role in this. Take the following experiment as an example. People were shown images of distinctly contrasting positive, neutral or negative emotional content – perhaps smiling babies or pictures of wartime destruction. They were then asked to recall them. Those who lacked enough sleep not only found recall in general more difficult, but the images they remembered were the negative ones. Lack of sleep makes us even more likely to focus on, and remember, the worst over the good. This paves the path to depression (we'll look at this in more detail in Chapter 8).

Too little sleep can drive us to unhealthy choices in other areas that are important to our health. When we are overtired we start to crave sugar and carbohydrates, we eat more in total and are less likely to exercise. As Robert Stickgold, one of the world's leading sleep experts, says, 'If you don't get enough sleep you are going to end up fat, sick and stupid.' However, he says, most of us don't connect the dots back to the number of hours we sleep.

KEY THREE: EXERCISING

Top tip Being grateful and sleep

Being in a grateful state of mind seems to help us get to sleep quicker, sleep longer and better as well as letting us feel more awake during the day. This was the finding of a study of 300 men and women aged between eighteen and sixty-eight years. Participants were encouraged to have positive and appreciative thoughts before sleeping rather than running over current worries. The 'three good things' activity we'll look at in Chapter 8 is a great brain-training tool to use before we sleep to help us switch off from worrying, become more appreciative and get a good night's rest.

Based on: Wood et al (2009)

Stress in life is a big cause of sleep loss. In the 2013 British Bedtime Study, around fifty per cent of people said that stress and worry kept them awake at night. Sometimes the factors that are causing that stress are out of our control. However, another study showed that having a more positive outlook and a greater sense of purpose in life helped people get a good night's sleep, despite their circumstances and troubles.

Sleep and functioning well

Babies and small children need to sleep a lot because they are learning during every waking moment. But as adults we need sleep too. Too little and we do less well on recall and straightforward skills tests. Other examples of the impact of lack of sleep include:

★ Driving after losing four hours of sleep has been shown to be like driving after drinking a six-pack of beer.

★ Sleepiness accounts for over 100,000 reported traffic accidents per year in the US. Estimates from Australia, England and a number of other European countries suggest that drowsy driving causes ten to thirty per cent of all crashes.

★ The more complex or creative the tasks or demanding the decisions we face, the worse the impact of lack of sleep.

Sleep can help our brains to work well. If we nap between learning something and having to recall it, we do better than if we stay awake for the same number of hours before recall. Sleep expert Stickgold suggests that for every two hours we take information in, we need an hour of sleep. 'The difference between smart and wise,' he says, 'is two hours more sleep a night.'

The amount of sleep we need is very individual and we may underestimate it. One of the world's experts on sleep says that the majority of adults need between eight and nine hours to allow sleep to fulfil its mysterious biological processes, deliver its health benefits and enable us to function at our best. Peak performers know this – top athletes, sports people and world-class musicians all recognise how crucial a full night's rest is – in fact research shows, on average, that they sleep for 8.6 hours per night. That's a lot more than most of us do.

 **Pause point...**

★ Think back to the last time you had too little sleep. How did that make you feel? How did it impact your interactions with others, your ability to think clearly and deal with issues and problems? How did you function at work? What other impacts did it have on you?

★ Now contrast that with a time you woke up refreshed – when you'd had a really good night's sleep. What difference did that make for you?

★ How many hours did you sleep? How does this compare to the length of your average night's rest? Do you feel rested after that amount of sleep?

★ What are your habits in the hour before you go to bed? How well is your bedroom set up for a good night's sleep?

KEY THREE: EXERCISING

Top tips Happier sleep habits

★ **Set your alarm for bed** It may be counter-intuitive, but going to bed and waking up at regular times helps to ensure you get the amount of sleep you really need. Sleeping in for a long time at weekends causes 'social jetlag' and is why waking up on Monday can be hard! Why not set your alarm an hour before you want to go to bed as a reminder to wind down for the night? (I'd suggest using a gentle sound, and a different one from the alarm you wake up to normally!)

★ **Go no-tech before bedtime** Our brain interprets the light emitted from devices as daylight, which makes us more awake, meaning it's harder to fall asleep. Anything interactive, such as playing games or checking email, makes us even more alert. So, if you find yourself tempted to check emails, texts, watch the end of a film or play your game a bit longer, ask yourself: 'In terms of my happiness tomorrow (and health longer term), what will be the biggest return from the next thirty minutes/hour (or so) – this activity or getting more sleep?'

★ **Watch what you drink** That nightcap may not be such a good idea after all! Alcohol helps us fall asleep quickly but it reduces the quality of our sleep, especially deep sleep, and can cause us to wake up earlier. Coffee, tea and chocolate (tobacco too) make it harder to sleep. Any liquid too close to going to bed can mean needing to use the toilet in the middle of the night. Try having these drinks earlier, at least an hour and a half before bedtime.

★ **Exercise in daylight** People who exercise regularly tend to fall asleep quicker, spend more time in deep sleep and wake less often in the night. Exercising outside, especially in the morning, can help set our body clock and make it easier to sleep at the end of the day (see opposite for more on why).

Important note: If you have problems sleeping and these persist despite trying some of the tips we suggest here, seek advice from your doctor.

See the light!
Daylight and happiness

Light is an often overlooked, but essential, ingredient in the complex mix of what we need to feel and be well. Natural light influences our physical well-being and our happiness. Most of us feel happier when it's sunny than when it's overcast. Seasonal Affective Disorder (SAD) is a recognised medical condition that some people experience in the wintertime, when there's a lack of daylight. Experiments show that people in offices work and feel better if they are near a window and so have natural light. Likewise, people in hospital heal faster if they are near natural light.

When our skin is exposed to sunlight, we produce vitamin D. That's why it's known as the 'sunshine vitamin'. Too little of it is also associated with low moods, poor sleep and depression. It's an important nutrient, too, for our bones and many other bodily processes. However, with our working schedules, indoor lifestyles and extensive use of sunscreen, vitamin-D deficiency is becoming increasingly common in the West. It's estimated that as many as half of us have too little. In fact, it's thought that our lack of exposure to daylight, and therefore lower levels of this vital nutrient, could be contributing to rising levels of sleep disorders and depression, as well as impacting our physical health.

Every cell of our body is programmed to tune in to daylight. It's in our DNA. The sun existed long before we did and, like most creatures, the rhythm of our bodily systems evolved to follow its pattern. Our bodies anticipate the rising and the setting of the sun over a twenty-four-hour period. This is called our 'circadian rhythm' and is borne out, for example, by us being more alert and hungry in the morning and starting to feel dozy and tired as it gets dark.

We evolved to structure our days according to the sun, rising with it and going to bed at sunset. It told our bodies when to eat and rest. However, since the invention of the lightbulb 140 years ago all that changed. We can now choose to get up and go to bed whenever we want, to work late when we need to and stay up all night and party if the mood takes us. Add caffeine into the mix, together with technology, and things start to worsen. Our bodies become confused because their natural pattern is disturbed. And as studies on people working shifts at night have shown, that is potentially detrimental to physical and mental health.

How much light do we need?

To get the most from sunlight we need to get the full spectrum of light. While natural daylight through windows does us some good, glass, like sunblock, filters out some of the wavelengths that daylight is composed of. We need to get outside and let the sunlight touch bare skin (our hands, forearms and head, at the very least). This may be partly why exercising outdoors has additional benefits for our well-being.

The amount of exposure we need varies, depending on the intensity of the sun (which varies according to our location and the time of year), our skin colour and the amount of skin exposed. However, as little as ten or fifteen minutes between the hours of 10am and 3pm without sunscreen in northern Europe can be enough to generate healthy levels of vitamin D (which is shorter than the time it would take light skin to burn in summer). We are all aware of the dangers of over-exposure to the sun and we need to be cautious of sunburn, especially at peak times, but getting some sunshine really does help us feel good – and it does us good too.

 Pause point...

★ How much time do you typically spend outside in daylight each day, in winter as well as summer?

★ If you don't regularly have at least fifteen minutes per day outside while it is light, how might you get more daylight on a regular basis – especially in winter? For example, consider walking outdoors at lunchtime or gardening, reading, eating or exercising outside.

To sum up

Here are five key points to take away from this chapter:

1 Incorporate more movement into your day – human beings are designed to move. It's essential for our physical and psychological health and it helps our brains to function well. Get your heart beating faster by doing at least 150 minutes of moderate exercise per week. And remember – more is better!

2 Stand up more – sitting is bad for your health regardless of how much you exercise.

3 What you eat affects how you feel – make sure you're getting the essential nutrients and limit your sugar intake.

4 Work out how much sleep you really need – and make getting enough a priority. It's vital for how well you feel/how effectively you function.

5 Love natural light – being out in daylight is important for vitamin D production, which is important for physical health and happiness.

Connections to other Keys

Other Keys you might like to explore in connection with Exercising:

★ **AWARENESS** (See page 108)
  Building your mindfulness skills can enhance your experience and the benefit you get from exercise and eating.

★ **DIRECTION** (See page 170)
  Setting some clear goals for the actions you need to take in order to move more, eat well and sleep better will make it more likely that you'll achieve your goals.

★ **RESILIENCE** (See page 198)
  Exercise and taking care of your body can enhance your resilience. There are other areas you can take action in too: learning some resilient-thinking techniques can help you sleep better.

★ **EMOTIONS** (See page 238)
  Exercise, eating well and being outside are some great sources of positive emotion – find out why this matters.

G
R
E
A
T
D
R
E
A
M

AWARENESS

Live life mindfully

There's an old saying that goes: 'Yesterday is history, tomorrow is a mystery, today is a gift. That's why they call it the present.' Well, science is certainly showing that taking time to notice the here and now can have a powerful impact on how happy we are. We call this being 'mindfully aware'.

Awareness: introduction

> 'Compared to what we ought to be, we are only half awake.'
>
> William James, *The Energies of Men*

A foundation for happier living?

Once hippie and now hip 'mindfulness' is popping up everywhere – as apps to download onto our smartphones, in our workplaces, schools, community centres, even in our doctors' surgeries. But is it just the latest fad or is it something more?

Well, it seems that mindfulness can literally change our minds – for the better. Practised for thousands of years in the East, forms of meditation started to emerge in the West in the 1960s with Zen Buddhist approaches and transcendental meditation, which at the time were considered to be 'fringe' activities. While there were some early scientific studies on the latter, it wasn't until the late 1970s that meditative practices started to be studied in earnest in the West as ways to improve and increase psychological health, and now the scientific evidence for their beneficial effects is growing fast.

There are now over 500 peer-reviewed scientific articles published each year on the mechanisms of mindfulness and its effects. And it's not just in ivory towers that interest is growing. A review of the UK press revealed only two mentions of mindfulness in April 2004, but ten years later there were 150 in that month alone.

The growing body of research suggests that there's something behind the hype. While some of the apps and courses may promise more than they deliver, mindfulness is not just a passing trend and no longer on the fringes of the field. It's a 2,500-year-old Eastern tradition whose time has well and truly come for us here in the West and which may significantly contribute to us being happier. More mindful awareness is something that everyone has a capacity for and could potentially benefit from. And perhaps, given the demands and overload of our lives today, we need it now more than ever before.

Mindfulness can certainly help as an 'emergency parachute' to use when we feel stressed; it can help us deal with our emotions and when we're down or if we have chronic pain. It's not about avoiding or eliminating sadness or difficulties, but changing our relationship to them. It's about freeing ourselves from the suffering caused by our own minds and experiencing ourselves, what's around us and the present, more fully.

And there's more. The intention behind the ancient tradition of mindfulness is to help develop and train our minds and ourselves towards optimal states of being – aware, insightful, joyful, interconnected and compassionate. So it seems that such a discipline can be a firm foundation for a happier life.

What is mindfulness?

Mindfulness is about the quality of our attention and awareness. A widely used definition originally coined by leading mindfulness expert, Jon Kabat-Zinn, is: 'paying attention in a particular way: on purpose, in the present moment, and non-judgementally'. It's these 'particular ways' that make our attention mindful. Let's unpack them a little more:

★ **On purpose** Mindfulness is a practice where we deliberately set out with the intention of paying attention to something specific such as our breath, or our body, or the sounds around us, or the thoughts and feelings we're experiencing.

★ **In the present moment** Our minds are very often occupied with thoughts or worries about the past or the future – what we've just done, what might happen, what's on our to-do list – that we don't notice what's happening in the here and now. Through intentional focusing of our attention on something that is happening in the present (e.g. our breath) it enables us to become less caught up in the 'noise' our minds generate. If our minds do wander we bring our attention back to our point of focus.

★ **Non-judgementally** As we're focusing our attention, thoughts,

GREAT DREAM

sensations and emotions will arise. Instead of reacting to these, it's as if we're a compassionate observer: we accept what happens as it is, not judging the things we become aware of as good or bad, recognising that thoughts are just thoughts, not facts, and that these come and go.

Our attitude to ourselves while we're practising, and what we notice, is important. We need to treat ourselves with kindness and be open and receptive to what we notice.

How do you practise mindfulness?

The way most people start to develop and then nurture their capacity to be mindful is through the practice of meditation. This means regularly setting aside an amount of time to intentionally focus our attention on something particular (such as our breath, body or sounds), noticing when our attention drifts off and bringing it back again and again and again.

Meditation is often practised sitting upright in a normal seat or chair, whether at home or work, or elsewhere. So there's no need to sit cross-legged or get into the traditional lotus posture unless you want to. We can also practise mindfulness in other ways, such as when we are walking or eating, and even cooking, driving and in our conversations with others. We'll look at some examples later in this chapter.

Through regular and intentional practice of mindfulness we become more mindful as a person (i.e. more aware) – seeing more fully what is around us, noticing what is going on in our bodies and in our minds. It can also help us to tune in to other people. We notice things that we usually don't notice or take for granted. It can give us a greater sense of calm and spaciousness, help us manage our emotional reactions and break unhelpful thinking habits. We develop a different relationship to our thoughts and emotions, learning not to get caught up in them or take them as fact – understanding that they come and go. With practice, we become more conscious of where our attention is and we become increasingly able to place it where we choose. This, in turn, helps us to gain more control over what we feel and do, and enables us to make wiser, healthier and more altruistic choices.

Clearing up some common misconceptions

Because it's easy to be confused about what mindfulness is (or isn't), here's some clarity on some of the most common points of confusion:

★ Mindfulness is integral to some faiths, but it's not a religious practice. It can be practised without religious dogma by anyone, regardless of whether they have a faith or not.

★ Mindfulness is not about clearing the mind. Trying to do that only leads to frustration as thoughts and images continue to come. The mind is great at reminding us of things or solving problems, so it's unrealistic to try to switch it off. Instead, mindfulness makes us more aware of the patterns of the mind, so we can choose what to act on and what to let go.

★ Mindfulness is more than stress management and is not just there to use when times get tough. Many people come to mindfulness because they're stressed and it can, and does, help with that. But it also goes beyond, helping us to see clearly and let go of some of our thinking patterns and behaviours that can contribute to our difficulties.

★ Mindfulness is not relaxation, but it can help us relax. Although it may not look like it to the outside observer, mindfulness is an active process. While relaxation techniques focus on letting go or switching off, in mindfulness we are alert. Its aims are different too. Like relaxation, it can help us deal with stressful situations, but mindfulness also seeps into our everyday life, bringing greater non-judgemental, conscious awareness of what we do, feel and experience.

★ Mindfulness is a way of training our minds and can help us be more effective, but it's more than a set of thinking skills or techniques. It is 'bigger than thinking'. It teaches us that thoughts aren't facts. Regardless of how profound, pleasant or destructive thoughts are, when we are mindful we can step back and observe our thoughts objectively, and this can lead to greater clarity, wiser insight and creativity.

★ Mindfulness isn't only for ourselves. It is generally an individual practice and it brings greater insight to ourselves, which in itself can have a positive impact on our interactions with others. More than that, one of the aims of mindfulness practice can be to help us develop more awareness of, and compassion for, others.

Old roots, new branches

Mindfulness has a long history and forms of it are found in a wide range of ancient spiritual and faith traditions from around the world, the most well known, documented and studied of which is Buddhism. In Buddhist traditions cultivating mindful awareness is at the heart of a wider system of psycho-spiritual development and transformation, with the aim of leading ultimately to freedom from suffering. Such freedom enables wholesome qualities of wisdom, joy, compassion and flourishing of ourselves and towards other people, other sentient beings and the planet, leading to a more profound happiness that doesn't depend on specific inner or outer conditions.

From the spiritual to psychological therapy

Despite the aim of traditional Buddhist meditation being to enable flourishing, the main focus of initial applications in the West has been to treat ill health, reflecting the emphasis of the health and psychology professions. Jon Kabat-Zinn is widely credited with bringing meditation practices into the mainstream in the West. He developed an eight-week-long programme called 'Mindfulness-Based Stress Reduction' (MBSR) to help chronic pain sufferers who were grappling with stress, pain and illness in their lives.

MBSR remains true to its Buddhist roots, but is free from religious or faith-based content so that it can be accepted and used by all. The aim isn't to teach people about Buddhism or even to make them into great meditators, but to 'offer an environment within which to experiment with novel and potentially effective methods for facing, exploring and relieving suffering at the levels of both body and mind' says Kabat-Zinn. The programme comprises a weekly two-and-a-half-hour group class (covering a range of different mindfulness practices), daily home practice, with a one-day 'retreat' towards the end of the eight weeks.

Studies of MBSR proved it was effective and since then its use has spread widely – a number of other mindfulness-based programmes and therapies based on, or building from, MBSR have been developed for the treatment of specific conditions, of which the most well known is Mindfulness-Based Cognitive Therapy (MBCT), which is designed to specifically help prevent recurrent episodes of depression.

From therapy towards flourishing

Mindfulness meditation programmes are now used as interventions for healthy people, for example to help people reduce and manage stress and enhance well-being.

Mindful Self-Compassion (MSC) is also gaining attention. This is a programme that enables people to be kinder towards themselves, designed to help build self-acceptance, recognising that we may tend to treat ourselves more harshly than we do others, which can undermine our emotional resilience and well-being (we'll be looking at this topic in more detail in Chapter 9). Mindfulness-Based Relationship Enhancement (MBRE) is another programme that is aimed to increase relationship quality and social well-being, primarily for couples.

Some even newer programmes are combining mindfulness specifically with positive psychological research on enhancing happiness (such as is covered throughout this book) and evidence seems encouraging. For example, one very early study showed that a group on a programme that included meditation and was designed to increase happiness showed a greater positive uplift than those receiving the happiness programme on its own.

Mind full or mindful?

> 'Half an hour's meditation each day is essential,
> except when you are busy. Then a full hour is needed.'
>
> Attributed to Saint Francis de Sales

Our minds are marvellous – capable of feats such as learning new things, coming up with ideas, analysing tricky problems, making up creative stories, anticipating issues and events, thinking and planning ahead, and remembering the past.

However, our minds can also work against us. They spend a lot of time thinking about almost anything other than what we're presently doing or what's going on in front of, or around, us. They jump easily to conclusions without seeing the full picture or switch onto automatic, so that we make assumptions about things being the same as they have been in the past. They can go into overdrive at the slightest trigger, repeatedly admonishing us with what we should, or shouldn't, have done, going over past events again and again or spinning off, imagining, inventing and worrying about what could happen in the future. All this can create unnecessary mental noise and clutter, and over time can lead to patterns and habits of thinking that don't serve us well.

In today's world of general overload, we have more competing for our attention than ever before. Many of us have lots to do in not enough time and a never-ending source of engaging distractions all around us, as well as through the media, our smartphones and various other electronic devices.

With all this, it's not surprising that our minds can go into overdrive and leave us feeling unhappy.

Try this! A mindful minute

Assuming, as you're reading this right now, you're probably somewhere where you can take a minute to try a simple experiment without being interrupted:

★ Sit with your feet both flat on the floor/ground (or stay lying down if you're reading this in bed).

★ The aim is to spend the next sixty seconds simply focusing on your breath – feeling the air come in as you inhale and go out as you exhale. Just that. If your mind wanders from your breath, no problem, just bring it back (you may have to do this many times).

★ When you're ready, set a timer to a minute. Put your phone in silent mode too so that you won't be disturbed.

★ If you can, close your eyes. If that's not possible right now (for example, you may be in a crowded train carriage), just soften your gaze on a neutral place in front of you.

★ Okay – press your timer and breathe… When the minute is up, think about the following questions: during the minute, how much did your mind wander away from your breath? Did you notice where it went?

Let's look at this some more…

Our wild and wandering minds

In the experiment above most of us, if not all, would have found our minds wandering many times, even in the space of a single minute. That's what our minds do naturally. We don't even need something external to stimulate all this mental activity, our minds just spontaneously wander a lot and the activity doesn't seem to be making us happy. That's what psychologists Matt Killingsworth and Dan Gilbert found. In an experiment using a smartphone app, they buzzed over 2,000 people asking them:

★ What are you doing right now?
★ How are you feeling right now?
★ Are you thinking about something other than what you are actually doing? If so, is it pleasant, unpleasant or neutral?

The results were curious:

★ Minds wandered almost fifty per cent of the time, regardless of what people were doing – working, talking with someone, exercising, listening to music, watching TV, cooking, eating or praying.

★ Regardless of the activity, people were less happy when their minds wandered – even if they wandered to pleasant thoughts this didn't lead to greater happiness. And if their minds wandered to neutral or unpleasant topics they were considerably less happy.

★ What people were thinking was found to be a better predictor of how they were feeling than what they were doing.

Mind-wandering can cause mindlessness. Multi-tasking is a culprit too. Have you ever had the experience of going into a different room to get something, only to find you've forgotten what it was? Or been in a conversation with someone but realised you hadn't listened to what they were saying? Or eaten a meal while watching TV or reading, without really tasting the food or knowing how much you've eaten?

Our minds can switch onto autopilot too. Have you ever made a familiar journey, like going to work, and arrived not being able to remember anything about how you got there? Or even intended to go elsewhere but found yourself on your usual route? Our minds very quickly identify regular patterns of action or thought and these become habits. Habits are handy: they enable us to get things done that we regularly need to do without clogging up our conscious minds. However, handy though our habits are, they sometimes trip us up, especially when our minds are overloaded or focused elsewhere.

Habits of mind don't only relate to actions, they apply to how we judge and interpret events and other people. We jump to conclusions based on a snapshot of evidence and make quick judgements about what is good or bad. Then we act on the basis that these are true, which can have knock-on consequences for how we, or others, feel. These are all examples of 'mindlessness'. And it can be very costly to us in terms of our health and happiness, and to make matters worse, when we're mindless we are, of course, unaware that we are being so because our heads are elsewhere.

Human doings or beings?

Sometimes it feels as if we are human 'doings' not 'beings'. Think for a moment. Do you know anyone who doesn't think they are busy? My guess is not many – if any at all.

A friend, Joe, worked out that to complete all the projects he needed, or wanted, to do would take him eighty years and that wasn't including anything new. Even though he was only thirty-six he felt that he had run out of time. Jumping from one thing to the next to keep the plates spinning, he felt out of control and completely overloaded.

The more stressed we are about what we have to do, the more our minds wander, worry and churn, focusing on what's wrong with us and our lives. This, in turn, makes us less effective and wears us down even more, leading to more rumination and stress. Unchecked, this can mean that we're less able to tackle things and it can lead to us going into a downward spiral. Think of a computer with lots of programmes open and running – it gradually becomes slower and slower. We may not notice this at first and we may even not realise we have things running in the background. The more programmes we open, the worse it gets. Sometimes we have to switch it all off for a few moments to get our device running faster again. We gradually learn ways of working so that we don't have so much open at once using up all the working memory. Likewise with our phones, the more apps we've got going the quicker our batteries run down. It's the same with our minds.

This is one way in which the practice of mindfulness helps. It enables us to disconnect from our doings and mental noise for a short while and that creates a sense of space. With that space we can step back and it helps us see more clearly what's really going on. And this greater awareness means we can make more conscious choices. With more choices we have more control, which is essential for human well-being. So mindfulness can be good for us in many, many ways.

Mindfulness is simple but it's not easy and it takes practice. It doesn't make all our problems go away, but it can help us to step off our 'hamster wheels' and separate fact from the fiction our minds often create.

A caveat

Mindfulness doesn't always work for everyone. It can also mean that we become aware of difficult feelings and thoughts. You may find it helpful to find a qualified mindfulness teacher or group to support you as you learn or practise (see Resources to find out how to find a qualified teacher). If you are suffering from depression, anxiety or another clinical condition talk with your GP before starting to practise. They may also be able to prescribe a specific course (sometimes available on the NHS).

 Pause point...

Reflect on a specific typical day in your life, perhaps yesterday...

★ How much time during the key activities of your day was your mind elsewhere?

★ How much time did you spend on autopilot during regular routines – e.g. time getting ready and travelling to work or school, time there, time when you got back home and time getting ready for bed?

★ How often were you so busy getting on with the things on your to-do list that you didn't notice what was going on around you?

★ How many hours of your day did mind-wandering, doing mode or mindlessness account for? How many hours are you truly 'present'?

In Matt Killingsworth and Dan Gilbert's mind-wandering study, people were only present and focused about half of the time. That means they were missing out on half their life. Indeed, Professor Mark Williams, one of the world's foremost mindfulness experts, suggests that there's a real sense in which becoming more mindful can double your remaining life expectancy!

See: Killingsworth, M. & Gilbert, D. (2010); Williams, M. & Penman, D. (2011)

Mindfulness & happiness

So far there is evidence that mindfulness can help us to be happier in a number of different ways.

Feeling good

Being more mindfully aware can help people to feel happier. People who are more mindful generally feel better about their lives and have higher levels of psychological well-being. They are likely to possess more hope, gratitude and vitality, experience more joy and be more resilient. They are less likely to experience depression, anxiety, stress or anger.

Attention to the present moment may encourage greater sensory engagement and enjoyment of life. People who are mindful certainly report that they have more positive emotional experiences and fewer negative ones and feel that they have greater levels of fulfilment generally. They are also better able to understand and repair bad moods and recover better from provocative negative events.

Dealing with stress

Individuals with higher levels of mindfulness tend to view demanding situations as being less stressful and are less likely to avoid dealing with them, meaning that issues are less likely to build up and they spend less time worrying about them. It is also associated with better-quality sleep.

When we are stressed we produce higher levels of the hormone cortisol, which gets the heart pumping faster and prepares the body to deal with the stressor. This is fine in the short term, but if levels are high for too long it is damaging to the brain and body. Experienced meditators can have a heightened initial reaction to stressful stimulus due to their greater awareness, but they recover more quickly. Indeed, mindfulness is associated with reduced levels of cortisol, and repeated practice may even reverse the negative effects that chronic stress has on the brain.

KEY FOUR: AWARENESS

In the workplace, mindfulness has been shown to be effective in reducing stress and burnout, more so than general relaxation programmes. Interestingly, it seems to help us to be both more relaxed and more alert.

Benefits have even been found among high-stress professions, such as the police, fire services and the military, which place intense physical, emotional and mental demands on people, often requiring them to make rapid life-impacting decisions under pressure. Mindfulness training was found to lower perceived stress levels, lead to quicker recovery of heart and breathing rates, a stronger immune response, better sleep and better working memory (important for making decisions under pressure).

Being kinder to ourselves

How many of the thoughts that you get caught up in are judgements you are making about yourself? How many of those are critical? Perhaps you chide yourself for what you just did or said, or should have done or said. Or you might have patterns of thought that tell you you're not good enough, you're too fat/thin/short/tall, not clever enough, don't work hard enough, are always messing up, have wasted your talents, have no talents or problems are all your own fault... or maybe a mix of them all!

Being so tough on ourselves can seriously undermine our happiness, well-being and health. Yes, we do mess up sometimes, and sometimes we may not be equal to everything we want to achieve, but often we're our own worst critic. And how we judge ourselves often isn't the way our loved ones, friends or a neutral observer would see things.

By ruminating on our flaws too much, we can start to believe they are facts rather than opinions. This can generate a sense of shame and unworthiness, which as well as making us unhappy can cause us to disconnect from what would make us feel better, such as seeing and nurturing our real strengths and talents, forming richer connections with other people and more fully experiencing life.

Mindfulness training can help us to become more compassionate towards ourselves, meaning we:
★ Treat ourselves kindly and without harsh judgement during difficulties.

★ Recognise that mistakes, failures and hardships are part of being human and need not cut us off from others.
★ Maintain, through mindfulness, a more balanced awareness of painful thoughts and feelings rather than avoiding, suppressing or getting caught up in them.

Being more self-compassionate isn't about deluding ourselves that we are always great, but not deluding ourselves that we're always bad either. It's about 'an open-hearted willingness' to face our difficulties and suffering, not turn away from it, including looking at what we don't like in ourselves with awareness, curiosity and kindness.

Self-compassion and mindfulness are connected, but separate, elements that each lead to higher well-being. Both are important. People who are meditators on a regular basis have been shown to be more mindful, more self-compassionate and have higher psychological well-being compared to those who didn't practise meditation. An increase in self-compassion has also been shown in depression-sufferers who participated in a mindfulness programme. As a result they were less likely to succumb to rumination and relapse into depression in response to sad moods.

A form of meditation, specifically focused on developing compassion for ourselves and others, is called Loving Kindness. We'll take a look at how to do this on page 139. We'll also look at ways to be more self-compassionate and accepting of who we are and to identify and nurture our strengths in Chapter 9.

Living a life we choose

Some psychologists propose that mindfulness leads to improved well-being and flourishing because it promotes greater self-regulation of behaviour and helps us take better care of our own well-being. And, indeed, mindfulness training has been shown to help people give up smoking, reduce binge-eating and lower alcohol consumption and illicit-substance use.

Mindfulness gives us fuller awareness of internal and external information, enabling us to make more accurate assessments of situations and therefore make more conscious choices. This leads to more flexibility, as we're not being driven by emotional reactions, impulses or autopilot, which, as we have seen, can cause us stress. Mindfulness can increase our sense of spirituality, help us become clearer about our values, strengths and interests, and do more that aligns with them. This is strongly associated with greater well-being and therefore happiness.

Not wanting what we don't have

One factor that is toxic to our levels of happiness is constantly comparing ourselves to others and wanting what we don't have, for example a fancier phone or car, designer clothes or a bigger flat or house. This is perhaps more than ever apparent today as we are bombarded by images and stories of people who seem to 'have it all' or be living 'perfect' lives.

A study of the financial desires of UK university/college students and US working adults indicated that higher mindfulness was linked to a smaller difference between what people had and what they wanted, and this was related to how happy they were. Importantly, this did not seem to be due to the level of personal or household income (albeit the group studied could be regarded as middle class). Further, for some people, as their mindfulness skills developed, the gap between what they had and wanted reduced and happiness increased.

Loving and being loved

As we saw in Chapter 2, our relationships with others are central to happiness, so how might mindfulness contribute to this?

If you think about it, if we are happier, feel better about ourselves and are better able to manage our emotions and impulsive responses, this is very likely to benefit our relationships and connections with others. How often have we reacted impulsively (especially to those close to us), to something someone has said, which has led to offence or has caused an argument that persists for hours or even days? Or have we been upset by something someone else did or said that niggled away at us and so coloured how we behaved towards them? Developing the ability not to get caught up in our instant reactions makes a difference. We'll look at this in Chapter 7. And if we are more aware, curious and non-judgemental, we are likely to be better listeners and notice subtle signals such as fleeting expressions that help us to see and better understand how others are feeling. We know that mindfulness increases our positive emotional experience, which, as we will see in Chapter 8, opens us more to others, makes us more trusting and even lets us get on with those from other cultures better.

If mindfulness leads to greater insight into and compassion for ourselves and simultaneously means we're less caught up in our own needs, we're more likely to be concerned and compassionate about others.

Scientific evidence to support the role of mindfulness in the quality of our relationships and connections with others is only recently emerging:

★ In romantic relationships people with a more mindful disposition report that they feel more satisfied and secure in their relationships, have increased feelings of empathy for, and greater acceptance of, their partner and deal more skilfully with relationship stress.

★ Students reported that meditation had a positive impact on their relationships. Young adults who were dating reported feeling happier in their relationships and experienced greater sexual satisfaction as a result of being more aware, reacting less to inner experiences and being better able to articulate their experiences.

★ Long-term couples who developed mindfulness skills in an MBSR-style programme specifically designed to enhance relationships, reported that they felt far more satisfied with their relationships and had higher acceptance of their partner, in part explained by the personal changes gained through mindfulness training.

★ Changes in the brain as a result of practising mindfulness are located in areas that are central to the regulation of interpersonal behaviour.

This all indicates the important role mindfulness could play in establishing and nurturing our connections with others, especially those close to us. Indeed one researcher suggests that as established relationships involve a significant reliance on automatic internal processes, mindfulness may be more valuable than other ways of improving relationships, since it makes us more conscious of these.

Making mindfulness accessible to young people through podcasts is now my mission. My friend, Anh, got me into it. Anh is a maths teacher, working with kids in really challenging circumstances, in an area that was the scene of riots. Anh had been practising mindfulness for a while and said that it really made a difference. I wasn't sure, but I let him drag me along to an Action for Happiness talk given by Jon Kabat-Zinn, the person who has really made mindfulness a big thing in the West.

The talk was interesting, but it wasn't until Anh asked Jon a question that my attention was really grabbed. Anh's hunch was that mindfulness could be helpful for the kids he taught and he wanted Jon's thoughts on this. What message could he give to kids from difficult backgrounds? Jon's reflection was that often those kids feel cut off and have 'no intimacy with the rest of the world'. Mindfulness could be of value to them, but it needed to be in their language, the language of their streets.

Jon suggested we make contact with the Mind Body Awareness (MBA) project in California, which had been teaching mindfulness to kids from the wrong side of the tracks who'd ended up in juvenile detention centres for a range of crimes. Apparently, the project had made an amazing difference. The kids learned more self-regulation, became less impulsive and less violent, and as a result, fewer of them were convicted again. It had helped these kids feel better about themselves and go on to have better lives. It struck a personal cord. I hadn't had the easiest of starts in life and I knew kids from tough backgrounds often weren't valued or cared for well by our society. If this could work for them, it had to be something special.

After the talk, I got in touch with the MBA project and asked if they'd be willing to be interviewed. The executive director, Roger Miller, said 'yes'. I also started practising mindfulness and I'm hooked. What was really ground-breaking for me was the difference it made to the way I related to my thoughts. I stopped caring so much about what people thought about me and worrying about whether I was good enough at work. I've become more focused on what's important and I'm also clearer about my personal goals.

Why does mindfulness work?

There are a number of different scientific theories that look at why and how mindfulness affects us emotionally and physiologically. It's complex and research is ongoing, but here are some potential insights that may help to shed light on this question.

Emotional spirals

As we practise mindfulness, the interaction between more positive emotional experiences, fewer negative ones and increased mindfulness seems to be mutually reinforcing, creating an 'upward spiral' of well-being, enabling us to be happier and to develop positive coping strategies when things go wrong. It's thought that these benefits come about, in part, through two intertwined psychological processes.

Firstly, mindfulness helps us to distance ourselves from our thoughts and see them neutrally. If we are feeling down we can interpret everything that happens to us in a negative light or assume the worst. We have already seen that our minds have a natural tendency to wander, and more so when we aren't feeling happy. One negative thought can go round and round in our heads, for example: 'I'm just not good enough' or 'He's so selfish'. The more these stay in our heads, the worse we feel. This is known as 'rumination'. Or we catastrophise – this is where something bad happens or a negative thought occurs and the mind gravitates to the worst imaginable outcome (e.g. 'Why did I miss that sale today? I'll probably lose my job. What happens if I lose my job? I'll have no money, we'll lose the flat, my wife will leave me, I'll end up on the streets...' Unchecked, rumination and catastrophising can lead to depression and anxiety. We'll explore this more in Chapter 7. Mindfulness teaches us to detach and step back from all this mental noise and not get caught up in it and so stop the chain reaction of one unpleasant thought leading to another – and another and another – and so on. The technical term for this is 'decentring'.

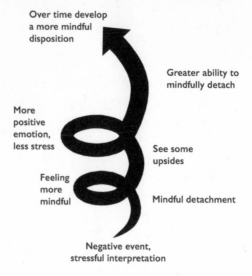

Upward emotional spirals counter downward ones

Over time develop
a more mindful
disposition

Greater ability to
mindfully detach

More
positive
emotion,
less stress

See some
upsides

Feeling
more
mindful

Mindful detachment

Negative event,
stressful interpretation

Adapted from: Garland, E. L., Farb, N. A., Goldin, P. R. & Fredrickson, B. L. (2015) Mindfulness Broadens Awareness and Builds Eudaimonic Meaning: A Process Model of Mindful Positive Emotion Regulation, Psychological Inquiry, 26:4, 293-314. With permission.

'Mindful coping'

Stepping back from unpleasant thoughts feels better – we're calmer and happier – which, in turn, opens us up and makes us more flexible in our thinking – facilitating greater mindfulness. As a consequence, when negative events happen we are more likely to be able to see a silver lining in them, reducing stress, unhappiness and enhancing positive feelings. Psychologists call this 'mindful coping' and it leads to considerably lower stress, greater resilience and more hope, which not only feels better, but has knock-on consequences for our health as well as other aspects of our lives. For example, say we're unfortunate enough to break a leg. Of course this would be painful and unpleasant, and we could get stuck on the downsides: 'It's so unfair I've broken my leg, it means I can't go out and I'm going to miss the fun, I can't play tennis, I'll be unfit and get fat, while everyone else is doing the opposite. I'm so fed up.'

The detachment of mindfulness enables us to take a different stance, helping us to cope better and feel happier, despite a bad thing having happened. So, in response to the scenario above, we're able to stand back, helping us feel better, which, in turn, helps us to find, or make, something constructive out of the situation, such as: 'Okay, if I can't play tennis in my spare time it'll be a good opportunity to catch up on all those books I've been meaning to read. I can also try out some new healthy recipes to help me manage my weight while I can't exercise.' This leads to less stress and more positive emotions. We'll look at other coping strategies in Chapter 7, and in Chapter 8 we'll explore the effects of positive emotions in more detail.

Mindfulness and the brain

In the past decade or so advances in imaging technology have meant that it's been possible to see how meditation practice impacts the brain – with remarkable results. Differences can be seen in the way areas of the brain are activated after practising mindfulness for only eight weeks. Over time, it can actually change the brain's physical structure – for the better.

★ When people are upset, angry, anxious or depressed, the brain area known as the pre-frontal cortex is activated more on the right side than on the left. When they are feeling happy, the reverse is the case and the left area is more activated than the right. Your ratio between the activity on the right and that on the left can predict your moods. Now it was thought that we each had a 'happiness set-point', a natural level to which we returned after good or bad emotional experiences. If you were lucky you were born with a set-point that was happy (and if you weren't, then – tough). The set-point would be the equivalent of your natural ratio of left-to-right pre-frontal activation.

Jon Kabat-Zinn, who developed MBSR, taught it to a group of workers. His collaborator, the neuroscientist Richard Davidson, measured the activation in their brains before and after the eight weeks of training. Incredibly, the activation of their brains had shifted to the left, even when they were exposed to sad music and memories. Studies of people who have meditated over a number of years show that there are structural changes in their brains, meaning that their ratios change and they are more likely to feel happy, energised and calm rather than sad, lethargic and angry.

KEY FOUR: AWARENESS

When Action for Happiness was launched, we designed a happiness challenge for the BBC. A group of volunteers in Scarborough was rounded up and their progress over the week was featured at breakfast time each day.

Among other things, that challenge included a short mindfulness practice, which participants found helpful. Researching that piece, journalist David Sillito came across a scientific study that found that this practice actually changed the brain after as little as a few weeks'. True to his profession, he decided to test it for himself.

So along with his friend, Fiona, who suffers from chronic pain, he enrolled on an eight-week MBSR course, and then asked neuroscientist Elena Antonova, at Kings' College, London, to take a 'before' image of their brains. Both duly attended the course sessions and practised in between, and they were curious to see the changes it might make. After eight weeks, it was back into the MRI machine.

In that short time clear differences were seen. Fiona had already found that mindfulness had helped reduce her pain 'a few notches' so that it didn't dominate her mind, and low and behold, her brain showed distinct differences in the areas that correspond to pain. Just to check that how the images were being interpreted was correct, David sent them to another independent neuroscientist. They confirmed Elena's analysis that the pain network in Fiona's brain was calmed through mindfulness meditation.

For David there were also changes, but these were a surprise. His brain showed reduced activation in the area concerned with the self. This supported the view that mindfulness makes us less focused on self-related mind chatter, opening us to what's around us in the present moment.

★ Mindfulness has been shown to enhance the functioning of the areas of our brain that help us manage our emotions and regulate the instant responses of the amygdala – the primitive area of our brain, which influences emotional reactivity and acting on impulse.

★ After intensive periods of mindfulness (e.g. a ten-day retreat) the network of connections between the prefrontal cortex and other areas of the brain associated with attention are strengthened. The prefrontal cortex has a number of important functions, including our 'executive function' – the area of the brain that helps us make decisions, solve complex problems, plan and set goals and regulate our behaviour.

★ After eight weeks of mindfulness training the density of 'grey matter' increased in participants' brains, compared to a control group. Higher grey-matter density is associated with higher performance of the area in which the grey matter is located. In this study, the areas of the brain associated with learning, memory, emotional regulation and being able to see things from different perspectives all showed greater concentration.

★ Another study showed that after undergoing an eight-week MBSR training, an area in the brain called the 'insula' becomes more activated and with sustained meditation practice it becomes enlarged. This is important since the insula is associated with our ability to feel empathy and compassion for others, and so regulates our sense of connectedness, a fundamental ingredient in well-being and happiness.

Towards a happier world

> 'If we are peaceful, if we are happy, we can smile and blossom like a flower, and everyone in our family, our entire society, will benefit from our peace.
>
> Thich Nhat Hanh, , *Being Peace*

Mindfulness can increase compassion for others

Greater mindful awareness could help us to make the world a happier place, and scientific evidence is emerging that this is indeed the case. For example, in an experimental study participants were divided into three groups, two receiving different types of mindfulness training and the third none.

Group 1 Received a weekly two-hour meditation class from an experienced teacher (instruction, discussion and thirty minutes' practice) for eight weeks, and a twenty-minute audio-guided meditation to do at home. These meditations concentrated on focusing and calming the mind (similar to MBSR training).

Group 2 Received the same type and amount of meditation training from the same teacher, but with an added focus on compassion.

Group 3 Was a control group, who received no training.

After eight weeks of training, all participants were invited, one by one, to the lab, ostensibly to complete some problem-solving tests (which they believed was the object of the experiment). Before entering the lab they had to wait in a room in which there were three chairs, two of which were already occupied. Naturally, each participant sat in the free chair. A short time later, a fourth person entered the waiting room using crutches and a medical boot, visibly wincing. Seeing that there were no chairs free, they leaned against the wall, clearly in discomfort. Neither of the two people already in the waiting room made any move to acknowledge the person with the bad leg or offer their chair. Unbeknown to the participants, the 'sufferer' and the two original people in the waiting room were actors. The point of the experiment was to see whether mindfulness training made a person more likely to act compassionately towards another, despite their being under unconscious social pressure not to do so, as exerted by the other people in the waiting room, who did not move. The results were dramatic. Participants in both groups receiving mindfulness training were FIVE times more likely to act compassionately and give up their chair than participants in the control group. It made no difference which type of training they received.

Mindfulness/behaving ethically and responsibly

Mindfulness also seems to increase our sense of environmental, ethical and social responsibility:

★ Happiness, mindfulness and behaviour seem to be related. People who are more mindful have been shown to be both happier and behave in ecologically responsible ways.

★ Mindfulness may also make us less likely to discriminate against stigmatised social groups. A study of one hundred adults receiving either a six-week training in loving kindness meditation; attending six weekly discussions on loving kindness, or nothing, found that only those receiving the meditation training showed decreases in unconscious bias towards people from other ethnicities/the homeless.

★ In another experiment, participants received either MBSR or interpersonal communication training (as the control). Before the training they received a moral reasoning and ethical-decision test comprising five difficult scenarios to which they had to determine the best course of action. This was repeated immediately after the training and two months later. Immediately afterwards, neither group showed change in moral reasoning and decision-making, but two months later the MBSR participants demonstrated improvement. These effects may also extend to the business community. A review on corporate social responsibility for the European Commission found that mindfulness training led to a greater probability of people behaving in a socially responsible way, whereas conventional executive education did not.

Ways to be mindful in your everyday life

You can practise mindfulness anywhere, pretty much any time. And the more you practise, the more you become naturally mindful. It becomes part of who you are. Most people trying it for the first time start with a short breathing meditation. Breathing is a core practice of mindfulness, which is good, since while you are alive you have your breath with you!

Getting started

Setting aside a short amount of time, if possible daily, helps you get used to the practice and you can gradually build up to longer sessions. Experienced mindfulness practitioners set aside between twenty and forty-five minutes per day for their practice. At first, don't try to do too much. Start with a few minutes – it's rather like wanting to start jogging. You wouldn't start with going on a ten-kilometre race, and if you did it could be very painful. You are waking up and training your brain.

Earlier in this chapter (see page 117) I asked you to try following your breath for just a minute. The point of that was to notice just how much the mind wanders. But just a minute of mindfulness is useful. It can be a quick and easy way to start, and you can easily do it several times a day. At first, sitting in a quiet place to do it is best. Once you're familiar with it, you can do it out and about/standing up. When you've tried the minute-long version a couple of times, try increasing it to five or ten minutes, focusing on your breath and noticing when your mind has wandered and bringing it back again. And again and again... Practise ten minutes of mindfulness once a day for two or three weeks. Then, over the following few weeks, gradually increase the time you practise, building up to, say, twenty minutes per day. Even as you become practised at doing longer sessions, the basic minute version can still be useful at times of stress or challenge. As leading mindfulness teacher Martin Boroson says, 'It only takes a moment to make a meaningful difference to your state of mind.'

Mindfulness basics in a nutshell

When I first learnt meditation, I have to be honest, I struggled. I just felt I couldn't clear my mind of thoughts – boy, was it busy and noisy inside my head, with thoughts coming up from the left, right and perhaps even off-centre! I felt it wasn't for me and gave up.

Years later, having studied positive psychology and so becoming aware of the research and the evidence of its benefits, I thought I'd try again. I signed up for an MBSR programme. On that course, the teacher imparted a simple pearl of wisdom that made all the difference for me…

'It's not about clearing your mind. That's impossible! Generating thoughts is what our minds do.'

The core skill is to notice when our minds have wandered from our breath and to bring our attention back. Over and over again.

The practice of mindfulness is about NOTICING when our minds have drifted off, as we're usually not aware of this, and then choosing to place our attention back to where we want it.

It's about not getting caught up in your thoughts, recognising that, like clouds, they come and go. When a thought arises you notice it, perhaps even label it – there's planning or thinking and then bringing your mind back to your breath. That's it. In essence, it's very simple, but actually quite hard to do. That's why it takes practice.

The three-minute breathing space – the hourglass

Sometimes, when we need it most, mindful awareness can disappear. Psychologist Professor Mark Williams (one of the world's leading experts on mindfulness) and his colleagues developed the 'Three-minute breathing space' specifically for when we are tired and stressed, under pressure and squeezed for time or can feel ourselves getting angry and emotional. The three-minute breathing space has three phases:

1 Acknowledging the comings and goings in your mind.
2 Focusing attention on a specific point of your body – the abdomen.
3 Expanding your attention to become aware of your whole body.

So your meditation starts wide, narrows and then expands wide again. Like an old-fashioned hourglass. See below for instructions. Try it twice a day for a week or two so you can call on it whenever you need to.

Try this! The three-minute practice

Whether you are sitting or standing, position yourself in a relaxed but upright posture. If you can, close your eyes.

First – notice what's going on inside

★ Bring your awareness to your thoughts. Notice them as passing events and try not to get caught up by them.

★ What emotions or feelings do you notice? Have a curious but 'warm' look at them, even if they are unpleasant. Don't try to change them in any way. Just notice that they are there.

★ What sensations do you notice in your body? Any tightness, tension or discomfort? Again be curious and 'warm', don't try to change the sensations in any way. Just notice that they are there.

Second – focusing attention

★ Focus on your breath and the sensations it creates in your abdomen, expanding and relaxing as you breathe in and out.

★ Each breath is an opportunity to come back to the present, bringing the mind back if it wanders.

Third – expanding your attention out

★ Gradually expand your focus on the breath in the abdomen out to your whole body, as if the whole of you is breathing.

★ If you notice an area of discomfort, look at it 'warmly'. Don't try to change it. Imagine, for a moment, breathing into and around it.

★ If your attention is being pulled into the feeling, return to an awareness of your body as a whole.

Based on: Segal, Williams, & Teasdale (2002). Williams, M., Teasdale, J. D., Segal, Z. V., & Kabat-Zinn, J. (2007) cited in Williams & Penman (2011)

A fuller experience – mindful eating activity

Many meditation classes include an eating meditation (see page 138) – often a raisin. The idea is to experience the food item fully – its smell, appearance (colour, shape, texture), its sound as you roll it between your fingers, then the feeling on your tongue, the tastes at the front of the tongue and then further back, the sound as your teeth bite, noticing how the taste changes. This is, of course, an exercise in being fully present in the moment. It also helps us see that there is a lot more to any experience than we are usually open to and notice. It's not uncommon for people who thought they didn't like raisins to decide that they really do, or who ate them regularly to realise that they really don't like them at all!

Top tips Mindfulness practice

Mindfulness and strengths expert, Ryan Neimiec, says the three most common obstacles to get in the way of practising mindfulness are:

1 Not having the time to practise

2 Forgetting to practise

3 Struggling with the practice because your mind keeps wandering

So here are some tips that can help:

★ Start short and build up. For the first few weeks try a few minutes per session, say ten minutes, and build up over time.

★ Be regular, get anchored. Set aside a regular time for practice. Anchoring to an activity that is already part of your daily routine can help with both fitting it in and remembering to practise, such as before you make your morning coffee or after cleaning your teeth.

★ Do some mindfulness rather than none. If you have a day where you really can't sit for the full time you'd planned, try to do something – even for just a minute or two.

★ Try something different. If you are struggling with your practice, try a different focus, e.g. mindful walking or eating.

★ Don't worry if it doesn't always go well – this is normal, so don't get frustrated with yourself or disheartened. Just keep at it.

Based on: Neimeic, R. (2015)

Try this! The full chocolate experience

Find a bar of chocolate (very dark chocolate is the healthiest!). The aim is not to eat the whole thing, just one small piece, very, very slowly, using all your senses and focusing on every tiny moment. Make sure you won't be disturbed for the next ten minutes or so.

★ First, look at the whole chocolate bar – notice the colour and pattern of the wrapper, its smell, its texture…

★ Slowly unwrap it, listening to the sounds and the sensations of touch.

★ Now break a small piece off. This is what you'll be focusing on for the rest of the activity. Start by really looking at it.

★ What different colours can you see in it? How does the light reflect off it? What does the texture look like? What is the shape like?

★ How does it feel in your hands? What does the shape and texture feel like? Is it the same all over?

★ Can you smell it?

★ Take a small bite – don't chew! Notice how it feels held in your mouth. What is the texture? How does that change in your mouth?

★ What can you already taste? If you move it around your mouth, does the taste change?

★ Then start to eat. Feel the texture and notice all the flavours as you chew the piece of chocolate slowly and as you swallow.

★ What do you notice once you've swallowed? Do traces of taste or texture remain? What else do you notice?

Take a few moments to reflect on this experience. What did you notice? What was new or unexpected?

Note: If you don't usually eat chocolate, you could try this exercise with a raisin or an orange segment.

138

Loving Kindness

This is a form of meditation specifically designed to develop kindness and compassion for ourselves and others. In Buddhism it's called 'metta' and it was initially introduced to the West by Sharon Salzberg.

Rather than focusing on your breathing or your body, focus on a specific set of phrases or wishes, which you repeat to yourself. An example of this to try is shown on page 140. Initially, this is focused towards you, then to someone you know well and care a lot about, then to someone you know, but not well, then to someone you find difficult – and then to all beings.

Practise this as long as feels right. You may want to start with just the first two stages, gradually expanding out, once you feel comfortable. In studies where people did a Loving Kindness meditation regularly (e.g. for thirty minutes each day for eight weeks), participants experienced increased positive emotions – joy, kindness, gratitude, hope, fewer negative moods, lower inflammation responses and greater immunity.

Making everyday moments more mindful

As well as having focused practice times, it's easy to find ways to weave mindfulness into everyday activities. The point here is to just simply be in the present moment, not judge or think. It's about being more fully aware – we may be surprised by how much more we can experience. It's also good mindfulness practice and it can be a welcome punctuation in the day. It need only take a few extra seconds or a minute or two to become aware of the information coming in through our senses.

Here are a few ideas:

★ Each time you step outside, look up at the sky and notice what's there – the sun, clouds or the stars. Notice all the different colours, shapes or textures. Notice the feeling of the air on your body, or the warmth or coolness or sensation of the wind. What else do you notice?

★ As you enter your home or workplace, be aware of sensations and feelings. How does the floor feel beneath your feet? What noises can you hear? What smells do you notice? What colours do you see?

★ Each day, notice an object of beauty such as a car, a building, a poster or something in nature. What do you notice about it?

Try this! Loving Kindness meditation

Sit with legs uncrossed, feet flat, relaxed but upright, shoulders relaxed/chest open. Focus on your breath. Imagine breathing into your heart. Focus on the four wishes for yourself and then, in stages, for others.

1 For yourself
★ Bring yourself into mind with warmth and kindness.

★ Warmly repeat these wishes slowly to yourself:
   May I be safe • May I be happy • May I be well • May I live with ease

★ While repeating each wish, bring your attention to it, slowly, as if there were ripples radiating out, like when a pebble is dropped into a pond.

★ If your mind wanders, bring it back to the wish, or your breath, and then back to the wish again.

★ Continue repeating rounds of the four wishes for a few minutes.

★ Pause between wishes to notice thoughts, feelings, sensations: acknowledge they're there, then let go.

Then take a few minutes to do the same...

2 For a loved one
★ Bring that person to mind, feeling the warmth that you feel for them.

★ Holding the person in your heart. For a few minutes warmly repeat the wishes for them:
   May you be safe • May you be happy • May you be well • May you live with ease

★ Pausing between wishes, notice what comes up. Let that come and go. If you get distracted, return to the wishes, continue repeating them.

Then do the same for...

3 A stranger you recognise, but who you don't know personally.

4 Someone you know who is suffering.

5 Extend the wishes to all beings – you, your loved ones and strangers.

Close by coming back to focusing on your breath. If you experience difficult feelings at any stage, bring your attention back to your breath.

Based on: Salzberg, S. (2011). Fredrickson (2013). Williams & Penman (2011). Neff, K. (2011)

★ Look up at some trees and notice how they are, their different shapes and colours. Look at the textures of their bark, branches and leaves. Notice how the leaves move and how they sound. Are there birds in the branches? Can you see sunlight through the foliage or drops of rain on the leaves? What insects are buzzing nearby? What else do you notice?

★ When you are going somewhere in the car, by foot or on your bike, notice how you are as you travel. Are you rushing to reach your destination? How does it feel? Where are the muscles in your body tight or relaxed? Which are working and which are not? How does your breathing feel – fast, slow, deep or shallow? Does it feel different when you slow down and take your time?

Try this! Mindful walking

Why not try this on a walk you often take, for example to work, school or college? This could be planned specifically. (You might want to walk a little slower than usual, so perhaps allow extra time.)

★ As you walk, notice how your shoes feel against your feet – are they hard or soft? Do they touch some areas but not others?

★ Focus your attention on the soles of your feet and how they feel as each, in turn, touches the ground – from your heel as it lands and through to your toes as you move to the other foot.

- Notice where your weight is
- Notice the texture of the ground on your feet and how this changes as you walk
- Notice how warm or cold your feet are
- Notice the noise your feet make as you walk…

★ Don't judge or worry about what you are experiencing or change the way you are walking as a result. The aim is simply to focus and notice.

★ If your mind wanders or gets caught up in thought, bring it back to your feet and notice the sensations of walking.

★ When you are doing something pleasurable such as taking a warm bath, petting your dog or cat, stroking your child's hair or sitting down for a moment of peace, be truly present. Really notice what it is you find pleasurable about the experience and how it makes you feel.

★ Listen to the sounds around you. What different sounds can you hear? What sounds do you notice close by? How do the sounds change as they get further away. What are the most distant sounds you can hear?

To sum up

Here are five key points to take away from this chapter:

1 The core practice of mindfulness involves consciously paying non-judgemental, kindly attention to a point of focus, such as the breath, and when the mind wanders from this, gently bringing it back again. The activity of noticing when the mind wanders and bringing it back again builds mindfulness.

2 Our minds naturally wander. We can spend time worrying about the past, planning the future or running on autopilot, meaning we're not fully aware in the moment. This undermines happiness and well-being.

3 We can get caught up in ruminating on worries or catastrophising about what might happen, making us less happy. Mindfulness teaches us to take a neutral stance as if we're an outside observer.

4 Regularly practising mindfulness changes the brain for the better, helping us to feel happier, calmer and less stressed; it can help us manage our emotions, be kinder towards ourselves and others; it can contribute to happier relationships and help us to be clearer about our values.

5 Mindfulness is simple but not always easy. In the short-term, many people find that it can help them feel calmer and more in control, but the bigger benefits come through persisting with practice over time.

Connections to other Keys

Other Keys you might like to explore in connection with Awareness:

★ **GIVING** (See page 10)
Helping others is an important source of happiness. Mindfulness can lead to us being kinder and more compassionate towards other people.

★ **RELATING** (See page 36)
Our relationships are central to our happiness and well-being. Being more mindful of our own reactions and those of other people can help us to help us feel more connected to others and nurture our relationships.

★ **RESILIENCE** (See page 198)
More mindful awareness helps us to notice our habitual unhelpful thought patterns and stop ourselves getting caught up in them, which can make us more resilient. It complements other approaches to building resilience that are explored in Chapter 7.

★ **EMOTIONS** (See page 238)
Mindfulness can be a source of more pleasant emotions that have beneficial consequences for our well-being. Mindfulness also helps us to tune into and manage our emotions.

★ **ACCEPTANCE** (See page 266)
Our expectations of ourselves can undermine our well-being. Mindfulness can help us to be more self-accepting and aware of our natural strengths and develop weaker ones. We can also apply our strengths to help us practise and develop mindfulness.

★ **MEANING** (See page 298)
Having a sense of meaning and purpose in our lives is important for happiness. Over time, the practice of mindfulness can help us understand our values and act in line with them, increase our level of compassion towards others, help deepen our sense of connection to something beyond ourselves and support behaving ethically and responsibly, all of which can increase the sense of meaning in our lives.

G
R
E
A
T

D
R
E
A
M

5

TRYING OUT

Keep learning new things

Love learning, love life. Learning can certainly be a rich source of enjoyment and happiness. Being curious, creative, open to trying out new things and getting absorbed in hobbies and passions helps us to keep our brain in shape, find fulfillment and get more out of life and ourselves.

Trying out: introduction

> 'The ways of creativity are infinite: the ways of formal learning are numbered. Restless, curious, playful, contriving, the innovative mind feeds on challenge, and makes its home in the province of mystery.'
>
> Robert Grudin, *The Grace of Great Things: On the Nature of Creativity*

When we think about 'happiness' it's very easy to focus on the short-term fix – things we find immediately pleasurable, especially when it comes to how we spend our hard-earned cash and precious free time. After all, pleasure feels good and helps us switch off from the demands of work and home and, as we will see in Chapter 8, that's important. But it's only part of the picture.

Happiness is also about a deeper sense of fulfillment, a sense that we're continuously growing and developing through putting effort into trying new things and challenging ourselves. Indeed the Ancient Greek philosopher Aristotle argued that the highest 'goods' were not about feeling good but about 'activities of the soul', in which we strive to achieve the best there is within us, discovering our unique talents and working to bring these to reality.

As humans, we have an inbuilt desire to learn, develop, be creative and grow that can continue throughout life. And this desire can truly help us to flourish. Learning is not only about acquiring formal qualifications, but more about what interests and excites us. It's about approaching our lives and what we do day to day with curiosity and a spirit of exploration, being open to trying new things – whether using our heads, bodies or hands – or all three. And being absorbed in hobbies, projects, passions and taking on new challenges can be a rich and important source of well-being and happiness.

TEN KEYS TO HAPPIER LIVING

Learning is not just for the young – it's about staying young in mind throughout life. Being curious and continuing to learn is always important and perhaps even more essential as the years go by to help us feel useful, connected and vital, and to keep our brains alert and active.

Trying out new things can help build our confidence and resilience too. Grappling with challenges and overcoming difficulties is part of learning, which in turn helps us tackle the problems of daily life. And the more we continue to learn, the more open to exploring and to new experiences we are likely to become.

Hardwired to be curious, creative and learning

We come from a long line of curious, creative learners. Every element of our lives, such as the way our homes look and are built, heated, furnished and decorated, the meals we eat, the clothes we wear, how we work and the tools and technology we use, is the result of curiosity, creativity and the knowledge and skills people have accumulated over millennia.

As a species we have had to explore, create and innovate in order to adapt, survive, progress and thrive – by stepping beyond boundaries and trying out new things. Our ancestors explored, grew and shared knowledge. Through that process they gained understanding and developed tools, skills and ideas. Their drive to explore was fuelled by both necessity and the rewarding experience of successful discoveries, finding out what worked and what didn't. Gradually, tales of discoveries – good and bad – were shared, and so our ancestors learned to be curious about each others' stories. Little by little they built on each others' findings. Those who made these new discoveries and developed skills were likely to be highly valued. And so, over time, as a species, we have become hardwired to experience pleasure when we have ideas, make new discoveries and are creative. In an ever-changing, uncertain world, curiosity and creativity helped our ancestors to survive, and today it seems that it's just as important if we're to thrive in our modern world.

Fundamental to flourishing

Aristotle continues his influence today. Martin Seligman, the catalyst behind the field of 'positive psychology', argues that having activities in our lives that absorb and challenge us is an important element of flourishing. Psychologist Carol Ryff has been studying well-being over the entire lifespan for many decades. She argues that two learning-related dimensions are vital for well-being: personal growth and mastery.

Personal growth

★ Feeling we are continually developing and growing, and having a sense of discovering and using more of our potential (rather than stagnating).

★ Being interested in, and open to, new experiences (rather than being bored or uninterested).

★ Learning and increasing our understanding of our self and the world, and using this to adapt, change and improve over time.

Mastery

★ Feeling a sense of competence in our external personal environment, managing its demands and making use of opportunities as they arise; choosing, managing and creating our personal environment to reflect who we are and what we value.

To some extent personal growth and mastery go hand in hand. Our external worlds don't remain static – there are always changes and new things to discover, which means we adapt, learn and grow in response to and, in turn, shape our external context. This ability to adapt to, and shape, our environments is an important part of resilience too.

Lifelong learning and happiness

'Learning is a treasure that accompanies its owner everywhere.'
Chinese proverb

When I first studied psychology, it was generally accepted that you 'couldn't teach an old dog new tricks', implying that by the time we reach adulthood our brain is set and it's pretty much downhill from there. Luckily, with the advances in neuroscience techniques, studies of the brain in the last decade or two have changed this thinking.

We now know that our brain can, and does, change throughout life. Even as adults, our brains are 'plastic' (meaning malleable). When we have new experiences and learn intentionally, we generate new brain cells

WHY THE *BAKE-OFF* MAKES US HAPPIER

What would contribute more to your happiness – eating a delicious cake or making it? TV programme *The Great British Bake-Off* suggests that there's something more than the pleasure of tasting a good cake, pie or pudding. The show is remarkably popular: over 15 million people (in the UK) watched the final of the 2015 series. And it's sparked a huge rise in home baking. But what's at the root of this interest about something as everyday as baking? What makes people switch on their TVs and afterwards get into the kitchen?

It's a lot about following the contestants' journeys as they learn. We watch as they are tested and stretched, challenge themselves and grow. We see them use their creativity, take on and build on judges' feedback, hone their skills and techniques, as they discover and develop areas of natural strength. We follow the contestants through successes and failures and emotional highs and lows. We see that the journey isn't easy. And we love to see someone who didn't expect to get far succeed. Perhaps they lacked confidence or belief in their abilities – so we feel, even share, their tears of joy in triumph.

For the most part, the contestants appear to be 'ordinary'. So if they can give it a go and improve, it helps us to realise that we can too, and so, perhaps, we decide to give baking a go ourselves.

So making cakes can extend far beyond the pleasure of eating them. It can be an ongoing source of enjoyment, challenge and creativity, as well as giving us a sense of connection as we share our creations with others.

and lay down new neural connections and even increase the volume of specific brain areas. This process may slow down a bit as we age, but it still continues. Yet if that's the case, why do we often seem to lose the natural curiosity and creativity we had as children?

Our brain is like a muscle and, as with our physical strength, it can be a question of 'use it or lose it'. We can start flexing our muscle brain at any time and there are benefits from doing so, but the longer we leave it, the harder it can become. Learning as adults, for fun and out of interest, rather than to get formal qualifications, makes us happier and more

KEY FIVE: TRYING OUT

resilient in many ways, such as:

★ Being more positive, optimistic and hopeful
★ Experiencing greater life satisfaction
★ Having higher self-esteem and more confidence in our own abilities, irrespective of formal qualifications
★ Creating a stronger social network
★ Being and staying physically healthier, experiencing less depression and anxiety, and therefore visiting the doctor less
★ Feeling more fulfilled and less dissatisfied in middle and old age.

It doesn't matter whether you have set out to reach great career highs or have chosen a different course – learning throughout life creates greater well-being and happiness. The benefits can be experienced by anyone, regardless of income, social or cultural background, gender or age. Studies are showing that keeping our minds active into old age is an essential ingredient in staying well, being happy and reducing the risk of dementia.

Mindsets for learning

Although we're all born with a drive to learn and develop our minds, for many different reasons this can get crushed or blocked – whether when we are children or as we get older. We may be put off learning completely or we may avoid certain things we'd actually like to learn by thinking, or saying, things like: 'I'm no good with numbers' or 'I can't draw/sing' or 'There's no point having a go, I'm terrible at technical things'.

Professor of psychology, Carol Dweck, and her colleagues at Stanford University, have spent decades studying this tendency in school children and adults, and say that our attitude to learning matters. The expectations we have about our capabilities and how good we 'should' be have a great influence on our actual ability and willingness to try new things and to learn. Dweck says we can approach learning with a 'growth mindset', allowing us to try fresh approaches, work through challenges and so improve, or approach learning with a 'fixed mindset', which can mean that we give up quickly or don't even try things in the first place because we're afraid to fail. The good news is that if we're aware of, and honest with, ourselves about our mindset to what we want to learn, we can start to change it.

Dweck uses the term 'fixed' because underlying these thoughts is a belief that our intelligence or capabilities have a fixed capacity. So if we struggle at something, or worse, fail, it's evidence that we're not clever or capable enough. So we get frustrated, feel incompetent and may even not try any more. Because if we don't try, we believe that no one will find out that we're not 'good enough' and we won't have to face this ourselves.

In contrast, in a growth mindset, we believe that we can learn and get better at things. It doesn't mean that we'll be great or perfect, but we can find ways to improve. This mindset regards difficulties as a normal part of anyone's learning process and opportunities to understand and build our skills. It means we're less likely to beat ourselves up when we make mistakes or block off potential sources of interest and it helps us to grow rather than stagnate.

Our mindset may vary depending on what we're doing or it may apply to most of what we do. Adopting more of a growth mindset generally helps us to overcome challenges, increase our enjoyment of learning and it means we're more likely to fulfill our potential.

✎ Pause point...

Think back to the last time you had difficulties when you tried something new, were struggling to get better at something or when something you tried failed. What thoughts went through your mind? Did you feel anxious or as though you wanted to just stop and avoid doing it ever again? Did you feel upset, incompetent, start to blame yourself or others, or find excuses for yourself? What if someone tried to give you feedback? Did you feel defensive, angry or crushed? Or if someone else was better than you at something that is important to you, did you feel envious, threatened or feel your confidence draining away?

If the answer to any of these questions was 'yes', these thoughts are indicators of a 'fixed' mindset. And if we're thinking like this, it gets in our way, making learning stressful, negatively impacting our curiosity, confidence and willingness to persist, put effort in and so improve.

Based on: Dweck, C. (2006), (2015)

Try this! Tune in to self-talk

Next time you want to try or learn something new, tune in to your self-talk and try making it growth-oriented rather than fixed. Here are some examples of the type of thing to listen out for...

Growth mindset self-talk		Fixed mindset self-talk
I'm not good at this yet	NOT	I'm not good at this
It feels hard – that's because I'm learning and stretching my brain!	NOT	It feels hard because I'm stupid/clumsy/not capable enough
One step at a time. It takes persistence and effort to get better	NOT	I tried my best and it wasn't good enough
What can I learn from this mistake to try next time?	NOT	I give up! There's no point trying. It'll never be perfect

If you want to see an example of this process in action, take a look at 'Austin's Butterfly' on YouTube. It's charming and one of my favourite video clips.

Adapted from: Dweck, C. (2015)

152

Finding our curiosity & getting more creative

> 'Curiosity… is the engine of our evolving self.'
>
> Todd Kashdan, *Curious? Discover the Missing Ingredient to a Fulfilling Life*

The starting point for learning and creativity

So curiosity may have killed the cat, but it's likely to do the opposite for you because curious people have been shown to live longer, have a higher quality of life, feel that their lives are more enjoyable, fulfilling and meaningful.

Curiosity is what drives us to explore and find things out. It's at the start of every idea we have or advance we make – big or small. It can lead us to discover our passions and interests and get deeper into them, and it's at the heart of a life that's creative and fulfilled. When we're curious we're present, alert, open and engaged.

Our curiosity moves us towards the novel, or the new, rather than away from it, whether it's to solve a problem, develop a new skill, play with or understand complex ideas, or get to know someone new. It drives us to ask questions, observe closely, manipulate or play with tools or techniques, immerse ourselves in research and persist despite challenges. It leads us to discover new things about the world, other people and ourselves. Through curiosity we can better tolerate the uncertainty that is part of new experiences or any learning journey, and so come to think and act in new ways. While some of us are more naturally curious than others, curiosity is a capacity which, with intention and practice, we can all develop more of.

KEY FIVE: TRYING OUT

Try this! Spark your curiosity

Intentionally spark your curiosity each day:

★ Look for things that are different/new as you go about your routine.

★ If you're on a journey you regularly make, look for something you haven't noticed before (e.g. look up at buildings, rather than just from your eye level or looking down at the pavement).

★ When something interesting catches your eye, be curious about it. For example, wonder why it's like it is, how it got there, how it was made or what else it could do or be used for.

See things differently, see different things

Look at the picture (right). What do you notice? Perhaps you saw the shape of the duck's beak or its eye, or another feature caught your attention... but did you also notice the rabbit facing right? Both creatures are there, but because you were asked to look for a duck, it's likely that this is what you saw, at least at first, because this is what you were focused on. We do this all the time. And while it helps us to make quick sense of what we're seeing, it means that we miss a lot – which could fuel our creativity and interest.

A simple example I've noticed in myself is when I'm trying to buy something different to wear. Despite actively looking, I'm still drawn to the style or colour I always wear. If all I want to do is replace something worn out, I've trained my brain well, but it's not so good if I want to break out and try something new.

Harvard psychologist Ellen Langer terms this effect 'mindlessness', which can get in the way of learning and creative thinking; she's conducted studies that show how. For example, in one experiment participants were introduced to the same range of objects in one of two slightly different ways. For the first group, each object was presented by saying what it *was*, for example, 'This is a rubber band' or 'This is a dog chew'. For the second group, the objects were introduced by suggesting what they *could* be, for

Try this! Test yourself

Let's put your curiosity to the test. Here's a picture of a duck. What do you notice about it?

example, 'This could be a rubber band' or 'This is could be a dog chew'. Later in the experiment, the 'need' for an eraser arose but none could be found. Only the second group was able to spontaneously suggest that the rubber band or dog chew could be used instead.

Likewise, a similar effect was found when two groups of children were introduced to the rules of a new game. The first group was given the rules and told, 'This is how you play smack-ball', while the second was told: 'This is how you could play smack-ball'. Both groups played according to the rules they'd been given, but after they'd had time to practise, the ball was surreptitiously changed to a much heavier one, which made it harder to play with. This caused the performance of the first group to be undermined but they stuck to their rules. In contrast, the performance of the second group didn't suffer – they didn't take the basics of the game as hard-and-fast rules, so they were able to adapt the way they played.

Incredible isn't it? Just a simple change to one or two words invited curiosity, rather than invoking mindlessness, and made a big difference to the possibilities people were able to see and the creativity they were able to apply. In fact, Langer calls her work 'the psychology of possibility'. 'It's so simple', she says. 'It's finding ways to be in a flexible state of mind in which we're actively engaged in the present and noticing the novel and the new and are sensitive to context.' In fact, some people refer to her work as 'creative mindfulness'.

KEY FIVE: TRYING OUT

Creative mindfulness increases enjoyment in learning, leads to better problem-solving and, indeed, to more creativity. Curiously it also seems to be really good for us too – reducing stress, damaging rumination, increasing self-acceptance and producing higher psychological well-being. It's a gateway into flow, too, which we'll look at on page 165.

Creativity and happiness

'Even though personal creativity may not lead us to fame and fortune, it can do something that from the individual's point of view is even more important: make day-to-day experiences more vivid, more enjoyable, more rewarding.' Mihaly Czikszentmihalyi, *Creativity: Flow and the Psychology of Discovery and Invention*

We can have beliefs about our ability to be creative that limit our thinking and stop us exploring. When I ask people to describe a 'creative' person, it's not unusual for them to say it's someone with artistic or musical talents and skills or who has ideas that change the world. Well, world-changing ideas are, by their very nature, creative, but they're also rare. While we may range in our level of artistic talent or creativity as a natural strength, any of us can learn to approach our life more creatively... and enjoy trying to do so.

Creativity is also not just about artistic pursuits. Of course, these can be great outlets for creativity (and a lot of fun), but they're not the only way our creativity can be found or applied. Having studied the rare phenomenon of creative genius for decades ('Big-C creativity', as it's known), psychologists are now starting to research 'little-c creativity', the application of creativity in everyday life. Creativity has been recognised through history and across cultures as something inherently valued and has long been something people do and pursue for its own sake – because it's something they enjoy, which gives them a sense of purpose, helping them solve problems and perhaps leading to a deep satisfaction. As psychologist and Quality of Life Therapy expert Michael Frisch puts it, 'In my work with both poor and affluent clients, I see many cases in which creative problem-solving or a creative outlet has a snowball effect', such as leading to a new passion or pastime, greater self-understanding and confidence, and being more energised across everything they do.

Try this! Default to 'yes'

When we're presented with opportunities to do or try something different, often our immediate reaction is 'no'. It's human to be wary of what's strange to us as this can protect us. But if we nearly always default to 'no' it can limit our creativity and learning.

So pick a day (or a week) in which you choose to default to 'yes' instead of 'no'. For example, you might say 'yes' to going to a different place for coffee, trying a food that's new (or which you decided you didn't like when you were a kid), watching a different sort of TV show or film, going out instead of staying in.

Who knows what you'll discover? Of course, apply common sense if something really is likely to be dangerous!

Thinking more creatively

We can apply creativity in almost any area we choose, big or small, for example: what and how we cook dinner; problems we need to solve at work; how we repair something at home; our relationships; or what, where and how we live, and the work we do.

There are two main elements to thinking creatively:
1 Getting out of habitual patterns of thought and the assumptions we mindlessly make.
2 Making connections between things that aren't usually connected.

Let's have a look at each of these.

1 Breaking out of our thinking habits

For the first element, there are tricks we can use to get out of our habitual patterns of thought and mindless assumptions. Psychologist Ellen Langer says there's always a different way of seeing something, if we consciously look for what's new, novel or changed in a situation or person. Simply ask: 'What would I think, see or hear if I stood in someone else's shoes?' Or 'What are the different ways in which I could look at this?'

There's a tried-and-tested creative-thinking technique, 'rules and revolutions', which works well too. If you're trying to solve a problem or come up with an idea for something, think of all the assumptions (rules) in your mind about that thing or the way it needs to be. Then think of ways to break these rules. It can be a quite fun idea to play with and you may find it opens up some new ideas.

The visual part of the brain is different from the rational, logical, part, so it can free us up to play with ideas, without an inner voice saying 'that will never work' too soon! Why not try thinking with your hands rather than with your head? 'Design thinking', as it's called, is becoming increasingly recognised to help people have more, and better, ideas. This subject is even being taught in some schools, taking the approaches designers use and applying them to solve practical problems.

One key technique is 'rapid prototyping'. When we're trying to get to grips with a problem or shape an idea, instead of thinking it through or writing pros and cons, you build a rough model of it. You don't need special skills or materials. You can use anything – play-dough or Plasticine, Lego or packaging from the recycling box. The point is that playing around, using our hands, helps us to think differently and see problems in new ways. It can free up the mind so that we have more and better ideas – and it can be fun too. Sketching out our thoughts and ideas visually can also be helpful, even if it's using basic stick figures and symbols or pictures torn from magazines.

2 Making new connections

It's been said that there are no new ideas, just new connections. Ideas happen when one thing is combined with another to make something new or when one unrelated thought triggers an idea about a project we're working on.

This is one of the reasons why curiosity and creativity are closely connected. The more we're curious, the wider the range of things in our unconscious memory that we can make connections between. One of the best examples I know is an idea that helped make early Apple computers ground-breaking. Having dropped out of college, Steve Jobs's curiosity led him to attend a calligraphy class. 'It was beautiful. Historical. Artistically subtle in a way that science can't capture, and I found it fascinating. None of this had any hope of any practical application in my life. But ten years later, when we were designing the first Macintosh computer, it all came back to me. And we designed it all into the Mac. It was the first computer with beautiful typography.' So you never know where your curiosity might lead.

Try this! Yes, and what if…?

New ideas are like delicate seedlings. They're fragile and need nurturing before we can see whether they'll bear fruit. Yet often we crush them the moment they appear, thinking or saying things like: 'That's stupid' or 'That'll never work'. So we close down ideas before we see where they could lead.

The next time you or someone around you comes up with an idea, think or say: 'Yes and what if…?' so that you add to, and build on, what they've already suggested. Try this with your own ideas too.

Living more creatively

'When a person says they have twenty years' experience, do they really mean one year's experience repeated twenty times?' Source unknown

Breaking out of some of our regular habits and daily routines can help to free up and fuel our creativity. It helps us to see the ordinary parts of our lives differently and to see different things, opening up more opportunities for interest, creativity and enjoyment.

Another of psychologist Ellen Langer and colleagues' experiments illustrates this beautifully. They asked skilled musicians to perform a well-known piece in two ways: firstly replicating the finest performance of the piece that they could remember and secondly playing it in the finest manner they could, but offering subtle nuances that only they would notice. The performances were recorded and played to audiences unaware of the instructions. The experiment was then replicated, varying the order the pieces were played in or listened to. The ability to use more creativity made a difference. Not only did the musicians enjoy playing more when they could personalise the piece, but their performances were rated by the audience as being better. However, we're generally creatures of habit. All too easily we can get stuck in a routine, doing the same thing the same way, year in, year out. Not only can this stifle curiosity and creativity, it can mean we stagnate and stop learning or growing, which, as we've seen, is important for our well-being, both physical and psychological. For this reason 'habit-releasers' can be helpful for depression, to help reignite curiosity and have some fun.

Doing something different

Habits are hard to break, even when we want to or know we need to for the sake of our health or happiness. There are three reasons for this, according to psychology professors Karen Pine and Ben Fletcher:

1 **Our brains are designed to automate** to make regular and frequent choices, decisions and behaviours automatic. This means they're quick and it frees our mind up because we don't need to consciously think.

2 **Our habits are cued by our normal environment** so if, when we get in from work, we always kick off our shoes, grab a glass of wine, switch on the TV and sit on the sofa, that chain of events is triggered as soon as we put our key in the door, even if we intended to practise the guitar or go for a run. Our key in the lock triggers the expectation of the wine/TV/sofa sequence as a 'reward' for getting through the day.

3 **There's a 'know–do' gap between habitual actions and thoughts about them** Our brain registers habitual actions seconds before the conscious thought of doing them, or deciding not to do them. Our habitual actions are triggered in the unconscious part of our brain, which works much faster than the slower, deliberative, conscious part that would help us break out of our routine.

Pine and Fletcher's research suggests that by building more behavioural flexibility or regularly 'doing something different', we are less likely to fall into habitual patterns of action and thought, and find it easier to get out of them if we do. So it helps us make choices that are better for well-being longer term, rather than opting for the instant, easy, though less satisfying, option of how we spend time. This flexibility will likely increase curiosity and creative potential too – leading to improved happiness.

Try this! Do things differently

How can you do something different? Complete the table below for different elements of daily life. There are no right or wrong answers. Just reflect on areas where you might try doing something different.

For each statement, tick the box that is most accurate.

	1 Not like me	2	3	4	5 Very like me
I take different routes to work/school/college each day					
I try to read different newspapers/browse different sites					
I watch/listen to different TV and radio stations					
I go out of my way to meet new people					
I go out of my way to try new activities					
I go out of my way to try new foods and recipes					
I go out of my way to visit new places					
I regularly spend time with people from different backgrounds and views to me					
I regularly spend time with people of different ages to me					
I like to read different types of books					
What I do at weekends varies a lot from week to week					

How could you try doing something differently?

★ Start with something that is easy to change

★ Try doing one different thing each day

★ Identify a trigger to remind you to make your change(s)

★ Use the curiosity prompts on page 154 to help you notice new things while you're trying different things

Doing things we love to do does us good too!

> 'There is no human competence which can be achieved in the absence of a sustaining interest.'
>
> Silvan Tomkins, *Affect, Imagery, Consciousness.*

Fuel for fun and fulfillment

When I run workshops, I often start by asking people to introduce themselves by sharing something they're passionate about doing outside of work. The sheer range of things that people do amazes me: riding vintage motorbikes, studying ancient history, maintaining canal barges, riding horses, coaching local kids' football, leading troupes of scouts, cake-baking, candle-making, learning languages, playing an instrument, writing poetry, rebuilding radios, breeding chickens, learning ballet, improving a golf handicap, fly-fishing – to name but a few.

So what motivates us to get stuck in to such activities after a hard day's work? On top of job, home and family, or other commitments, you might think all we'd want is a rest, but people pursue all kinds of things in their spare time that involve hard work and learning. Why?

Psychologists agree that learning is a natural human tendency. It's there from birth. Children are actively curious, inquisitive and playful, which leads to learning and so to development. As we grow up, and as adults, what interests us still drives us to explore – whether that's new ideas, meeting new people or in the things we do. But as adults there are many things we have to do or learn, at work and at home, that we're not naturally motivated towards. We may do them for many reasons: because we have to, to gain external reward or recognition, or even for self-approval.

Our type of motivation matters. It's the 'energy' or 'fuel' that drives our intentions, actions, which can, if we're motivated in the right way, sustain them over time and keep us learning. Psychology is showing that the more we can become curious about what we're doing and find something that interests us in it or which we value, the better it is.

When what we choose to learn or do feels like 'us' and/or we're interested in it, we value it for its own sake rather than for what it leads to. This has various effects: not only does this benefit us if we have to persist at it, we're more likely to do it well and more creatively, and it also enhances our happiness, well-being, vitality and confidence.

As adults, to sustain and support this type of motivation (called 'intrinsic' or 'autonomous' motivation by psychologists), three basic conditions or core 'psychological needs' have to be met in some way:

★ Control – how we want to learn needs to be freely chosen and/or align with who we are, our values, beliefs and what we feel is important.
★ Competence – we need to feel some sense of effectiveness, confidence and progress (e.g. we have to have a sense of how to go about it and confidence in our ability to learn and overcome challenges).
★ Connection – it helps us in some way to feel connected to, or cared about, by others.

If these needs aren't met or if they are frustrated, over time this may negatively impact our learning and the time and effort we put into it. It can also reduce our enjoyment and undermine well-being longer term.

Given that there are always things in our lives that we wouldn't naturally be drawn towards doing, having interests that we choose to pursue and learn outside the workplace is an important source of well-being and part of a flourishing life. That's why studies have found that our enjoyment and sense of vitality is higher during our free time, when we have more choice and opportunity to do what we love doing. So rather than deplete us when added on top of our other commitments, it seems that freely chosen hobbies, interests and passions can be great sources of increased energy for us.

Hobbies, passions and interests

Our hobbies are a great resource of personal growth and mastery, giving us the opportunity to explore, play, be creative and develop and use our potential. Because we're interested in them and find them enjoyable, this gives us energy to stretch and challenge ourselves. In addition, they give glimmers of insight into ourselves as 'real' people. Psychologist Brian Little proposes that our 'well-doings' – that is our personal projects, the things that we choose to do and pursue over time – help to define who we are as well as being important for well-being.

Tuning in to what it is about the things that you're naturally drawn towards doing can give clues about your natural strengths and help you find your passions. The more we're able to use our strengths, the more we're likely to flourish. We'll look at this more in Chapter 9.

Psychologist Robert Vallerand studies our passions: those activities in which we have a deep interest, which we love to do and invest time and energy in. He's also researched the idea that how we spend our free time is central to who we are. Our passions feel truly 'us' and become a core feature of our identity. They are something he terms 'harmonious passions'. People who have a harmonious passion typically experience greater enjoyment in life and higher psychological well-being. Their enjoyment of their chosen activity leads them to engage in the activity frequently, often over years, or even a lifetime, which in turn leads to sustained well-being and even prevention against ill health. However, he distinguishes these harmonious passions, which are good for us, from obsessive passions, which are not. Obsessive passions are those that are compulsive because they are not driven by inherent enjoyment of the activity itself, but, for example, by a need to prove our worth (to others or to ourself). While these activities can provide excitement and can occupy much of our time and energy, they have also been shown to undermine our well-being since they can control us rather than us controlling them. An obsessive passion for gambling would be a good example of this.

In terms of dealing with failures and mistakes, the nature of our passion also seems important. While the well-being of people with harmonious passions seems protected, even if they experience failure in what they're

✎ Pause point...

★ What are your favourite hobbies, interests and passions?

★ What, and how, do they contribute to your life and happiness?

★ To what extent do you prioritise them in your free time?

★ What hobbies/interests/passions did you enjoy as a child?

★ Is there an activity you'd like to start doing again or is there something new you'd like to try?

doing, that's not the case for those who have an obsessive passion. For them, failure has a significant impact on their well-being.

Finding our flow

'The best moments in our lives are not the passive, receptive, relaxing times... The best moments usually occur if a person's body or mind is stretched to its limits in a voluntary effort to accomplish something difficult and worthwhile.'
Mihaly Csikszentmihalyi, *Flow: The Psychology of Optimal Experience*

Our hobbies, interests and passions: things that we're intrinsically motivated by, can be a great source of 'flow'. Flow is a state of deep focus on, and absorption in, something we're doing. It's when we lose a sense of time and of ourselves, and we're oblivious to what's going on around us, sometimes even to people who are talking to us. This state is sometimes described as 'being in the zone'. It's something we're all capable of, says psychologist Mihaly Czikszentmihalyi, who identified the term and whose work sparked decades of research on flow states.

'Being in flow' is a common phenomenon. People report experiencing it while they are doing all sorts of things, for example, playing chess, dancing, rock-climbing, painting, drawing, writing, singing in choirs, playing music or games, cooking, making or fixing things, doing crafts or playing sports.

Flow is closely connected to learning and creativity. Flow experiences involve an optimal, delicate balance of challenge relative to our skills.

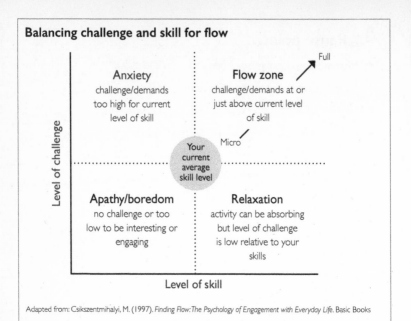

Balancing challenge and skill for flow

Level of challenge (vertical axis)

Anxiety
challenge/demands too high for current level of skill

Flow zone
challenge/demands at or just above current level of skill

Full

Micro

Your current average skill level

Apathy/boredom
no challenge or too low to be interesting or engaging

Relaxation
activity can be absorbing but level of challenge is low relative to your skills

Level of skill (horizontal axis)

Adapted from: Csikszentmihalyi, M. (1997). *Finding Flow: The Psychology of Engagement with Everyday Life*. Basic Books

When we're in flow the level of challenge revealed in what we're doing is at, or just above, our current average skill level: we know where we are aiming for in the activity and as we try different actions or moves, we get an instant sense of whether these work or not. Gradually, as our skills increase, we need to increase the level of challenge to remain absorbed – and so we learn. The experience of flow is rewarding in itself so that we want to persist and repeat it. Little by little, we increase our mastery of what we're doing. When we're in flow we're completely focused on what we're doing. Our mind isn't wandering or worrying. Being in flow enables our creativity to emerge. Because we're so absorbed, we're not giving ourselves a running commentary on how well we're doing, we're not filtering our ideas or what we 'should', or 'shouldn't', try next.

There seems to be a range of flow-type experiences – from 'microflow', when we're getting to grips with something new and are learning how to do it, through to full, or deep, flow experiences, when we're at such a level of mastery that we don't have to think about what we're doing and it's as if we merge with the activity. People often describe being in full, or deep, flow as times when they've felt they've been at their very 'best'.

TEN KEYS TO HAPPIER LIVING

Being in flow is strongly associated with happiness and well-being. As we're experiencing flow, we're not usually aware of feeling anything, but afterwards we have a sense of deep satisfaction. We're using our full ability in that moment – in terms of our attention, skills and capabilities.

Of course, there are activities that we can get completely absorbed in that involve some skill but which don't challenge us. Often people find such activities relaxing and enjoyable but not stretching, which might explain why mindfulness colouring books have become so popular. These are what are called 'passive leisure' activities because we're not actively 'doing' anything. They're 'easy' and great for switching off and relaxing, but they can't give us the mastery, creativity or well-being benefits that we can get from being in flow and the chance for us to be at our best.

A caveat
We can get hooked on activities which get us into flow in unhealthy ways that undermine our well-being (as we can when our passions are obsessive). For example, video games are often designed to get us into flow states. That's why they can be so absorbing and, for some people, addictive. It's a question of whether we're choosing or controlling what we're doing or whether the activity is, in fact, controlling us.

How to get into the flow zone
The more we are intrinsically motivated in life (as we looked at on page 163), the greater our curiosity, mindfulness and persistence, the easier it is for us to get into flow states. Luckily these are all areas where we can increase our capabilities. Here are some ideas to try:

★ **Get out of your comfort zone and actively try things out,** this will either help you find new interests or get deeper into ones you already have. It's how you'll find that optimal balance between the challenge or demands of what you're trying and your current level of skill.
    You don't have to push yourself too far – aim for enough challenge to keep you on your toes, but not so much that it makes you anxious.

★ **Get curious and flex your focus 'muscles',** practising mindfulness is a great way to do this. Look at activities/resources in Chapter 4.

★ **Create the context for flow,** set aside regular time for an engaging hobby or interest. Don't multi-task! Make sure you've got the things you need for what you're doing, switch your phone off and get stuck in.

★ **Know what you're working towards.** Have a goal for what you're doing. Know what you're trying to accomplish in what you are currently doing. It could be learning a song for a concert, preparing a new recipe in time for dinner or assembling part of a model you're making.

Think about it Your flow experiences

Think back to a time when you were in the 'flow zone': you were so absorbed in doing something that you lost all sense of time. This should be something that engaged you and used your skills, and then afterwards left you feeling good and that you had stretched yourself.

★ What were you doing? What were the conditions that enabled you to get into the zone?

★ Think about what you currently do in your spare time. Where would you position these activities on the chart on page 166?

★ How could you increase the number of flow experiences in your life? Perhaps through the hobbies and interests you currenly have or by exploring something new?

To sum up

Here are five key points to take away from this chapter:

1 Being curious, creative and learning is natural and can lead us to sustained happiness and greater confidence. Such things are essential for a flourishing life. We may be interested in different things and creative in different ways and to differing degrees.

2 Our mindset towards learning matters. If we have a growth mindset and don't expect to always get things right or be perfect all the time, it helps us to see mistakes as opportunities to understand better, tackle challenges as we learn and help us fulfil our potential.

3 Curiosity is the pathway to our creative and learning selves. Noticing the novel and the new, thinking about possibilities rather than rules, and making connections between ideas and observations can help us find solutions to problems and give us yet more new ideas.

4 Do something different. Our habits may feel comfortable and help us to get things done, but they can stifle curiosity and creativity and can undermine our resilience. Trying things out and doing different things fuels learning, helps us think in new ways and helps us adapt and use more of our creative potential. It can be fun too!
5 Following interests to find hobbies to pursue in free time can be a rich source of well-being in life and mean we're more likely to find our flow!

Connections to other Keys

Other Keys you might like to explore in connection with Trying out:

★ **RELATING** (See page 36)
Trying new things, learning and pursuing hobbies and interests are great ways to meet and connect with other people.

★ **DIRECTION** (See page 170)
Having and setting goals can help us focus on what interests us or what we want to learn and explore, and help us feel a sense of progress, competence and mastery.

★ **RESILIENCE** (See page 198)
Learning, thinking creatively and building our behavioural flexibility can help to boost our confidence to deal with difficulties and overcome challenges. It helps us adapt and be resourceful, and that's important for resilience.

★ **EMOTIONS** (See page 238)
Spending some of our free time actively doing and pursuing things we enjoy — our hobbies, interests and passions — are a great source of feeling good, which can do us good! Learning, being curious and creative can be fun too.

★ **ACCEPTANCE** (See page 266)
Learning and exploring our interests and creativity helps us understand and develop our strengths, build our confidence and can help us fulfill our potential.

★ **MEANING** (See page 298)
Learning, creativity and pursuing our interests and passions can give life meaning and help us find our sense of purpose.

KEY FIVE: TRYING OUT

DIRECTION

Have goals to look forward to

Goals give us direction. They're the stepping stones
from where we are today to our hopes for the
future. And it's not just achieving them that's
important for happiness – but choosing, planning
and working towards them too.

Direction: introduction

> 'How we think about the future — how we hope —
> determines how well we live our lives.'
>
> Shane J. Lopez, *Making Hope Happen: Create the Future You
> Want for Yourself and Others*

This chapter is about hope and how this gives us direction in our lives. When we're hopeful about the future, we're likely to be happier. But I'm not talking about wishful thinking or something undefined, but rather about having a sense of direction and plans to help us to get from where we are now to where we hope to be. This enables us to turn our needs and our dreams into reality.

As well as being a type of outlook or disposition, hope is also a psychological theory. It can be used practically too as a framework to help us think about, and plan, how we'll achieve our goals, both the big, longer-term ones and the smaller, shorter-term, ones too. And unlike some approaches to goals, it's not just about rational thinking — our hearts and emotions are part of the journey too.

Humans have an innate capacity to imagine and create mental images of how things could be and so we're drawn towards the future. So it follows that how we think and feel about future possibilities and goals are part of how happy we are today. Indeed, the capacity to maintain an optimistic sense of the future is considered a defining feature of us as a species.

What is hope?

'Everything that is done in the world is done by hope.' Martin Luther

Psychologist Rick Snyder developed 'Hope Theory'. Curiously, the idea for it was initially sparked by his research into the excuses people gave

✎ Pause point...

What are you hoping for?

★ What goals are you working towards at the moment?

★ Which goals are the most important for you and why?

★ Which goals are you most excited about or energised by?

★ Which goals do you think will be the most straightforward and the most challenging?

★ What are some of the obstacles that you'll need to overcome in order to reach your goals?

when they'd made mistakes or had done poorly at something. Along with their reasons as to why things hadn't worked out, he noticed that people also hoped to do better in the future. In other words, they had a potential motivational force that was the opposite of making excuses. This observation inspired decades of research exploring what hope really was and how people could turn their hopes into reality.

Dr Snyder defined hope as the process of thinking about not just our goals but also about the pathways we can take towards them and our beliefs about our capacity to get there. In his terms, hope is a 'positive motivational state' made up of three core elements:

★ **Our goals** What we'd like to obtain, attain or achieve.
★ **Our psychological 'energy'** The 'driving force' in hope. It's our motivation for the goals and energy to get started and continue (Snyder called this the 'will power' of hope).
★ **Pathways** How we'll achieve our goals and our beliefs that we can find paths to them and deal with obstacles along the way (Snyder called this 'way power').

When we're working towards an important goal things rarely go smoothly. Often we'll go up and down or back and forth in our feelings about our goal and our beliefs in our ability to achieve it, at times experiencing a range of emotions varying from frustration to joy. Sometimes we might need to find new pathways from those we'd originally envisaged and we might even find we want, or need, to refine or reshape our goal.

The more our goals are aligned with our interests, passions and values, the more motivated we are to strive to achieve them. Our experiences of similar or related situations from the past shape the goals we set and our beliefs that we can achieve them. Likewise, our emotional experience of working towards a current goal and whether or not we achieve it, in turn, will shape the goals we set in the future.

In this chapter we'll look at each of the core elements of hope in more depth and the practical actions we can take to help us find it and turn our dreams into goals, and so into reality. But before we do that, let's look at why this all matters in terms of our happiness.

Feeling good about the future and happiness

Have you ever met a happy person who wasn't hopeful? Yet psychologists used to think that being optimistic, or hopeful, was naïve or misguided (or even potentially indicative of psychological ill health). After all, life can be difficult and we all inevitably experience some disappointments. Well, studies are now showing that people who have an optimistic or hopeful outlook actually do seem to be happier and less likely to be depressed.

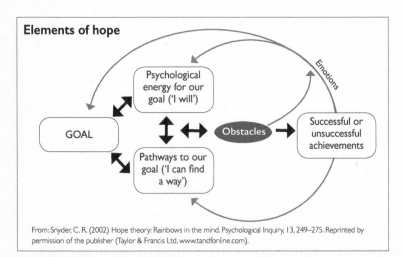

Elements of hope

Psychological energy for our goal ('I will')

GOAL

Obstacles

Pathways to our goal ('I can find a way')

Successful or unsuccessful achievements

Emotions

From: Snyder, C. R. (2002) Hope theory: Rainbows in the mind. Psychological Inquiry, 13, 249–275. Reprinted by permission of the publisher (Taylor & Francis Ltd, www.tandfonline.com).

Not only do they experience more pleasant emotions and fewer unpleasant ones, they're also more likely to have higher life satisfaction, higher self-esteem and greater confidence that they can achieve what they set out to.

Some psychologists have specifically studied optimism and others, like Rick Snyder, have studied hope. The two areas are related but in psychological terms they're not exactly the same. Optimism is generally tending to expect that things will work out well or positively and even if things aren't currently going well that they can become better in the future. Hope goes beyond a general sense of feeling positive about the future as it also incorporates our thoughts and beliefs about how we'll actually get there. It's thought that optimism and hope are complementary in supporting our well-being, hope being most helpful in situations where we have some control, and optimism serving us at times when we don't.

Our personalities vary in their level of natural optimism or hopefulness. Some people tend to believe that the future will work out well, while others assume the worst. Of course, most of us are somewhere in between. We all experience times in which we feel hopeful or optimistic and can take action to help us think and act, so when needed even the most pessimistic among us can benefit from sometimes seeing the ups as well as the downs in life. The ideas and actions we'll explore later in this chapter can help to do this. Before that, let's explore the various potential benefits in a bit more detail.

Relationships Feeling optimistic seems to help us fare better in our relationships, which, as we've seen in Chapter 2, are central to happiness. Optimists are less likely to be lonely and tend to work harder at their relationships and have a more constructive approach to dealing with problems. They perceive that they have greater social support and have been shown to have wider, more diverse, social networks, which in turn helps maintain, even increase, their optimism.

Resilience Hope and optimism help us to build and maintain our 'reservoir' of psychological resources and so help us cope better in tough times. This means we're less likely to be stressed or burn out and we'll experience less anxiety. It's thought that optimists and hopeful people are more likely to take an active rather than a passive approach to dealing with their problems and are less likely to dwell on issues. This makes us more emotionally resilient (see Chapter 7).

Managing our time and efforts Optimists and hopeful people are more likely to persist with tasks and they tend to perform better (e.g. at school or college, in sports and professionally) than their pessimistic, or less hopeful, counterparts – even if their capabilities are equal. Optimists seem better at managing conflicting goals, prioritising the more-important over the less-important ones and balancing effort across these – knowing when it's worth investing effort and when it's not.

Physical health Optimists or hopeful people are more likely to be physically healthy and tend to live longer. They have stronger immune responses, even when they are in high-challenge situations. Indeed, optimism seems to have a protective effect against a number of diseases and conditions. Optimists are also more likely to look after their health, for example by eating healthily, exercising more and smoking less, and they are also more likely to take part in and persist with treatment programmes.

Are there downsides to being optimistic or hopeful?

A number of past studies suggested that most of us have an 'optimism bias', in that we generally think that things will work out better, and that negative events are less likely for us than for the average person, even though mathematically this isn't possible! It has therefore been suggested that if we're unrealistically optimistic this could cause us to take inadvisable risks.

However, there seems to be little evidence that there are many situations in which pessimism is the best stance to adopt. One exception is gambling, since pessimists are better at cutting their losses and therefore lose less money. In contrast, the potential benefits of an optimistic or hopeful outlook are many. Hopeful people are more likely to find more, and different, ways to achieve their goals and so persevere through difficulties. Optimism also seems to help even when obstacles crop up. If we are optimistic that we'll achieve success, we're more likely to keep up the effort. If we're doubtful, we tend stop trying. If we stop trying, but still value the goal, it can cause us distress. As world experts in optimism, Charles Carver and Michael Scheier, point out, in difficult times taking the perspective that 'although things are bad now, they will get better' is likely to lead to better functioning in the present than believing that things will stay as they are.

So feeling good about the future seems, on the whole, to be good for us, but of course we need to keep our feet on the ground. So perhaps being a 'realistic optimist' is what we need to aim to be!

Lack of hope and unhappiness

Not feeling hopeful is a common symptom of depression. People with depression tend to believe that they don't have what it takes to achieve the goals they hope for. A recent study suggests that it's not necessarily that people with depression think that good things won't happen at all, but more specifically that they feel that good things happen for others rather than for them. It appears that this isn't permanent. The study also found that people who'd experienced depression in the past but who weren't ill currently had similar expectations for the future for themselves as people who'd never been depressed. Their will- and way power (see page 173) was also higher, but it was not as high as for those who'd never been depressed. So hopeful thinking had been restored to some degree. Researchers therefore suggest that finding ways to increase the elements of hope (see page 174) could have potential benefits as part of therapeutic treatment.

Goals & happiness

'Goals are the means by which values and dreams are translated into reality. Happiness does not just happen. It has to be earned by thinking, planning and the constant pursuit of values.'

Edwin Locke, *Oxford Handbook of Positive Psychology*

Goals connect our present to our future. At a basic level, we're all naturally driven by them. Take being hungry as an example. Your goal is to find food to eat and you feel better when that goal is achieved, that is, when you've eaten. Most of our daily needs could be said to be goal-directed in this way. It therefore, perhaps, makes sense that our goals could be an important key to happiness.

Psychologist Sonia Lyubomirsky, a leading researcher in how we achieve happiness, says working towards meaningful life goals is one of the most important ways to become happier. Such goals could be connected with work, our families, communities, personal projects, passions and interests – anything that is personally meaningful and valuable.

Working on goals we're interested in and engaged by can be pleasurable, but there are a number of further reasons why setting, committing to and pursuing goals has a positive impact on happiness:

★ **Goals give us direction,** a sense of purpose and help us achieve meaning. They're integral to having a sense of engagement in life and feeling a sense of growth and accomplishment.

★ **Goals give us a sense of control over our daily lives,** through taking accountability for making them happen, whether through putting together a timetable, setting deadlines or learning new skills.

★ **Goals help us structure time in the short and long term.** One of the certainties in life is that time is limited and it's easy to waste it. The process of identifying and committing to our goals helps identify our big priorities in life and the shorter-term goals to get there. They help us prioritise available time and apportion our effort and energy.

★ **Goals boost our confidence,** progressing towards and reaching our goals, helping us feel effective and capable.
★ **Goals can be something to look forward to,** giving us enjoyment in anticipation.

For our goals to enhance our happiness, it's not just working on or achieving them that's important, it's also about how we plan them. Building our goal-setting and planning skills has been shown to have a positive impact on well-being.

✎ Pause point...

Identify a goal for action to increase your own happiness and/or that of others. Use this to practise the ideas we'll cover as we progress through this chapter. You'll learn ways of crafting and planning your goal that will make you much more likely to achieve it.

What makes a goal good for happiness?

'What man actually needs is not a tensionless state but rather the striving and struggling for a worthwhile goal, a freely chosen task.' Viktor Frankl, *Man's Search for Meaning*

In our busy lives it is likely that we'll have a whole host of goals – things we need or want to do at home or at work. But when it comes to happiness, not all goals are equal. Some goals are thrust upon us as things we have to do, for example at work (a set target of increasing sales by ten per cent) or at home (replacing a broken oven). We'll have chosen others because they are inherently interesting. Which type would be most energising and most likely to enhance our well-being?

What our goals are and why we're doing them matters, influencing:
★ How well we maintain our efforts in pursuing our goals.
★ How likely we are to be successful in achieving them.

★ The happiness and well-being we experience through working towards, and reaching, those goals.

Psychologist Kennon Sheldon says the goals that are most likely to lead to happiness and well-being are those that we feel we really 'own', have been chosen by us, that fit with our values and personality and are personally meaningful. He suggests we can think about the 'why' and the 'what' of our goals with three tests:

First test (Why?) Is it a passing whim or does it reflect our enduring

Try this! Reflecting on my current goals

Choose three goals that you're currently working towards, whether personal, work-related or connected with something else. Perhaps choose goals that are taking quite a lot of time or headspace for you at the present time. (You could include your goal from the pause point on the previous page.)

Now think about the extent to which these goals fulfill the following criteria for you:

Part I Name each of your goals	Goal I	Goal 2	Goal 3
Tick which of the statements below best reflects your reasons for pursuing this goal: I'm focusing on this goal because…			
A Someone else wants me to or my circumstances mean I have to			
B I'd feel ashamed, guilty or anxious if I didn't ('I should')			
C I believe it's an important goal to have			
D It aligns with my values and who I am as a person			
E I get a lot of enjoyment and/or stimulation from it			

Developed based on: Sheldon, Abad, Ferguson, Gunz, Houser-Marko, Nichols & Lyubomirsky (2010), Gagné & Deci (2005)

interests/values. Following transient whims can mean we squander energy and end up confused about our aims.

Second test (Why?) Where's the driving force for the goal coming from? Is it something other people want us to do or something we feel we have to do? Or is it something we've freely chosen, reflecting what interests us/our values?

Third test (What?) What is the nature of the goal? How does it satisfy our core psychological needs for: control – we have some say in how we'll work towards it; competence – it helps us to feel competent and

Part 2	Goal 1	Goal 2	Goal 3
In which ways are these goals helping to meet the following needs for you? You might want to make a few notes:			
Feeling connected – It is helping me feel meaningfully connected to other people by…			
Feeling competent – It is helping to build my feeling of competence and is giving me a sense of progress by…			
Feeling a sense of control – I am able to choose what and how I am working towards this goal by…			

Reflection

★ What is your main reason for each these goals?

- If they are E, D or C, then that goal may contribute to your well-being. (E is the strongest reason, but D and C are good too).

- If your top-of-mind reason doesn't feel right, try the 'why, why, why' activity. Ask yourself why it is important, then ask why again and again – until you get to the reason that feels right.

★ To what extent are each of these goals meeting your psychological needs for connection, competence and control? The more these needs are met, the better it is for well-being and goal achievement.

KEY SIX: DIRECTION

effective and we can see progress; connection – it in some way helps us feel connected to others (see also page 163). The more these needs are satisfied, the more likely we are to persist in working towards our goals, and overcome obstacles. And in the process enhance our well-being. Where our goals thwart these basic needs it can have the opposite effect.

The Why and What: our goals and well-being

Goals we freely choose and want to do because we find them inherently interesting and/or they align with our personal values are said to be 'intrinsically motivated'. If the driving force for a goal is more external, for example – something we feel we have to do or want to do for external reasons (such as for approval, popularity, money or appearance) are called 'extrinsically motivated' (we touched on this idea on page 163). There is evidence that goals which are extrinsically driven can have a less positive impact on our well-being (and can even be detrimental) than more intrinsically driven goals – for example focusing on things like nurturing relationships, helping others or achieving personal growth. Clinical psychologist and goals expert Professor Andrew MacLeod highlights the fact that if we're unhappy it's easy to see why we might reach for concrete goals such as money, but since these goals are external, they're limited in their contribution to well-being and so can reinforce feelings of ill-being instead. To help us reach a bigger, more intrinsic goal, we may have intermediate goals for something external, like money. In this case, the 'why' behind the external goal helps.

We're likely to be more motivated to work towards and persist in the face of obstacles if our goals are intrinsically motivated and support our core psychological needs, however, studies have also shown that if we don't achieve them, it can have a bigger negative impact on our well-being than not achieving more extrinsic goals. It's likely that we'll have different goals across the spectrum from extrinsically to intrinsically motivated: from ones that others impose on us to those we've freely chosen. The more we can find ways to meet our basic psychological needs in working towards either type of goal the better it is for our well-being and the more likely we'll achieve them. But if our goals are mostly extrinsically driven, it can be bad for our longer-term happiness and well-being. So how do we find goals that are better for us?

Finding our personal goals

> 'A wise person knows which goals are ultimately fulfilling and which only offer the illusion of fulfillment and thus will order his or her life accordingly.'
>
> Robert Emmons, *Flourishing*

If you put a mix of sand and pebbles into a jar and shake them for a while, you'll notice that the big pebbles eventually come to the top and the finer grains of sand fall to the bottom. There's a logical reason for this, based on physics, but the process seems a bit magical too. For me that image represents the process of identifying our goals. There are some helpful, logical steps we can take and through those what's most important in terms of our priorities rise to the surface.

There's a lot of 'stuff' that can go into our 'jar' when we're identifying good personal goals – what our strengths are, our interests and values, our dreams, as well as our feelings about these and our personal circumstances, to name but a few. Becoming clearer on these will help us identify our overarching life goals and purposes (like the biggest pebbles that find their way to the top of our jar) and then we can start to break these down into medium-sized and medium-term aims (smaller pebble sizes) and, in turn, into the small, short-term steps (grains of sand) that help move us towards what we want for ourselves and our life. Not all the goals we set will be big and meaningful. Often we'll have intermediate 'stepping stones', or sub-goals, which help us move towards what we're aiming for. For example, if we have the dream of being a doctor, then we'll need to pass certain exams in order to get there, even if some are in subjects we don't especially like. Being able to see a clear link to our main goals is important.

KEY SIX: DIRECTION

We might also need 'maintenance' goals to take care of our well-being (and others') as we pursue difficult or longer-term aims. As an example, a big current goal for me is to write this book. To help me think clearly and to maintain my physical health I have the maintenance goal for exercising for thirty minutes each day.

Finding our big goals is a process that takes time and reflection – just as shaking the jar to sort the stones will only work if you've left space at the top. We need to allow ourselves space to reflect, think and feel what's most important for us. And evidence suggests that effort and time is an investment which will pay back in term of happiness and well-being.

So where do you start? I'd suggest by getting out your notebook or some paper (your 'jar', metaphorically speaking). Over the next few weeks start collecting 'clues' and writing down various bits of information. Some of the other chapters in this book will be particularly helpful:

Chapter 5 may have inspired you to identify hobbies, interests and passions that you love.

Chapter 8 Reflecting on the themes of your daily 'Three good things' activity often reveals clues as to what's meaningful and enjoyable for you.

Chapter 9 looks at your strengths. These give great clues to what you're likely to be drawn towards, value and find intrinsically interesting.

Chapter 10 is all about meaning, purpose and priorities. Your reflections from those activities are very useful here.

You will start to get a sense of the things that feel most important and engaging for you, which will be helpful for the life goals exercise on page 185.

How challenging should your goals be?

We often hear advice to set ourselves BIG or s-t-r-e-t-c-h goals, but while these may motivate some people, this doesn't necessarily suit everyone.

Psychologists have found that if people are prone to being anxious they can prefer to take an approach called a 'defensive pessimism' for important goals. This means deliberately setting low expectations for their performance and, prior to undertaking the task, devoting a lot of

Try this! Writing about life goals

There is a large body of evidence that the process of writing can be beneficial. By expressing our thoughts in words and structuring them in a coherent narrative, this helps our brains process and structure our ideas. It's been shown to be helpful to assist people in clarifying priorities and goals and at the same time boosting happiness.

Instructions:

For twenty minutes per day over the next four days or so, think and write about your 'best possible future self'. Think about your life in the future. You've worked hard and everything has gone as well as it possibly could. You've succeeded in accomplishing all your goals. Think about different parts of your life. Write about what you imagined in as much detail as possible. Write by hand or electronically. The aim is for you to be able to write freely – so choose the method that enables that.

Having carried out this activity for a few days, what has emerged for you? What goals stand out?

Based on: King, L. A. (2001). The health benefits of writing about life goals. Personality and Social Psychology Bulletin, 27(7), 798-807.

time and mental energy playing through everything that might happen or go wrong. In contrast, 'strategic optimists' set higher goals for themselves, actively avoid too much reflection before undertaking the task and often run through thoughts of how good things could be during it.

Neither approach is better than the other. Both defensive pessimists and strategic optimists perform equally well if they pursue their preferred approach. If, however, either types are prevented from doing what they feel comes naturally to them, or they are required to do the opposite, their performance is undermined and their anxiety is increased.

So we need to find what works for us.

Top tips Crafting your goals

Many studies have shown that the way we craft our goals can have an important effect on how likely we are to put them into action, persist and achieve what we set out to.

★ **Be specific**

This is the number-one goal tip. Identify what, where, when and how much/how many. This helps you think through what you need to do and know when you've achieved it. For example:

• An unspecific goal: I plan to exercise more.
• A specific goal: I'll go to the gym for 45 minutes, three times a week.

★ **Know your 'why'**

Have a clear reason why you are pursuing your goal, what a positive outcome will be for you and how it meets your core psychological needs (connection, control, competence – see page 181). This increases your commitment to your goal and means you're more likely to achieve it. You'll feel better as a result.

★ **'Will do' not 'Won't do'**

We can frame our goals as something we want to move towards ('approach') or something we want to stop ('avoid').

There is evidence that 'approach' goals are more energising and effective than 'avoidance' goals. For example, if we want to change our snacking habits in order to lose weight:

• An avoidance goal: 'I'll stop eating chocolate as a snack.'
• An approach goal: 'When I'm peckish I'll snack on carrot sticks.'
  It's important to look at the underlying reason for the goal too, to see if that is 'approach' or 'avoidance'. For example, 'I want to lose weight to feel healthy' (approach) or because 'I don't want to be embarrassed in front of other people' (avoidance).

★ **Growth goals, 'not being seen to be good'**

We looked at growth and fixed mindsets in Chapter 5. The same thinking applies to framing our goals. Setting goals that emphasise getting better rather than 'being the best' means we are likely to persist and deal with obstacles, get less anxious when things aren't going how we want, and learn from mistakes. Goals that are linked to 'being seen to be good' can be motivating but may mean our self-worth is contingent on how others see us and we are more likely to give up if we don't achieve them – even if we have a near miss.

• A 'being good' goal: 'I must get the top mark in maths.'
• A growth goal: 'I want to build maths skills by learning percentages and get a better mark than I did last time.'

★ **Write down and share your goals**

If you write your goals down you are more likely to achieve them. You're reinforcing/committing to them in your mind. Sharing them with others builds even greater commitment and accountability. Why not share your goals with someone you trust and agree to share a progress report with them on an agreed date?

Based on: Grant Halvorson (2010); Sheldon & Houser-Marko (2001), Sheldon (2002); Gollwitzer (1999), MacLeod (in press); Adams Miller & Frisch (2009); Norcross & Mrykalo (2002)

Identifying the pathways to our goals

> 'You can get there from here.'
>
> C.R. Snyder, *The Psychology of Hope*

Contrasting our dreams and reality

People who have tried the Writing about life goals activity (see page 185) have said it not only helped them think about where they want to get to in future, but what they need to do today to help that future come true.

Some self-help advice suggests that if we really visualise what we want, it will happen. Visualising the future can be enjoyable, but unfortunately research evidence suggests it's not enough on its own. We also need to put effort and attention into planning how to make it happen, the pathways we need to take to achieve our goals.

There is a good way our positive visions of the future can be put to use. Psychologist Gabriele Oettingen studies an approach called 'mental contrasting' and this is helpful for identifying the pathways to our goals. Firstly you focus on your goal, really visualising in detail where you want to be or what you want to achieve, then you compare the details of your vision with where you are now. This helps you think about the different areas of activity, or sub-goals, you'll need to achieve your bigger goal. For example, David's big goal is to change his career path. He's been working in an administrative role for a retail organisation, but he really wants to get a job in the charity sector and he's particularly drawn to the idea of working with homeless people. He visualises himself working at a centre for the homeless as part of a team, where he's really able to understand the clients and their situations, helping to build their confidence by working with them on practical steps to find a better future. Comparing this vision to the reality of his current experience, David realises that although he's already done some volunteering, he could take on more in order to understand the sector and the challenges facing homeless people. Also there may be some specific skills that would be useful for him to develop, such as counselling. So he decides to set himself some medium-term sub-goals:

★ To get a regular evening volunteer position at a local homeless shelter.
★ Explore training courses on counselling.
★ To follow some of the charities that he'd like to work for on social media, to keep up with their news and issues.
★ Ask friends, family and others if they know of anyone working in the sector who he could call to find out more about it and how he could usefully use his current skills, and if there are any others that would be helpful to develop.
★ To organise a sponsored sleep-out to raise funds for the shelter and get some sense of what it feels like to sleep rough.

Now there's a lot on David's list. His intermediate sub-goals will take time and effort to achieve, but by going through this process not only has he got a clearer, more realistic, view of how to achieve his bigger goal, he can also assess whether it's something he really does want to do – or not. Was it just a fantasy or a whim, something that's just not realistic for him right now or is it something that he's really excited about working towards? So it's a reality check, both in terms of the what and the how. If it is something he really does want to do, evidence suggests that this process can energise us and strengthen our commitment to it. Dr Oettingen calls this 'motivational intelligence'.

Identifying obstacles

'There are many paths to a goal and none of them is free from obstacles.'
Shane J. Lopez, *Making Hope Happen: Create the Future You Want for Yourself and Others*

'If–then' planning

Whatever our goals, inevitably things can get in our way. We will be better able to stay on track if we think about what those obstacles might be in advance and make a plan for how we'll deal with them if they arise.

Psychologist Peter Gollwitzer says this helps to set up a connection in our mind between each obstacle and our plan to overcome it, so should these arise, the action to deal with it is automatically triggered.

These obstacle and action pairings are expressed in terms of 'if–then' plans, i.e: 'If (obstacle) happens, then I will (action)'. For example, if my goal is to jog each morning for at least thirty minutes I might encounter various obstacles: it might rain, I may feel too tired or not have enough time – the 'ifs'. I can now identify the actions. I'll take in each case.

If...	Then...
It's raining	I'll check the weather forecast to see if it will be dry later in the day and go for a jog then. If it is going to rain all day, I'll do thirty minutes of yoga at home instead.
I feel really too tired/lazy	I'll put on my running kit anyway and go for a walk. It usually wakes me up and if so I can break into a jog and if not at least I will have done some moving about and seen a bit of daylight!
I feel I don't have time as my chapter deadline is very close	I'll remind myself that I always think more clearly after a run, even if I only do fifteen minutes.

Scenario planning

There may be multiple ways our bigger, overarching goals could materialise. Creating different potential future scenarios for these can have several benefits:

★ It gives us greater mental flexibility and wider options for how we can achieve our bigger goal. If we know what we are aiming for, but aren't fixed on a single outcome, we're likely to be open to more opportunities that come our way.

★ In this way, it may be protective for our well-being as people experiencing depression are more likely to tie their happiness to specific goals. For example, they are more likely to think or say, 'I'll be happy when...' or 'I'll be happy if...'

★ It also helps us identify sub-goals that will be useful for any of the specific scenarios, which means they may be a priority for action, to move us closer towards our big goals, regardless of which opportunities present themselves.

Here's an example:

Big goal: To help people reach their potential		
Potential scenario 1 Become a life coach	**Potential scenario 2** Build a career as a training and development professional in an organisation	**Potential scenario 3** Develop a website service that helps people identify their talents and set goals to achieve them
Common sub-goals: Get a qualification in the psychology of adult learning and career development		
Examples of specific sub-goals:		
• Investigate options for training as a coach • Identify a business model for coaching practices and how to attract clients	• Identify organisations that have good training and development departments • Apply for learning and development jobs in organisations • Identify different types of training roles and career paths in organisations	• Design website and tools • Identify potential web programmers • Develop a business plan and budget

Where there's the will there's a way

> 'A journey of 1,000 miles starts with one step.'
>
> Ancient Chinese proverb

So we've got a goal or two we're really interested in, meets our psychological needs (see pages 180–1) and we can see the way to get there, but what makes us actually get started… and keep going? That's the 'energy' that fuels us – our motivation to meet our goals. Sometimes, however excited we are about our goals, it can still be hard to get started. Well, psychologists have been discovering some useful ideas that really can help.

1 Find ways to use your strengths

In Chapter 9 we'll explore how you can identify your strengths. Strengths are a source of energy for us. They are our natural capacities for thinking, feeling and behaving… and what motivates us. When we're using our strengths we tend to enjoy what we're doing more, learn easily and do better. Crucially, using our strengths is energising rather than depleting, meaning we're more likely to persist towards our goals. Indeed, research is showing that using our strengths is associated with better progress towards our goals as well as greater well-being.

Your strengths can also suggest what types of pathways to your goals are likely to be more enjoyable and effective for you. For example, if you have a strength of teamwork, then finding ways of working with others to achieve your goal may be better for you than working towards them on your own. Or if creativity is one of your main strengths, you'll be most likely to prefer to develop your own ideas rather than following a tried-and-tested route.

KEY SIX: DIRECTION

Our strengths can also help us consider the obstacles we might cause to our own progress. Because our strengths are so natural for us and we enjoy using them, we can sometimes use them inappropriately or too much. For example, if you have the strength of creativity, you could spend too much time generating ideas to help you reach your goals and so not leave yourself enough time to put your ideas into action.

Top tip Identify your top strengths (see Chapter 9) and find ways to use them to achieve your goals. Also think about how your strengths could trip you up and what you'll do to prevent this.

2 Be clear on when and where

Psychologist Peter Gollwitzer discovered that if we create a clear plan for *where* and *when* we will take action, we are much more likely to do what we intended, especially for more challenging goals or actions. For example, in one study, just before the Christmas holidays, he asked students to identify two goals they wanted to complete during the upcoming break – one easy and one difficult (examples included: writing a seminar paper, settling a family conflict or participating in sports). He asked half the students to identify specifically when and where they'd actually work on each of their goals – two-thirds of this group actually reached their difficult goals, whereas only a quarter of those who hadn't set when–where intentions did so.

In a similar study, he set two groups of students the task of writing an essay on what they did on Christmas Eve no more than forty-eight hours after the day. But only one group was required to identify specifically when and where they'd be when they completed this assignment. For example: 'I'll complete my essay on the morning of December 27th (when) by taking my laptop to my local coffee shop (where)'. Three-quarters of this group wrote their essays, whereas only a third of the other group did.

Top tip You are more likely to do what you intend to if you identify specifically when and where you'll take action. So for each step towards your goal, identify your when–where intention.

3 There's power in tiny steps

Harvard psychologist Teresa Amabile and colleague Steven Kramer did a study of people working in teams on specific projects in their organisations. At the end of each working day over the duration of the project, each participant completed a confidential survey on their mood, motivation level, what they'd worked on and what stood out in their mind from the day. They discovered that the factor which made the biggest difference between good and bad days was experiencing a sense of progress. This wasn't about successfully reaching the ultimate goal or achieving big leaps towards it, but taking tiny, frequent steps forward. If we go back to our core psychological needs, this makes sense. Even tiny steps forward help us to feel competent and give us a sense of progress.

So if you find yourself stuck or are having difficulty getting started because the goal seems overwhelming, break it into smaller sub-goals. Think about what you could do to move yourself one per cent closer to your goal. Or if you feel frustrated because you haven't got enough time, find a micro-step you could take. Spending as little as five minutes could be enough to help give you a sense of momentum and an emotional boost. For example, in five minutes you could brainstorm some ideas, make a list to get organised, do some research online or make a call to someone who can help you with your goal.

Top tip Think small. What could you do in five, ten or twenty minutes to help you progress towards your goal? What could you do that would move you one per cent closer to it?

4 Hang out with the right people

In the first two Keys we looked at how important feeling connected to others is for our well-being. This can be an important source of encouragement, moral support and help. So when planning your goal, it's a good idea to identify your supporters and how you'll have regular contact with them, and people who could be a source of help. Remember that asking for help can give the helper a well-being boost, so don't be shy about seeking help when you need it (see Chapter 1).

Connecting with others can help us in other ways to achieve our goals. Curiously, it seems that goals can literally be catching. Psychologists have found that we tend to subconsciously adopt the behaviours and goals of the people we're in close contact with. For example, if all your friends are studying hard to pass their exams, you are more likely to do so too. This suggests that connecting with people who are working towards similar goals may be a great way to help us to maintain momentum on top of the well-being benefits we get from connecting with people with shared interests (it also may mean not hanging out with people who aren't motivated or who take us off track).

In Chapter 5 we looked at how trying things out is a great way to build confidence in our capabilities and what we can achieve. Another good source of building confidence is to watch and learn from others who are experts in what we want to do. Who do you know who's a role model for achieving goals? If there's no one around in your circle of contacts with the experience you're looking for, ask contacts they know who might know someone. It usually doesn't take long, through such outer social circles, to track someone down.

Top tip Identify specific people you can connect with around your goal for support, encouragement, help and to learn from.

5 Acknowledge and act on significant doubts

Working towards important goals isn't always easy and we may have days where we might question our own capability or even whether we're doing the right thing.

If we know we're prone to certain patterns of thinking that can drain our energy, such as getting frustrated if things aren't going to plan, we can apply the if–then approach we looked at (see pages 188–9). For example: 'If I start feeling myself get very wound up about my lack of progress, then I will take myself out for a walk to calm down and phone an encouraging friend. In Chapter 7 we'll look at resilient thinking – the ways our thinking can undermine us, and what to do if it does.

LAURA: FROM DREAM TO HOPE TO REALITY

Laura had been going to Crete to teach every summer. Right from her first visit, she loved the light, the sea, the barren landscape... and she liked village life. She promised herself that one day she'd buy somewhere of her own there. Back home she started to save. Each summer she worked on building relationships with the people in her favourite village and started to learn Greek. After a few years, she'd saved enough for a small building plot. High on a mountainside, with views out to sea, it had just enough space for a house and garden between three ancient olive trees. But there's an expression in Greek which means 'slowly, slowly' and that's how things progressed. Laura wasn't worried – it was a long-term goal and it gave her time to save.

Eventually the land was secured and after many meetings she'd found an architect who could help her realise her dream. Plans were drawn up. She had just about saved enough cash when a currency crash meant she could no longer afford to have the house built. She needed to find a new pathway to her goal. In the meantime she could still enjoy the land – so for a few summers she camped or stayed nearby. After lots of research she discovered a designer/maker who was building eco-cabins. This seemed like the perfect solution – a cabin was much cheaper than a house and it could be built in the workshop then positioned. They just needed to find a way to get the cabin to Greece. Again plans were drawn up, but this time a different sort of problem got in the way. Laura discovered she had a life-threatening illness and needed surgery and treatment.

Now the goal of building a home in Greece took on new importance. It was a focus for hope. She found a way to transport the cabin by sea, the village mayor helped her get a water supply and a date for installation was set... a month after her surgery. While her friends and partner were worried that this was too optimistic, it worked for Laura. She was determined to make it to Crete and watch her cabin arrive. But she realised that to reach that goal, sheer determination wasn't enough, she needed to take care of her well-being pre- and post-op and she called on friends to support her.

She made it! Last summer she was able to stay in the little place of her dreams, looking out over the sea.

KEY SIX: DIRECTION

Occasionally, we may find that our goal is not working for us and we need to step back and review it to see if it really does align with who we are, what we want to do and what's meaningful in our life. If the goal isn't working for us, we might be able to adapt or we can re-craft it so that it does. For example, there could be different ways of achieving the same ultimate goal (see page 189). Can we use our strengths more in working towards it?

Sometimes we may decide that the goal no longer fits or that despite trying it's just not realistic or possible for us at this time. Indeed, the ability to recognise and disconnect ourselves from goals that aren't working for us has been shown to be a sign of well-being. If that's the case it's important to remember the old maxim: 'Nothing ventured, nothing gained' – if we don't try we don't learn. So reflect on the insights you've gained from the experience and how you can build on the learning and achievement to work towards a new goal that feels like a better fit.

To sum up

Here are five key points to take away from this chapter.

1 Feeling optimistic and hopeful is an ingredient of happiness associated with many benefits. While we may differ in our natural outlook, we can learn ways to remain realistic and positive about the future.

2 Goals are an important way in which happiness happens. They link where we are now to our future. It's not surprising, therefore, that having and working towards goals is good for well-being.

3 Not all goals lead to happiness, but some can. Goals which reflect our enduring interests and values and which we've chosen rather than are obliged to do are most likely to lead to happiness. If we choose how we work towards them, feel a sense of progress and they help us feel connected to others – that's good too.

4 Planning how we'll meet our goals is an investment for happiness, and psychology is showing that there are some simple tips to make it much more likely we'll achieve what we're aiming for.

5 Maintaining momentum is important, especially since things will inevitably get in our way. Using our strengths, visualising when and where we'll take action and thinking through likely obstacles and how we'll tackle them are all tools to try. And even tiny steps forward help.

Connections to other Keys

Other Keys you might like to explore in connection with Direction:

★ **GIVING** (See page 10)
  • Asking for help when we need it as we progress towards our goals can be a boost not just for us but for the well-being of our helper too.
  • Likewise we may be able to help others reach their goals too.

★ **RELATING** (See page 36)
  Other people are important sources of support, encouragement and motivation (and we can be for them too).

★ **RESILIENCE** (See page 198)
  Working towards important and long-term goals needs resilience, as inevitably we'll encounter obstacles along the way.

★ **EMOTIONS** (See page 238)
  Identifying the different sources of feeling good in your life can reveal clues as to what's meaningful and enjoyable for you and help you to identify your goals.

★ **ACCEPTANCE** (See page 266)
  Your strengths give great clues as to what you find intrinsically interesting and rewarding, and so help you identify your goals. Your strengths are also sources of energy to help you achieve them.

★ **MEANING** (See page 298)
  This chapter will help you find what your purpose and priorities are as a basis for identifying your goals.

Note: All the ideas for action covered in all the Keys may provide you with ideas for goals you want to work towards.

RESILIENCE

Find ways to bounce back

Difficulties are part of life. We all have them (and sometimes we create them!). Building on our natural resilience, science is showing that there are skills and thinking tools that can make a difference, even in the toughest of times.

Resilience: introduction

> 'Fall down seven times, get up eight.'
>
> Japanese proverb

It might seem strange that a Key to happiness is resilience. As I have touched on throughout this book, a happy life doesn't mean one that is completely free of difficulties. Stress, pain, loss, trauma – tough times are part of life. So being better equipped to face and deal with these is important, even essential, for happier living.

What is resilience?

The word 'resilience' comes from the Latin verb *resilire* meaning to jump, leap or spring back. In everyday usage 'resilience' describes the ability to 'bounce back' from difficulties or 'bending not breaking' under pressure.

Although there's no one definition of 'resilience' in psychology, most experts concur that it's our ability to successfully cope with, adapt to, or deal with adversities and persevere in the face of challenges. These adversities can range from the daily difficulties, pressures or stresses we all face through life events and trauma. Some see it as a dynamic process where we use our abilities in flexible ways, as circumstances change, to enable us to maintain normal psychological/physical functioning. Experiencing difficulties can throw us off-kilter and resilience is the process by which we can get back into balance. Resilience means we find ways to come to terms with, and come through, adversities in spite of their threats to our well-being.

In the past, resilience was considered to be about surviving and being less likely to suffer psychological ill health. While this continues to be accepted as part of it, experts now find that beyond coping and surviving, resilience can mean we learn, grow and thrive as a result of experiencing hard times.

Being resilient doesn't mean we won't ever experience tough times or that we'll feel good all the time. Challenges, difficulties and threats to our well-being are inevitable in life. While some of us may have more to deal with than others, no one's life runs absolutely smoothly. Neither does resilience mean putting up with bad situations or never asking for help. Quite the opposite. It's about recognising when times are hard and focusing on what we can do, control or change, acknowledging difficult feelings and managing them and knowing who, or where, to get support from.

Being more resilient helps us to manage stress better, bounce back from difficulties faster, believe things can, and will, get better and that there are things we can do to make a difference. It can also help to prevent us causing difficulties for ourselves through how we think. So it helps to buffer the damaging impact that difficulties and traumas can have on our physical and psychological well-being, lowering our risk of depression and anxiety, enabling us to age more successfully and increase the likelihood we'll develop and grow as a result of trauma.

We all have resilience and can develop more

Let's start with the fact that we're all resilient. This isn't a rare quality found in a few, extraordinary people. It's a natural human state. We wouldn't be here otherwise. Dr Ann Masten, an expert in the subject, describes resilience as 'ordinary magic', something we all have. This is a good thing. Studies suggest that more than fifty per cent of us experience severe trauma, a life-threatening event, at some point in our lives and the majority of us experience tough, life-changing challenges, such as the death of a loved one, loss of a job or relationship, or a physical accident. Yet fewer than ten per cent of those go on to develop post-traumatic stress disorder (PTSD). And all of us are used to dealing with stress and minor difficulties in day-to-day life.

We may vary in how naturally resilient we are in specific situations or at certain times, but Masten argues that resilience isn't a static characteristic or personality feature, but comprises many factors, internal and external. Each person and each situation is different. Although genetic factors and upbringing certainly influence our resilience as adults, what's becoming clear from research is that we can increase our capacities for it, through how we think and the actions we take, so that we're less likely to be derailed or descend into depression when the going gets tough – and we're better able to bounce back if we do.

These are exciting times in resilience research. The merging of psychology, biology, medicine and neuroscience is paving the way for greater understanding about how resilience works in our minds, bodies and behaviour and how it can be increased. While this scientific path is relatively young, it is showing that there is a range of skills, tools and approaches that can help us when we face difficulties.

We can't always predict or control what life throws at us, but we can build our skills and nurture our resources to help us respond flexibly, deal with challenges effectively, recover more quickly and even learn and grow in the process. What's more, these same skills can help us manage the fear of taking on new opportunities and so can help us to develop in other ways too.

 Pause point...

Think back to a challenging time in your life:

★ Who and what helped you get through it?

★ What positive thing did you learn about yourself as a result of it?

★ How has that helped you deal with subsequent challenges?

The ingredients of resilience

There isn't a single prescription for resilience that works for everyone or in every situation: a range of different 'ingredients' contributes to it – a mix of skills, attitudes, behaviours and resources that we can draw on flexibly to respond as particular situations require. The other nine Keys for happier living that we're exploring in this book are all ingredients of resilience too. So, as the old saying goes, perhaps prevention is better than cure. Taking care of our well-being in the good times will help us deal with our problems, cope when times are bad, help us take on new challenges and even perform better when we are under pressure.

Many studies of resilience look at people who have been through trauma without experiencing sustained psychological ill health afterwards, whether that was a difficult childhood, being caught in a natural disaster, accident or being a victim of crime or warfare. At the time, of course, the experience would have been extremely difficult for each individual. They would have experienced fear, anxiety, hurt or sadness just like anyone else would in that situation. But what made the difference to those who were able to cope better during the experience and adapt as a result, eventually returning to normal functioning?

Resilience experts Drs Dennis Charney and Steven Southwick and colleagues have identified the most important ingredients of resilience – areas where we can take action to learn, feel and be stronger. Let's look at these, why they help and how they connect to the ten Keys in this book.

A Using active coping strategies

Feeling we're doing something is better than feeling we're doing nothing. Active coping strategies are those where we face our difficulties and focus on what we're able to actively do or control, even if it's only small. This could be seeking to resolve the problem somehow, changing our perspective about it, focusing on the silver lining, looking after our bodies, asking for help – or something else.

Drs Charney and Southwick discovered amazing stories of active coping strategies in even the most extreme situations. For example, prisoners of war in solitary confinement teaching themselves complicated mental arithmetic, recreating detailed memories of school days or building an entire house, nail by nail, room by room, in their minds (which the prisoner went on to build in real life on release). By contrast, passive coping is where we feel resigned to the problem and think there is nothing we can do. So we ignore or deny the issue or find ways to blunt our emotions, such as through drinking too much or drug abuse, or distracting ourselves in some other way. While these strategies temporarily remove the experience of difficult feelings, it can lead to a sense of helplessness and, as a consequence, a heightened risk of depression. Finding ways of taking action gives us a sense of agency and control – an essential ingredient for psychological well-being. This boosts our mood, helps us to feel more optimistic and confident, and reduces our fear and stress levels. Importantly, it disrupts the processes in our brain that lead to depression.

Examples of active coping in action:
★ 'I sort out what can be changed and what can't'
★ 'I make a plan of action when confronted with a problem'
★ 'When things look hopeless, I find something I can do'
★ 'I try to find help when I need it'
★ 'If what I try doesn't work, I try something else'
★ 'When I'm under pressure I give myself encouragement'

The good news is that the ideas for action in this chapter and throughout this book can all contribute to your toolkit of active coping approaches.

B Thinking resiliently

This is our ability to tune in to our thoughts, assess their accuracy and reframe or replace them with more accurate, helpful or positive ones. It's a core resilience skill, whether we're dealing with big life challenges or small daily stresses. It also means we avoid adding to our problems through the way we're thinking. If we're stressed and tired it's easy for thoughts to get stuck or out of control – perhaps we ruminate on our problems, magnify the issues, catastrophise, overly blame ourselves or others, or believe the issues will spread to other areas of our life and that we have no control over them.

Concepts and techniques originally developed for therapy are now being used proactively to help build resilience, prevent psychological ill health and limit the damage we can do to ourselves.

Examples of thinking resiliently in action:
★ 'Is there a more helpful way of looking at this situation?'
★ 'I try not to beat myself up too much when things go wrong'
★ 'I play mental games to stop unhelpful, unpleasant thoughts intruding'
★ 'I challenge myself to find alternative explanations for why things happen'
★ 'Am I exaggerating this problem?'

We'll look at how to think more resiliently later (see page 213).

C Use optimism and humour

Positive emotions and moods have power, even, or especially, in the face of stress and difficulties. They have important psychological and physiological benefits, impacting our minds and our bodies. We'll look at this more in Chapter 8. They help us to cope well, replenish depleted emotional resources and recover more quickly after tough times, such as feeling gratitude for what we have, rather than only sadness for what we've lost.

Maintaining hope, finding glimmers of light or seeing potential positive outcomes despite difficulties decreases the likelihood of stress-related illnesses compared to those with a more pessimistic outlook. This doesn't mean being unrealistic but rather engaging with the reality of our problems and focusing on what we can do rather than what we can't. Unlike 'blind optimism', realistic optimists don't filter out risks – they filter out unnecessary, unhelpful negative information. In this way having a more optimistic approach enables us to adopt active coping strategies.

Maintaining a sense of humour in dark times is a common feature of resilience. It helps to lift our gloom, diminish fear, threat and tension, and reduce the negative impact of stressful situations. It also helps to connect us to others in tough times – another ingredient of resilience.

Examples of optimism and humour in action:
★ 'I try to see the funny side of difficult situations'
★ 'I look for something good or positive in negative situations'

Importantly a more optimistic interpretation of events can be learned through resilient-thinking approaches (see page 226). Mindfulness can help us find moments of calm, which we looked at in Chapter 4.

D Nurture relationships and help others

In tough situations it's usually better together – feeling we have social support is an important ingredient of resilience. Knowing that there are people we can turn to when we need them helps to buffer us against stress, deal with fear and anxiety, and come through even major traumas, so can protect us from psychological and physical ill health. It's worth noting too that social isolation is a common contributor to psychological disorders, and it can also be a cause of them.

Resilient people rarely face difficulties alone if they can avoid it. Actively seeking support from those close to us or professionals is also associated with better outcomes and is an active coping strategy. The ability to bond with a group with a shared mission and experiencing mutual care is a core feature of the emergency and armed service professions and is considered essential in dealing with the complex, and often extreme, situations they face as part of their work.

Resilience experts Drs Charney and Southwick highlight the value of having 'role models of resilience' as a way of building our 'coping self-efficacy'. Whether these are people we know personally or characters from the media, film or fiction, learning how they've dealt with problems can be helpful to apply in our own lives. They can also be a 'virtual guide', helping us in moments of challenge by thinking: 'What would [name] do?'

Interestingly, helping others is also a common feature of resilient individuals, who recognise that connecting to others helps us to find meaning and contributes to our own healing. The experience of trauma and difficulties can make us more compassionate towards others and it's often said 'altruism is borne of suffering'. Indeed there are countless stories of people who have suffered terribly going on to do what they can to help others – so good can truly come from bad.

Examples of nurturing relationships and helping in action:
★ 'I know who I can turn to for help'
★ 'I see asking for help as a strength, not a weakness'
★ 'I get emotional support from others'
★ 'Helping others through tough times helps me too'

Helping others has twice the benefit – if it's good for our resilience, it is likely to be for others too. Chapters 1 and 2 looked in detail at why our connections with others matter for our well-being and resilience – have a look back at those actions and try them out.

E Look after your physical well-being

Physical activity can be an instant stress-reliever and a great source of positive emotions. This means that not only does regular exercise help to reduce and prevent depression and anxiety and increase our confidence so that we are better able to deal with difficulties, it literally makes our brains more resilient. This builds our cognitive capacities for things like planning and decision-making, boosting areas of our brains responsible for stress regulation and helping to repair the damage stress does in our brains, meaning that we're less susceptible to it. Getting enough sleep and eating well are important too.

If there is a great deal in life that we can't control, taking care of our physical well-being, even in a small way, is often something that we can do to help us feel in control and actively cope.

Examples of taking care of physical health in action:
★ 'I get out for a walk to clear my head'
★ 'Exercising helps me sleep'
★ 'I make sure I eat healthily and regularly'

In Chapter 3 we looked at how the different ways of taking care of your body also take care of your mind, including lots of ideas to get started.

F Have a sense of values, purpose and meaning

Having a strong moral compass – a sense of purpose or clear values (whether personal, spiritual and/or originating in following a religious faith) – are common features of resilience. If these are robust and hold up when challenged or when all else seems to fail, they have been shown to be protective, enabling us to focus on what really matters, serving as a guide for action, helping us make sense of what's happening and so pull us through.

Examples of having values, purpose and meaning in action:
★ 'I keep focused on what's most important in life'
★ 'My beliefs give me strength'
★ 'I search for the bigger meaning in what's happened'

In Chapter 10 we'll unpack this idea, looking at why values, purpose and meaning matter and how we can find them – if they're not clear for us.

G Know, use and actively develop your strengths

Sometimes it takes tough times to show us what we're really made of. Indeed, there is a growing focus on the value of challenges to help build and nurture 'character'. But let's not wait until we face difficulties to discover what's best about ourselves. Research shows that when we better understand our strengths and weaknesses, it helps to build our confidence, find different ways around problems and appreciate and draw on the strengths of others – all of which contribute to greater resilience. Understanding our strengths can also be a clue to our values and help us find our purpose. And resilient thinking can mean we focus more on where we're okay rather than where we fail.

Examples of strengths in action:
★ 'Using what I'm good at gives me confidence to tackle difficulties.'
★ 'I know the areas I find challenging, so I look for ways around them... or get someone to help.'
★ 'I know that what doesn't kill me can help me develop my strengths.'
★ 'Knowing I have strengths I can draw on helps me face challenges.'

In Chapter 9 we'll look at ways to identify, develop and use our strengths and find out how to be more self-compassionate so we don't undermine our own resilience by giving ourselves too hard a time!

H Keep learning and challenging yourself

In a large study people were asked how they coped with the biggest challenge in their lives. Eighty-two per cent said they drew on strength developed from past stressful experiences. So a key way we can build our resilience is by challenging ourselves to try new things, experiment and learn. As we master new skills and have novel experiences, we see ourselves progress, our sense of self-efficacy grows, which can boost our ability to solve problems creatively.

Being resilient doesn't mean we're not scared by difficult or new situations, but that we're willing to 'feel the fear' and try anyway. When we try new things we often also experience some fear. By getting through the fear and progressing we learn to look it in the face.

Gradually increasing the level of challenge in whatever we are doing builds our confidence and ability to deal with difficulty – it's called 'stress inoculation' and is used in some resilience training. Using our strengths in new ways can also help us to do this, applying them in different situations and challenging ourselves in our physical activity is a great place to start.

Examples of learning and challenging yourself in action:
★ 'I like to put myself in new situations'
★ 'I learn from trying new experiences'
★ 'Little by little I set myself new challenges at home or at work'
★ 'I make plans for how I can work towards a goal'
★ 'I can find ways around obstacles to reach my goals'
★ 'Can I push myself five per cent further?'

Chapter 5 looks at why trying new things and learning are important for well-being and resilience throughout our lives and gives ideas for actions to try. Learning and challenging ourselves takes and builds discipline – practising mindfulness can do this too, which we covered in Chapter 4.

 Pause point…

What are your beliefs about stress?

★ Is it generally a good or a bad thing?

★ Does it undermine your health or give you vitality?

★ Does it inhibit or enhance learning?

★ Does it help you to perform better or mean you do worse?

★ Is it something to be avoided or can it be harnessed?

Based on: Crum, Salovey & Achor (2013)

Is stress a friend or a foe?

We talk about stress a lot and it gets a lot of press – articles forever offer us stress-busting tips. But should we always want to get rid of stress? Or could we find better ways to manage, or even harness, it for our good? Sure, stress can be harmful: many common illnesses, including heart disease, Alzheimer's and psychological disorders have stress as a risk factor. But it's also a part of life that's pretty hard to avoid. And there's a paradox. Stress is the body's natural response to a difficulty or challenge, physical or mental. And challenges can be good as well as bad, for example competing in a sport, working to a deadline or learning something new.

Stress prepares us to meet challenges by creating changes in our bodies and brains, including storing/mobilising energy resources, increasing alertness and preparing us for action (in extreme situations fight, flight or freeze). It enables us to focus, increases memory functioning (which helps us to learn from these situations), gives us a burst of energy (ensuring a steady flow of glucose to the brain) and helps keep our bodies' functioning in balance. This response evolved to deal with short-term exposure to danger and difficulties, after which our bodies and minds returned to normal. However, our present lifestyles mean that we can be in a constant low (or high) state of stress. This means the amygdala in our brain continues to trigger the release of the stress hormone cortisol, regardless of high levels already in the body. The stress response becomes generalised, i.e. not just in reaction to a specific stressor, and so is potentially damaging – physically and mentally. For example, this has been associated with storing fat around the abdomen, higher blood pressure and impaired cognitive functioning. It can also lead to anxiety and depression. But it turns out that the way we think about stress might have a major impact on how harmful it is.

A national survey in the US asked over 28,000 people how much stress they had experienced in the past year: a lot, a moderate amount or relatively little; and also how much they perceived that stress had an effect on their health: a lot, some, hardly any, or none. The results showed that either experiencing a lot of stress or believing it harmful had a negative relationship to health outcomes. But a combination of both was worse. Those who scored highly for having a lot of stress and believing

WHEN JULES WAS CREATIVELY RESILIENT

'When I was first diagnosed with breast cancer I was devastated. Friends offered supportive comments: "You're strong, you can fight it". While bolstered by their empathy, I realised that each of us held different perspectives on the news and reacted to it in our own way. To me it didn't feel like a "fight" or a "battle" that I must win, but a time when I needed to nurture my body and help myself heal. A "fight" implied "us" and "them", but in reality it was all me! Something in my body had gone awry and I needed help to get things right again.

I decided to look beyond the present. I created an image of how things would be one year on, when I'd finished treatments. The first time I did this, a large bumble bee flew past the window and became my emblem of the future. Friends began to bring me cards depicting bees or little model bees, so it also became a sign that I wasn't alone. And I kept reminding myself that things could always be worse.

When I was recovering between chemo sessions, I started to look at what the illness might be trying to tell me. I was in a really pressured job, so I decided to downshift to a simpler role and also take up painting. I found a local painting group and I loved it. It helped me focus on something other than the treatment regime, giving me time out and space for mental and physical recovery.

Unluckily, five years later I received a second cancer diagnosis. I promised myself that when it was all over I'd dedicate more time to art. I applied to do a part-time foundation course. When I started the course I found the work really helped me come to terms with what had happened. During my first year the cancer became central to my art as I explored my reactions to the illness and the physical impact of the treatment, which meant I had to come to terms with a new identity. This culminated in my final project, where I focused on the scars from eight operations. I decided to commemorate my scars by turning them into objects of beauty. I made moulds of them and created delicate porcelain ornaments. At the end-of-year show people were drawn to them despite their origins. I got top marks for my work and sold all the pieces. I went on to do a full art degree and a ceramics course. It's now what I most love to do and I thank my illness for helping me (re)discover the real me!'

that it was very harmful had a much greater risk of dying prematurely eight years later. In another study, psychologist Alia Crum and colleagues found that people who saw stress as being enhancing showed fewer negative health outcomes than those who saw it as being debilitating. Both Crum and Kelly McGonigal, a health psychologist, argue that instead of always trying to eliminate stress, we need to view it differently.

Crum suggests these three steps:

1 **Name it** Rather than ignoring, denying or dwelling on stress, simply acknowledge it. By doing this, it seems we can switch activity in our brain from the primitive, emotionally reactive, amygdala to the prefrontal cortex – involved in slower, conscious, decision-making. Resilient-thinking approaches we'll look at next or mindfulness practice (see Chapter 4) help us name our stress without worrying about it.

2 **Recognise it means you care** We get stressed because, at some level, we believe something important is at stake. Resilient thinking helps us to identify beliefs/thoughts/interpretations that underly our emotions and check whether they're accurate – or not. If it's something that it's helpful to care about, we can view the stress as positive.

3 **Harness it** The stress response is designed to galvanise us into action, so using that extra energy, alertness/focus for the task at hand.

Recognising and harnessing the energy of stress is another element in our resilience tool kit. But sometimes it's not so easy, for example where stress is prolonged – such as if we are caring for a disabled loved one. Both Crum and McGonigal suggest that acceptance rather than dwelling on it is key (step 1): finding ways of seeing positive meaning in it also helps, such as focusing on caring because we love someone or learning something from it.

In times of chronic stress finding ways to take action to take care of ourselves, however small, is important. Every little action helps and can enable us to feel a bit more in control. For example, the one-minute or three-minute breathing spaces (see Chapter 4), getting outside for a brief, brisk walk or asking for help. Techniques, such as progressive relaxation, where we work up through our bodies, slowly tensing each part in turn and then releasing it, can also help us switch off from our problems.

Foundations for resilient thinking

> 'I have been surrounded by troubles all my life long, but there is a curious thing about them—nine-tenths of them never happened.'
>
> Andrew Carnegie, *An American Four-in-Hand in Britain*

Albert Ellis, the grandfather of cognitive behavioural therapy, wrote that we are remarkably good at disturbing ourselves. As a therapist, he saw that the way people thought, their habits and patterns of thinking, could contribute to unhappiness and lead to anxiety and depression. He developed ways to help his clients counter their conditions by learning new ways of thinking, which, with awareness and practice, could become healthier habits.

With the advent of positive psychology, it has been realised that these healthier thinking habits are skills that are not only beneficial in the treatment of psychological ill health, but could be used to help prevent it happening and enhance well-being. Let's look at some of the foundations for more resilient-thinking habits.

The power of our instant thoughts

Imagine this situation. You're working from home and you're not feeling one hundred per cent well. You realise that you've run out of milk so you ring your partner or housemate and ask them to get some on their way home. Hearing them open the front door, you think: 'Great, I've been looking forward to a cup of tea.' You come out of your room to say hello, only to see that they haven't bought any milk.

How do you feel in that moment? What thoughts are running through your head? As a result, what would you say or do?

Take 1

Like many people, especially if you're under pressure or under the weather, you might feel angry or upset, thinking something along the lines of: 'They're so selfish, they couldn't be bothered to stop and get the milk, even though I asked them.'

As a result, instead of smiling and being pleased to see them, the first thing you greet them with is a sarcastic criticism: 'So you couldn't be bothered to pick up some milk for me. You're just so thoughtless.'

Upset by the fact that you haven't given them a chance to say hello, let alone explain, before being moaned at, they respond defensively. Before you know it, a row escalates that clouds the whole evening. The hostile atmosphere perhaps even impacting the kids or other housemates. Both of you go to bed tense and irritated and neither of you sleeps well, so that you're below par the following day.

Take 2

Now rewind to the moment your partner or housemate walks in the door and you see that they haven't bought any milk. The same instant interpretation (that they couldn't be bothered to buy it) pops into your mind and you feel yourself getting angry. But instead of immediately chastising them, you remind yourself to pause for a split second to check that your instant interpretation is actually true.

Sure, there's no milk – as far as you can see. But they could have left it in the car or maybe they'd intended to head back out to the supermarket, popping in to pick up the shopping bags and to see if there was anything else you needed. Or perhaps something had gone wrong for them at work or on the way home.

You realise, at that moment, that you don't know for sure what the reason is. It might, indeed, be that they couldn't be bothered, but it could equally be any of the other scenarios. Yes, the person might have been thoughtless in the past, but at that particular moment you don't have evidence either way. So why not give them the benefit of the doubt or be open to finding out more?

So the emotions you initially felt, anger and upset, subside and you're able to say with a warmer tone: 'Hi there. How was your day? Did you have a chance to pick up some milk?' Well, it could be that they had forgotten, but you've given them a chance to say: 'I'll go and get some now' or one of the other scenarios unfolds. The incident then passes without much further thought. You have a pleasant, relaxed evening together and sleep well that night.

We can see how the scenario in Take 1 could undermine happiness that evening and if repeated or perpetuated could undermine well-being over time. In contrast, in Take 2 a pleasant evening at home, feeling supported by each other, would be enjoyable and help sustain mutual well-being.

That split-second pause you took in Take 2 to check the evidence for your interpretation of the situation made all the difference between a good evening and a bad one and the follow-on consequence that then ensued. Let's unpack this a bit more.

The essence of more resilient thinking

Our emotions are driven by our in-the-moment interpretations. We have more control over these than our emotions, but we often don't even realise we've made a judgement, let alone stopped to check it's right.

Consider the sorts of things we might think or say when someone or something triggers an emotional reaction in us. For example: 'He makes me so angry' or 'It makes me feel really guilty' or 'She's really upset me'. It's as if the control over what we feel is with the person or event that triggered that reaction in us.

In reality, however, it's not the other person or the event that caused us to be angry, sad or guilty – or whatever emotion we felt. Our feelings are, in fact, triggered by our instant interpretations of the situation, often our 'guess' about why something happened or what might happen next. Our in-the-moment interpretations are instant and automatic – not the product of rational thinking! The thing is, these thoughts happen so fast and our emotional reactions even faster, that we don't even recognise that this chain of events is happening – we just feel what we feel.

Our emotional reactions are hard-wired, primitive and instinctive, which makes them especially hard to control. And in situations we perceive as adverse, our emotions can be strong.

Psychiatrist Viktor Frankel famously said: 'Between stimulus and response there is a space. In that space is our power to choose our response. In our response lies our growth and our freedom.' But often we don't realise that a space exists or that we might have more choice over our responses than we might think. If we can pause for a moment between the trigger event and our emotional response to it, it allows us to tune in to our instant interpretations and check how accurate they are, we'll have more choice over what we feel and do as a result.

The concept is easy. In the heat of the moment it can be harder than it sounds and there are some common pitfalls to watch out for. But as we become more aware and understand the thinking that underlies our reactions, we increase our power and freedom to choose how we respond. And that is an important source of personal resilience and well-being: it impacts others too.

Our emotions can set off a chain of reactions

Emotions are more than just feelings. They set off a chain of reactions in our bodies, rapidly preparing us to act in certain ways. So our emotions drive what we do next. For example, if we feel anger our bodies prepare to retaliate; if we feel fear, our bodies prepare to fight or flee. Rapidly our muscles get tense, adrenaline starts pumping, we're more alert to further sources of anger or fear and we can lash out or act in defence without thinking. And how we respond has knock-on consequences for us and other people. The way we react triggers responses in those around us.

As we saw in Take 1 (see page 214), unchecked, our instant interpretations led to emotions and actions that set off a chain of consequences for ourselves and others that lasted for the whole evening and potentially had an impact beyond it.

We may go on to seethe for hours, ruminating not about what's just annoyed us, but all the other ways our partner has annoyed us in the past. So the event, in our mind, gets bigger and takes up more energy and attention. It may then cause us to react inappropriately or disproportionately to what the other person does subsequently – even if that's to say sorry! So in this way, an incident can grow out of control, potentially impacting our relationship and even spreading beyond it.

Appropriate emotional reactions rather than no emotions
Resilient thinking isn't about never being angry, sad, fearful or guilty. Absolutely not. It's about making sure our response is appropriate.

To be sure that we're angry or sad for a good reason, we need to tune into the space between the trigger and our emotional reactions and the interpretations that are driving what we feel. If we understand these we can check they are accurate and so make sure our responses are appropriate. Tuning into our interpretations also helps build our self-awareness and understand ourselves better. If there are themes to our interpretations whenever our emotions are adversely triggered, it may give us insights into our deeply held beliefs or values (see Chapter 9). It could also indicate that we're falling into interpretation pitfalls that could undermine our resilience and well-being longer term.

Our emotions give us clues to our interpretations

Psychological research on emotions shows there are typical pairings between specific feelings and the actions they tend to cause our bodies and minds to prepare for (called 'action-tendencies'). I've found an awareness of these pairings very helpful in getting to understand my own reactions and why they happen.

When I first learnt that it was my interpretations that were driving my emotional reactions, I found it hard to put a finger on what my underlying thoughts were whenever an emotional reaction was triggered in me. My emotions kicked in so quickly and often so strongly that it was difficult to tune in to the essence of my instant interpretations.

The table overleaf lists some of the typical interpretation–emotion pairings. These pairings helped me work backwards. Tuning into the emotion I felt and the likely essence of the underlying thoughts helped

Interpretation–emotion pairings		
Interpretation 'essence'		**Emotion**
I'm in danger	⟶	Fear, frightened
I've been done wrong to	⟶	Anger, annoyance
I've done something wrong	⟶	Guilt
I've lost something (this could be tangible, such as a physical thing or a friendship, or something intangible, such as an enjoyable experience or even self-worth)	⟶	Sadness, upset, dejection
I'm not good enough or I'm not as good as	⟶	Embarrassment, shame
Based on: various sources, including: Briers (2009), Reivich (2010), Reivich & Shatté (2002)		

me become clearer about why I was feeling how I was. And then I could check to see whether that interpretation was accurate or not. At first I did this after the event, and gradually my awareness grew so that now I am more able to do it in the moment, rather than being subsumed by what I am feeling.

An understanding of these interpretation–emotion pairings can also give us clues as to how other people are interpreting situations. For example in Take 1 (see page 214), when we were critical of our partner or housemate, perhaps they were upset or sad because their instant interpretation was that they'd lost your trust and then anger because that wasn't correct – they had thought about getting the milk (but there were other reasons why they hadn't bought it).

Check your interpretations!

'There is nothing either good or bad, but thinking makes it so.'
William Shakespeare, *Hamlet*

As we've seen, an important part of resilient thinking is to know that our instant, automatic interpretations aren't always accurate. We're really good at jumping to conclusions when we only have a snapshot rather than the full picture or if the situation is ambiguous. These quick

✎ Pause point...

Think of a time when an event or situation triggered an adverse emotional reaction in you – the more recent the better!

★ What emotions did you experience?

★ At the moment your emotions were triggered, what were your underlying interpretations? (Often these are about why something happened or what will happen next.)

★ If there was a sequence of emotions, such as guilt and embarrassment, can you think back to what the sequence of interpretations was?

conclusions we jump to can be helpful – better to err on the side of caution if we're in real potential danger. For example, if a vicious-looking dog is heading straight for us or we feel someone too close behind us when we are walking alone along a dark, empty street.

But often our instant interpretations aren't accurate and may be unhelpful – or could even be harmful. If we act on them without pausing to check them, it can set off chain reactions in ourselves and others, taking up emotional energy and head space, impacting our relationships and unnecessarily undermining our own and others' well-being.

Pausing just for a split second enables us to tune into our instant interpretations, check their accuracy by looking for evidence for and against them, and challenge them if they are irrational or unhelpful.

We need to check whether we've jumped to conclusions by asking ourselves questions such as:
★ What evidence do I have that my interpretation is correct or true?
★ How helpful is this interpretation for me and others?
★ What are other ways of looking at this?
★ Is there evidence for alternative explanations?
★ Is this an interpretation I often jump to?

KEY SEVEN: RESILIENCE

This sounds a lot to do in a few seconds, but it can be done. And if we don't have enough evidence we can seek some, such as in our Take 2 example on page 214. It might be, of course, that our instant interpretation is correct, and the way we feel and act in response is appropriate.

Sometimes, even by pausing and tuning in to check our interpretations, we realise that we don't have enough evidence to know whether they're accurate or not. In that case it's best to give the situation the benefit of our doubts and choose an interpretation that is least likely to hinder or harm, or is most likely to be helpful. For example, a real 'red-button' trigger for me is people driving too close behind me. I remember one incident where a car drove right up, almost to my bumper, then pulled out and back in again very close in front. After initial fear, causing me to slam on my brakes, I felt a surge of anger, and I had an urge to teach the driver a lesson by doing the same thing to him. My underlying interpretation was that he was an arrogant idiot who didn't care about anyone else. This might well have been true, but at that moment I had no way of knowing. I felt het up and had I acted, my interpretation unchecked, it could have caused an accident. Alternative explanations could have been that something important had gone wrong for him or he was in the midst of an emergency. Though this was perhaps unlikely, I had no way of knowing. But in the moment, finding a different way of interpreting the situation instantly lowered my anger and I was able to let it, and him, go – a more helpful response for me and potentially less harmful for others too.

 Pause point…

★ Do you have any emotional 'red buttons': events or situations that trigger a strong adverse reaction in you?

★ What are your instant interpretations or thoughts about these triggers – perhaps why they happen or what they might lead to?

★ Are your interpretations helping, hindering or harmful to you? How else could you interpret them?

★ How can you remind yourself to pause and check next time this red button is pressed?

Interpretation pitfalls and traps

Even in a situation where our instant interpretations seem clear, we still need to pause and check them. We may think we see things accurately, but we often don't. As human beings we have a number of natural pitfalls that get in the way of making accurate interpretations. They're natural and automatic and we can all fall into them.

Three common pitfalls are:

1 **We see what we're looking for** If we are looking for something, it's likely that's what we'll see, but we'll also miss other details, which may be just as important. Psychologists call this 'selective attention'. For example, have you ever looked for something that you have a mental picture of but not been able to find it? Say you're trying to find a book and you remember it having a yellow cover. You know it's around somewhere, but you just can't find it. Frustrated, you stop looking and try again a little later. You find it! It was right in front of you all the time. You just didn't see it because its cover was, in fact, blue.

2 **We see what we want to see** This is known as the 'confirmation bias'. This means that once we've interpreted a situation one way:
   ★ We look for, notice and remember evidence that supports that particular interpretation.
   ★ We're less like to notice evidence to the contrary.
   ★ We're more likely to interpret ambiguous information as supporting our interpretations.
   ★ We stop looking once we find evidence to support our thoughts.

3 **We can get trapped by habitual interpretation patterns** We may have particular patterns of thinking that, because of our natural tendencies for selective attention and the confirmation bias, cause us to interpret many trigger events and situations in that way. Over time this can really undermine our resilience. Let's look at an example in the thought experiment on page0

Thought experiment Picnic in the park

Imagine you're a parent out for a picnic in the park with your young daughter, Drew, aged four. You're tired because things have been so busy recently, so you are looking forward to a couple of hours' break and hopefully bumping into other parents in the playground afterwards. You find a good spot to stop and eat and while you get the sandwiches out, you give your phone to Drew to hold. As you're getting the picnic laid out, you suddenly notice Drew playing a game of catch with your phone and hear a smash as it drops to the ground. Of course, your immediate reaction is to be annoyed, but then...

★ What would be your automatic thoughts (immediate interpretation) of why this happened or what could happen next?

★ How would this have caused you to feel?

★ What might you then do as a result?

★ What could that lead to?

In the thought experiment above, what interpretation first came into your mind? Was it something like one of the Common interpretation traps (see opposite)?

Based on this interpretation, what do you think you'd feel and have done as a result? For example:

★ Shame and guilt about your abilities as a parent and so avoided other parents in the park that day.

★ Ruminate on all your partner's faults so that by the time you got home you felt annoyed with them, so snap at the first thing they said.

★ Sadness that your child didn't respect you and your possessions, which then reminded you of other situations when someone hadn't thought about you.

★ Crossness with Drew so that you shouted at her for being so careless, causing her to burst into tears.

★ Hopelessness that there was nothing you could do to change Drew. Feelings of depression all afternoon, ignoring Drew and others.

★ Hopelessness and feelings of being overwhelmed by all your problems.

Common interpretation traps

Trap	Thought experiment example
Personalising Blaming yourself – believing you are usually the cause of every problem.	It's my fault. I've brought her up so badly. I've failed as a parent.
Externalising Blaming others or 'it' – usually believing that other people or circumstances are the cause of every problem.	It's all her father's fault. He spoils her.
Mind-reading Assuming that you know what another person is thinking, or expecting another person to know what you are thinking.	I should have known that would happen. She should have known not to do that.
Labelling Judging another's (or your own) worth, ability or motivation on the basis of a single situation.	She's so selfish. I'm stupid.
Black-and-white thinking Thinking that things are either completely good or bad, successful or a failure.	We've ruined this child.
Shoulds and musts When you have overly rigid 'rules' or excessively high expectations for how you or others 'should', 'shouldn't' or 'must' behave.	A good parent shouldn't get upset with her child.
Believing it's permanent Believing the 'problem' will be there forever, that you have no control or there's nothing you can do. Use words like 'always' or 'never'.	• She's just like that. I can't do anything to change her. • I'll never be a good parent.
Believing it can spread Believing that an incident in one area of your life will spread out to all, or most, other areas. Use words like 'all' or 'everything'.	• Her little brother will be like that too. • Just like me to have a selfish child. Everything I do turns out badly.

What could have been the adverse knock-on consequences of any of these reactions for you, Drew, your partner, your connections with other parents? Of course your interpretation could be accurate. But if we have a pattern of interpreting events in the same way it can become a self-fulfilling prophecy and also indicate an unhealthy, deeply held belief – for example, always blaming ourselves when things go wrong might indicate a belief that we're no good or that we must be perfect.

Toxic traps and downwards spirals

Interpretation traps are common. Most of us fall into them from time to time, especially if we're tired or under stress, causing knock-on consequences, which impact our own and others' happiness.

If we regularly fall into these traps it could potentially undermine our well-being and resilience longer term. It means we'll continually look for evidence to support those thoughts and unconsciously ignore evidence to the contrary, therefore reinforcing the trap and perpetuating our feelings, actions and the consequences as a result. Unchecked, this can create self-fulfilling prophecies, causing us longer-term unhappiness.

If our interpretation patterns combine multiple traps it can amplify the impact on our resilience. The following combinations have been shown to be particularly toxic:

★ Personalising + Believing it's permanent + Believing it will spread
   → can lead to hopelessness and feeling bad about yourself

✎ Pause point...

★ Do you recognise any of the interpretation traps on page 223 as ones you tend to fall into?

★ What are the situations that cause you to get trapped? Can you think of a recent example?

★ Do you have a particular interpretation-trap pattern?

★ How would you change or stop this pattern of interpretation? What's the evidence for and against your interpretation? What other interpretations could there be? What might be a more helpful way of interpreting the situation?

Some prompts to help you escape from your interpretation traps:

★ **Personalising** Look for how others, or the context, contributed to the situation.

★ **Externalising** Look for how you might have contributed to what happened.

★ Externalising + Believing it's permanent + Believing it will spread
   → can lead to persistent anger and a victim mentality

Psychologist Dr Martin Seligman found that the way we interpret the
causes of everyday setbacks can have a significant impact on our ability to
cope and deal with difficulties, our physical health and our persistence in
the face of adversity. He looked at three key types of interpretation trap:

★ **Personalising** When bad things happen, resilient thinkers tend
   to focus on causes outside themselves. For example, if they miss a
   deadline they will look at the computer issues they had or the other
   pressing jobs they had to do, rather than only beating themselves up
   for being late.

★ **Believing it's permanent** When things go wrong, resilient thinkers
   see it as transitory, perhaps thinking: 'It didn't work this time, but
   next time it will be better.' Someone with a less-resilient thinking style
   might think it will always be that way: 'It didn't work this time, and it's
   never going to.'

★ **Mind-reading** Check whether what you think another person is
   thinking is correct and/or be clear about what your own thoughts/
   needs/intentions are.

★ **Labelling** What's the reason for their (or your) behaviour in this
   specific situation?

★ **Black-and-white thinking** What less-extreme interpretation is more
   likely?

★ **Shoulds and musts** How could you counter your interpretation?
   For example: no one's perfect; everyone makes mistakes sometimes;
   nothing's right all the time.

★ **Believing it's permanent** What could change? Is there something
   you can do?

★ **Believing it will spread** Put boundaries around it. What's the
   evidence in this specific situation? Is there an example where you did
   the opposite in another part of your life?

★ **Believing it will spread** When something goes wrong in a resilient thinker's life, they put boundaries around the issue, limiting it to that specific area. For example: 'I went the wrong way; I find following directions hard.' We can undermine our resilience if we see the problem as spreading out to everything: 'I went the wrong way. That's typical of me – I'm no good at anything.'

This isn't about being unrealistic or not taking responsibility when problems occur, but about being realistic and flexible in our thoughts about why these issues happened. If we are stressed or feeling 'down', we can all too easily fall into the traps of thinking that everything is our fault, can't be changed and that trouble will spread to all areas of our life. This makes us feel hopeless and can start a downward spiral towards lower resilience and even depression.

Building your resilient-thinking skills

The first step towards more resilient thinking is awareness. And having read this chapter so far, you now know that your instant thoughts and interpretations are driving your emotional reactions to a trigger event. As we've already seen, our emotional reactions happen very fast, so at first just remember to pause, just like Viktor Frankel suggested (see page 216). Sometimes that's enough for us to moderate our responses in a way that is better for our well-being (and others' too).

To build your resilient-thinking skills, it's helpful to go back over past incidents when your emotions were triggered and unpack what your underlying interpretations were and the feelings, actions and consequences they led to. At first it can be easy to mix up thoughts (i.e. interpretations) with feelings, so watch out for that. Then think about how you could have checked your interpretations. See page 222 for an example from the thought experiment we looked at earlier.

This retrospective review builds awareness and helps us to get used to the relationships between triggers and our interpretations and reactions (emotions and what we said/did as a result). It also helps us to start to see any traps we might fall into in particular situations.

Reviewing a trigger event (example)

TRIGGER (stick to the facts only)

* Gave Drew my phone to hold.
* She took it, played catch with it and then dropped it.

INTERPRETATION

She should know better. I'm such a bad parent, I've brought her up so badly.

REACTIONS

EMOTIONS	ACTIONS
What you felt	What you did or said as a result
• Annoyed	• Snapped at Drew
• Shame and sadness	• Walked home not wanting to meet the other parents in the park

CONSEQUENCES

Did this reaction help, hinder or harm?

Drew was upset and instead of the afternoon being enjoyable, I didn't meet up with my friends, the other parents, so I felt isolated and down for the rest of the day.

How could you check your interpretations?
(e.g. What's the evidence for and against? What other explanations are possible?)

* Although, like all young kids, she has her moments, Drew's generally quite a careful child, so I must be doing something right.
* I normally remind her to be careful when she holds my phone, but I forgot today – it's probably because I'm tired..

This skill takes practice. So if you don't manage to check your interpretations the next time your emotions are triggered, don't get frustrated. When you have a calm moment, unpack what was going on for you and look out for it next time.

In Chapter 4 we looked at mindfulness. That's a skill that can help us notice what's going on for us without getting caught up in our thoughts and emotions, and so help us think and act more resiliently.

Try this! Practising resilient-thinking skills

1 Looking back

Think of a specific situation in the past (ideally as recent as possible), which your emotions were triggered by. Unpack it by following the Drew example on the previous page.

★ Trigger – what specifically was the trigger? Try to stick to the facts – what a neutral observer would see.

★ Interpretations – what were your instant interpretations?

★ Reactions – emotions: what you felt – and actions: what you did, or said, as a result.

★ Consequences – did this result reaction help, hinder or harm? How could you check your interpretations?

2 Unpacking practice

Over the next few days, unpack five events in this way. They don't have to be big things. For example:

★ A trigger could be noticing someone you know in the street, but they walk straight past you even though you wave at them. Your instant interpretation might be something like: 'They didn't want to stop and say hello because I'm just not interesting enough' and your reaction as a result makes you feel sad and so want to avoid people.

Other quick, handy resilient-thinking tools
Take a break from your thoughts

Sometimes we get stuck on the same thoughts going round and round in our head and we just can't seem to stop them and switch off. This can drain our energy and stop us from sleeping, so undermining our well-being. It could be simply that we've got too much to think about because we're busy. Or we might be ruminating on a worry, something that's upset us or another negative thought, going over and over it. And as we do so the thought can get bigger and bigger or it expands into other, similar, thoughts. Over time, rumination can lead to anxiety and depression.

You decide to start jogging around the park, but when you get there it is busy with lots of fit people already running. You think to yourself: 'I'm such a lump, I'll never be as fit as them.' You feel embarrassed and so turn around and go back home.

Unpacking several incidents in this way will help you tune into your instant, automatic interpretations and identify any traps or patterns you might be falling into.

3 Reflection
Looking back over the incidents you've unpacked:

★ How helpful were your interpretations in terms of how they made you feel and what you did as a result?

★ Did you fall into any interpretation traps?

★ Was there a pattern to your interpretations?

★ If each of these situations happened again, how could you check or challenge your interpretations? (See the Pause point on pages 224–5 for prompts.)

  • What alternative interpretations might there have been?

  • What other evidence could you have looked for?

It's not about ignoring our worries but taking a break from them. The aim is to distract your mind and interrupt the thoughts going around in your head. To do this you need to give your mind something else to think about that's absorbing but not too demanding. Thinking and memory games can work well such as those listed in the box on page 230. These may sound silly, but they can, and do, work. I use them when I'm struggling to get to sleep and I usually find I've nodded off before I get to the end of whichever game I'm playing.

Such distraction games can also be helpful in situations when we're anxious – perhaps waiting to go into an appointment, exam or go on stage to perform in a play or to give a presentation.

Try this! Distraction games

Number games – these might be a bit more engaging than just counting sheep! For example:

★ Count backwards from 1,000,000

★ Count backwards from 1,000 in threes, e.g. 1,000, 997, 994… etc.

★ Practise multiplication tables

Alphabet games – for example:

★ Pick a category, e.g. animals, fruits, famous footballers, place names – anything! Then come up with an example for each letter of the alphabet. For example: fruits: apple, banana, cranberry… etc.

★ Pick a letter and then a category, e.g. famous actors whose names begin with G: George Clooney, Gérard Depardieu, Gary Oldman…

'How many?' games – for example:

★ Pick a category and see how many examples you can remember in two minutes, e.g. parts of the body, TV soap-opera stars, capital cities

Imagination games – for example:

★ Make up limericks

★ Make up fantasy sports teams – especially two opposing sides!

Some other ways to distract your mind

Other distraction techniques that can also be helpful are:

★ **Laugh** Years ago a friend, Sarah, trained as an accountant. This involved doing many tough exams and she got pre-exam nerves. To deal with that anxiety, Sarah had a fun tactic, which turned out to be a good one. As she waited outside the exam room, she would immerse herself in a joke book. Not only did it help her to stop worrying, but it put her in an upbeat frame of mind, ready to focus on the exams.

★ **Look closely** Pick up a small object, such as an interesting pebble, and study it intensely. What shape is it? What does it feel like? How does it sound or taste? What colours can you see in it? What could it be used for? Apparently, actors use a technique like this when switching between characters, scenes or emotions.

* **Write it down** Jot down worrying or recurrent thoughts as soon as they occur (such as when our minds are buzzing because there are things we need to remember or do). It gets them out of your mind and onto paper and can give help us feel we've started to deal with them.
* **Worry time** If you've got a lot going through your mind, set aside a specific time, maybe 30 minutes or an hour, as 'worry time'. If worries come up outside that time limit, remind yourself that you have set a time for worrying later, perhaps making a note of the thought.

Get things back in proportion

Some of us are natural catastrophisers. When something goes wrong, we don't limit our worries just to that particular issue, our minds go into overdrive, spiralling from that incident to the worst possible thing that could happen. Even if the worst-case scenario is so far-fetched that it's not likely to happen, our levels of anxiety are significantly increased. Let's look at the example in the box on pages 232–3. If you don't tend to catastrophise, you may think that this example is extreme. But in the mind of a catastrophiser, it's not. And it's easy to see how thoughts and worries like this can wear you down, especially if you are tired or under pressure. So how do you stop this train of thought in it tracks. Distraction techniques (see page 230) can help, but even more effective is to make yourself work through some rational questions:

* When I've got through bad situations in the past, what helped me?
* Relative to all the bad things that have happened to me in the past or which could happen in the future, how bad is this, really?
* If what's going through my mind is the worst-case scenario, what would the best-case scenario be (e.g. your mistake highlighted a change that needed to be made to the process and led to big savings for your organisation. You'll get a big promotion and pay rise. Your partner will be really proud of you. You'll be able to buy a house, etc.)?

Somewhere between the best and worst case is the most likely scenario, so what can you take action on to prepare and deal with that? Taking the example on pages 232–3, perhaps email your boss over the weekend asking to see her first thing Monday, to offer some ideas on how to resolve the issue.

Catastrophising Imagine this!

It's Friday night. You're relaxing at home after a busy week. Suddenly a thought about an ongoing work project pops into your mind. You realise you've make a serious mistake with some figures you've prepared for your boss, which she has presented at an important meeting this afternoon. The thought of your mistake starts to gnaw away at you. You start to think…

'What if she didn't notice my error and committed us to something we can't deliver? She'll be really angry with me.'

'Or maybe it really embarrassed her at the meeting: her team isn't doing quality work.'

'Surely she would have rung me if there had been a problem.'

'It will mean my promotion won't happen.'

I bet she was so angry she's waiting until Monday to give me a dressing down.'

'If it's caused a serious problem, I might even be sacked.'

'If I'm sacked I won't get a reference and then I won't be able to get another job.'

'That will mean I won't be able to pay the rent.'

'That means we'll lose the house.'

'My partner will probably leave me.'

'I'll end up all alone and sleeping on the streets.'

'There won't be any point going on'...

You feel increasingly anxious and don't sleep well all weekend. You're distracted so don't enjoy family time as much as you would do normally, and by the time Monday morning comes round your well-being and resilience are at an all-time low.

Usually when you're researching something, it's great to put it to the test, but that wasn't the case for Lucy. Passionate about positive psychology, she had already integrated much of it into her life. With resilience, however, the true test came only in the darkest of times.

Lucy, Trevor and their three kids live in New Zealand. They had a great life: good friends, a close-knit local community, interesting work and a beautiful landscape. In spring last year all that changed. A mountain-biking trip with another family didn't go to plan. Lucy, Trevor and their two sons had driven down early and were waiting to be joined by their daughter, Abi, and her best friend, Ella, both aged twelve, travelling with Ella's parents. But they didn't arrive – a police car came instead. There'd been a crash and the girls had been killed instantly when a car drove through a stop sign straight into their car. 'Trying to take the news in,' said Lucy, 'I knew the battle was on for our survival. That first week I remember moving around on autopilot, feeling sick and struggling to breathe. But I also remember having a voice in my head that kept telling me to choose life, not death. We had no choice in Abi's death, but I felt instinctively that we did have choices over how we responded to it. We had two beautiful teenage boys to live for – they needed us here and now – so I was determined that I was not going to let death rob me of the good things we had left. We could try to grieve in a functioning way using the tools I'd studied, or let it overwhelm us. Over the next few weeks and months I developed a new life goal, one of "mainly functioning".'

'I made a lot of use of resilient thinking. To every action, decision or thought I asked: "Will this help or harm us in our goal?" For example, we chose not to attend the driver's court hearing. Having his image in my mind wouldn't help and might harm, so we chose to meet our boys' teachers instead. I remember driving past the media huddled outside the courthouse. They were desperate for a soundbite, wanting us to blame the driver – it felt good to drive by knowing we'd decided not to get swept up in a blame game and were choosing to focus energy and attention where it mattered most to us.

Knowing how vital supportive relationships are for resilience, and imagining how hard it was for family and friends to know what to say or do, I decided to ask for help directly rather than expect them to mind-read – whether that was something for supper or company when walking the dog. This wasn't always easy, but I was aware how much I needed help and kept reminding myself that their offers were genuine, reaching out strengthened our bonds.

A short while later the terrible Malaysian Airlines tragedy put our loss into perspective: one poor family had lost not one but all three kids: we still had two. Our boys were fourteen and sixteen at the time of Abi's death, so we owed it to them to focus on what we had, rather than what we'd lost.

The power of using our strengths has blown me away. We've discovered that forgiveness is a strength we share as a family. On the way back from the lake on the night it happened, our eldest son said: "We're not going to blame the driver are we?" I remember the relief at hearing those words, which began a growing conviction that forgiveness, not blame and hatred, was the only way forward. I didn't want any more misery to come from this already terrible situation.

Love has always been my signature strength, so although it hurt to see other mums and daughters, I knew I needed to spend more time, not less, with friends and their kids – and on the first anniversary of the crash sixty friends joined in a run to celebrate the girls' lives.

Finally there's mindfulness – I've used it a lot to focus on the present, not slip back to the past or worry about the future. If I find myself wondering "How will I feel on Abi's 18th birthday?" I remind myself to wait, rather than think about it now. Feel the pain as it comes, be true to it in the moment, but don't go hunting out future pains now.

Our experience has really tested the resilience skills I teach. I've found that, even in the darkest times, they work. Even when life is bleak, we can still choose how we think and react and what we do. It's now my mission to help others realise that we are all hard-wired to cope with death and to pass on the tools of resilient grieving.'

Dr Lucy Hone has written about what she's learned in a blog: www.1wildandpreciouslife.com and her book *What Abi Taught Us: A Roadmap for Resilient Grieving*, Allen & Unwin (2016)

KEY SEVEN: RESILIENCE

To sum up

Here are five key points to take away from this chapter:

1 We are all naturally resilient and we can learn skills and ways of thinking and behaving that boost our natural resilience.

2 There are lots of ways to support and boost our resilience and help us deal with stress – the ideas for each of the Keys will also help our resilience and can be useful in managing our stress.

3 Don't get stressed about being stressed – either take action to manage it or harness it to motivate yourself into action.

4 Our patterns and habits of thinking have a big impact on our resilience and well-being and can mean we undermine our own resilience!

5 There are five basic principles of resilient thinking for use when our negative emotions are triggered:

★ In the moment, how we feel is driven by our instant thoughts/interpretations about the trigger – usually these are about what caused it and/or what might happen as a result.

★ How we feel impacts what we immediately do next and that has knock-on consequences.

★ Our instant interpretations aren't always helpful or accurate, which can lead us to experience unnecessary or unhelpful emotions and so take actions that can in turn lead to consequences that have a negative impact on ourselves and others.

★ Our interpretations are often inaccurate or unhelpful because we don't have enough evidence about the situation or we've fallen into a common interpretation trap.

★ If we pause... and check the evidence for (and against) our interpretations we can make sure what we feel and do as a result, is appropriate or make choices that are helpful rather than being potentially harmful.

Connections to other Keys

The other nine Keys will help you build your Resilience by offering you active coping strategies, but here's a quick summary:

★ **GIVING** (See page 10)
- Helping others helps us to take our mind off our own problems and can give us a sense of purpose and meaning.
- Asking others to help us when we need it is a resilient tactic.

★ **RELATING** (See page 36)
Things are generally better together – strengthening connections with others helps us feel supported and so boosts our resilience.

★ **EXERCISING** (See page 76)
- Taking care of your body means you take care of your mind.
- Physical activity can be a stress-reliever, a source of positive emotions and it helps you think more clearly. It can help you sleep better too.

★ **AWARENESS** (See page 108)
Mindfulness can help you find moments of calm in times of stress and help you regain perspective in difficult times.

★ **TRYING OUT** (See page 144)
Learning and challenging yourself regularly will help you have confidence and think creatively when you face difficulties.

★ **DIRECTION** (See page 170)
Setting, and working towards, goals – even one step at a time – helps us persevere and deal with problems and obstacles.

★ **EMOTIONS** (See page 238)
In tough times we can find moments to be grateful. These reduce stress, give a psychological boost and help us persevere.

★ **ACCEPTANCE** (See page 266)
- Identifying and using our strengths is our backbone in troubled times.
- Being kinder to ourselves and not beating ourselves up when things go wrong stops us from undermining our own resilience.

★ **MEANING** (See page 298)
Having a sense of purpose, clear values and meaning help focus us on what's important and provides a guide for action in difficult times.

EMOTIONS

Look for what's good

We evolved for a purpose – to help us survive and thrive. It's not only negative feelings that count; science is showing that beyond feeling good, pleasant emotions can do us good too. Yet we're wired to focus on what's wrong rather than what's going well. Luckily, studies are showing that some simple practices and actions can help put that right.

Emotions: introduction

> 'Emotions determine the quality of our lives.'
>
> Paul Ekman, *Emotions Revealed: Understanding Faces and Feelings*

We are emotional creatures

Emotions, positive and negative, are part of what makes us human and have helped us survive as a race. They're signals that something's right or wrong – they help us communicate this. But there's more to them than meets the eye. Emotions are central to happiness and recently science has shown that feeling good isn't just a side benefit from things going well, it's actually an important ingredient of it. It seems that pleasant emotions don't just feel good, they actually do us good too and have important consequences for our well-being, our development and our resilience. Although we may want to avoid them, difficult or uncomfortable emotions can't always be dismissed from our thinking about happiness either, they're part of the mix too and can give us insight into what we're thinking and where we might need to take action. Every chapter in this book includes actions that can help us feel good and manage our emotions better, and in this chapter we look deeper at why this matters – and other ideas to try too.

What are emotions?

Psychologists agree that emotions are a core feature of the human mind and that they're much more than just feelings. They're actually quite complex responses to our immediate (initially unconscious) perceptions about a situation or event that involve co-ordinated changes in our body, motivation and behaviour that help us deal with what we've perceived.

There are typically three core components to an emotion:
★ Our feeling – our individual experience of a situation or trigger.
★ An external expression of what we're experiencing (facial, bodily, verbal – or all three).

★ Physiological changes (e.g. changes in our heart rate, breathing and muscle tension). These physiological changes aren't generally in our conscious control but we often become aware of their impact (e.g. sweating, panting, goosebumps).

It is thought that physiological reactions prepare us to act in certain ways, depending on the type of emotion, for example: fighting, running away, crying or laughing. These responses are sometimes called 'action tendencies'.

Our immediate unconscious interpretation then gives rise to our facial and physiological reactions and subsequent actions. This can be why we may experience emotions as happening to us rather than being chosen by us. However, once we become conscious of the emotion we can reappraise the situation and so manage our emotional reaction to it. This is the basis for resilient thinking that we looked at in Chapter 7.

An emotion tends to be brief unless the trigger or our interpretation of it continues. Emotions are evoked by events happening in real time or they can be triggered by our memories or thoughts of past or future situations. And they're usually about something which, at some level, matters to us. In contrast to emotions, moods tend to last longer – hours, days or weeks. They typically feel more general and have fewer specific triggers and prominent reactions. We'll typically experience emotions as being in the forefront of our minds, whereas moods tend to be background.

 Pause point 1...

Make a list all the different emotions you can think of.

★ How many would you describe as positive and how many negative?
★ Are the positive ones always a good thing?
★ Are the negative ones ever useful?

We'll come back to these points later.

★ Look back at your list of emotions from Pause point 1 (see page 241.) Where would you place them on the chart, based on whether they feel good or bad and energising – or otherwise?

★ What do you think might be the underlying purpose behind each of these emotions?

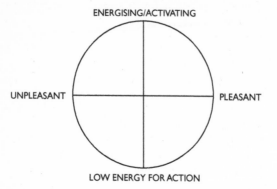

Adapted from: Posner, J., Russell, J. A., & Peterson, B. S. (2005). The circumplex model of affect: An integrative approach to affective neuroscience, cognitive development, and psychopathology. Development and Psychopathology, 17(3), p.716. Cambridge University Press. Reproduced with permission

242

Why do we have emotions?

It's believed that whether they feel good or bad, emotions evolved to help our ancestors survive. Feelings described as good, pleasant or 'positive' evolved to motivate us to approach and take advantage of potentially safe opportunities and to signal that things are going well. In contrast, feelings we'd call 'bad' or 'negative' motivated us to avoid potentially harmful situations. So even though unpleasant emotions don't feel great, they can still be helpful.

Whether pleasant or unpleasant, emotions differ in the level of energy for action they activate in us. Some emotions, for example fear or anger, create a high degree of activation. Likewise, attraction can energise us to build new social bonds and relationships. Of course, our level of activation will also be influenced by the intensity with which we feel the emotion in any given situation. Other emotions, such as joy or sadness, are associated with lower energy for action – either signalling things are going well, so we should stay as we are, or to help us avoid further loss.

Types of emotional experience

Initiated by Darwin, scientists have proposed that common themes in our evolutionary history led to core emotional responses that seem to be hardwired in most human beings. Psychologist Paul Ekman identified six 'basic' or 'universal' human emotions: fear, anger, sadness, disgust, surprise and joy/happiness. He proposed that these are expressed facially in similar ways around the world and so are recognised in different countries and cultures. The universal recognition of these basic emotions enabled us to communicate at a basic level without a shared language or culture. Beyond these basic emotions there is a much wider range of emotions that we can experience and which overlap, for example: love, connection, optimism, disappointment, anticipation, pride, guilt, shame, jealousy, contempt, interest, boredom and excitement.

Emotions aren't always distinct and sometimes we can feel more than one at the same time. Individual experience also varies: no two situations and no two people are identical. Even though the six basic emotions are common, reflecting similar reactions to shared themes, we still vary on specific triggers and reactions. For example, you and I might both get angry if we perceive someone doing something we believe is wrong, but our triggers might be different. Your trigger might be your spouse leaving laundry around because you believe being tidy is respectful; my trigger might be my spouse chastising me for not picking up clothes because I like to sort laundry at a later time to suit me. Even if we both get angry for the same reason, our intensity of response can vary. It might be a mild irritant for you but a red-button trigger for me, our responses being shaped by who we are and past experiences. These factors combined give rise to an infinite number of variations in emotional experience, albeit with many shared themes. This is why emotions can be tricky to pin down in ourselves, let alone communicate to others.

Emotional 'false alarms'

What we feel is a result of our instant interpretations or judgements of an event or situation and these aren't always right. In a split second we take into account whether an event or a situation is:

★ New or familiar
★ Pleasant or unpleasant

★ Predictable or unpredictable
★ Helps, or gets in the way of, what we are trying to do
★ Caused by ourselves, others or circumstances
★ Controllable
★ Aligned, or not, with social norms or personal values

It's not surprising, then, says psychologist and emotions expert, Randolph Nesse, that we sometimes have emotional 'false alarms'. This is because we're programmed for rapid emotional responses that err on the side of caution, meaning that our emotional reactions can be triggered when there's only a hint of potential danger, for example feeling anger or fear when there's no real need. This happens, says Nesse, because in evolutionary terms the 'costs' of the false alarms are low in terms of energy expenditure and time – relative to the 'costs' of fighting for survival. He argues that this is a key to understanding why we may develop conditions such as anxiety and depression, which in his view stem from an ingrained, very sensitive, response to potential dangers.

Our language of emotions matters

Our awareness, understanding of, and ability to, communicate and manage our emotions and the needs they represent is important for our psychological well-being. Being sensitive to emotions in other people is also fundamental and essential to building good connections with them. Research suggests that the more specific we can be in differentiating, naming and describing our feelings, the less likely we are to be overwhelmed by them and the more we're able to deal with them, regardless of how uncomfortable or intense they are. For example, if we're afraid of spiders – when we see one, we may simply say 'I feel afraid', whereas a more specific response might recognise a wider range of emotions such as disgust and curiosity as well as fear. When people were trained to better recognise their emotional responses, they experienced less anxiety and were more able to approach the spider. This was more effective than telling themselves that the spider was safe.

The better our ability to be specific about our emotional experiences, the less likely we are to be susceptible to unhealthy or potentially harmful ways of managing difficult emotions, for example through binge-eating, drinking or aggression, and the more likely we are to make less-biased moral judgements in fraught emotional situations. The good news is it seems we can increase our emotional vocabulary.

Some languages have words to describe particular emotions that don't exist in another. It seems that there are some culturally specific emotions, demonstrating how nuanced emotions can be. Here are some emotions that the English language doesn't have specific words for:

★ The Danes and the Dutch can capture a particular sense of warmth and cosiness or a sense of togetherness with family or friends with the words *hygge* (Danish) and *gezelligheid* (Dutch).

★ *Pena ajena* in Spanish is roughly translated as 'foreign embarrassment' or 'sympathetic shame': what you feel when you observe another person's embarrassment.

★ *Gigil* in Tagalog (national language of the Philippines) describes resisting a strong urge to squeeze someone or something because it's either really sweet or frustrating (think super-cute baby or puppy or a persistently irritating child!).

★ *Hiraeth*, in Welsh, means a deep longing for home, but more than homesickness it has an essence of the Wales of the past, such as your childhood home.

Emotional intelligence and well-being

Psychologists Peter Salovey and John Meyer developed the concept of 'emotional intelligence', popularised by Daniel Goleman. This is our ability to accurately detect, express and manage emotions in ourselves and others. The better able we are to do this appears to have many benefits for well-being and happiness, including better moods, better relationships, helping others more, higher self-esteem and better work performance. It may help us to reduce or manage emotional false alarms too.

Emotional intelligence looks at the degree to which we can:
Perceive emotions:
★ Accurately identify, differentiate and express our feelings and emotions in ourselves and the needs underlying them.
★ Identify emotions in others.

Use emotions:

★ Redirect and prioritise our thinking to facilitate our moods.

★ Use our emotional states to facilitate particular tasks or thinking.

Understand emotions:

★ Understand the complexities of emotions and the relationships and transitions between them.

★ Understand contradictory emotions.

★ Understand causes and consequences of emotions.

Manage emotions:

★ Our ability to be open to both pleasant and unpleasant emotions.

★ Monitor, reflect on and detach from emotional states.

★ Manage our emotions as motivation for appropriate and useful action.

Try this! Noticing and naming emotions

How many emotions did you list in Pause point 1 (see page 241)? Let's see if you can increase your 'vocabulary'.

Your emotions:

★ Over the course of a day, pause for a moment each hour.

  • Notice and name any emotions you are feeling.

  • How intense are those feelings for you? (Perhaps use a scale where 1 is low intensity and 10 is very strong/intense.)

  • How easy is it for you to name and express your emotions?

  • Are there any situations where you feel neutral – i.e. no emotions one way or the other? What characterises these situations?

★ What bodily sensations are associated with these emotions for you?
  • Where are these physical sensations and how strong are they?

Emotions of others:

★ When you interact with others, take time to notice what emotions you perceive in them. What are they doing or saying that signals those emotions?

★ When you watch a film or TV drama, what emotions do you notice?

  • How are people expressing those emotions – verbally, facially, bodily?
  • What words are they using to describe emotions?

Emotions & happiness

Beyond simply feeling good

Feeling good feels good, it goes without saying, but that's not all, it also appears to do us good and helps us to do well too. Numerous studies have shown that when we're in a pleasant emotional state, even if it's fleeting and a result of something small, it seems to make a difference. We're not talking about big life-changing positive events, such as getting a promotion or winning a prize. We're talking about the small everyday moments that give us a mild, momentary sense of feeling good. For example, studies show:

★ Doctors given a small gift of a bag of sweets made faster, more accurate, diagnoses.
★ People shown a comedy video clip were more productive on a work-type task than counterparts shown a neutral or unhappy clip.
★ People who received a small gift were more likely to spontaneously help others.
★ People who were either shown an uplifting film clip or given a small gift showed:
  • Improved performance on creative problem-solving tasks.
  • Better recall of neutral and positive information.
  • More flexibility in their approaches to solving problems.

So it seems that feeling good might not just be an output of doing something enjoyable or doing well, it might be an input to it. Indeed, regularly experiencing pleasant emotions (along with infrequently feeling unhappy) is now considered a feature of mental health and flourishing.

It's curious, then, that for more than a century pleasant emotions weren't considered a topic worthy of rigorous study. Yes, they felt good and that was nice, but they were thought unlikely to serve any important purpose. In the 1970s, the psychology of emotions began to be taken more seriously. But the focus was only on unpleasant or negative emotional experiences, since it was believed that only these mattered from an evolutionary perspective, being crucial for survival, and of course a core purpose of psychology was to alleviate suffering. However, in the last two decades or so, this view has changed with the work of psychologists Alice Isen and Barbara Fredrickson and their colleagues. It now seems that feeling good isn't just a pleasant by-product, it also has important functional, developmental and survival benefits both in evolutionary terms as a species and for us as individuals.

Feeling bad is stronger

Reflect on the emotions you listed on Pause point 1 (see page 241). How many pleasant and unpleasant ones did you list? On the chart in Pause point 2 (see page 242), was there a difference between how energising pleasant and unpleasant emotions were? If you found you'd listed more unpleasant emotions than pleasant ones it's no surprise. Even among the six basic emotions, only one is enjoyable. In fact, there appear to be more words for negative emotions in English than positive ones (sixty-two per cent to thirty-eight per cent respectively – how did your ratio compare?).

We have what's known as a natural 'negativity bias', meaning we're hardwired to notice and more likely to remember what's wrong rather than what's right. Not only this, but psychologist Roy Baumeister and colleagues found that our emotional reactions to negative or unpleasant events in different areas of our life tended to be much stronger and last longer than pleasant ones. For example they found:

★ We pay closer/longer attention to negative information than positive.
★ Having a bad day is more likely to spill over to reduce people's well-being the following day.
★ People are more upset about losing $50 than they are pleased about gaining the same amount of money.
★ Major traumatic events have a longer-lasting negative effect on people's lives than major positive events, such as a lottery win.
★ Following couples over a decade, marriages with higher levels of negativity/distress in the early years predicted higher rates of divorce.
★ People are more concerned to avoid bad feedback than they are to maximise good feedback.
★ People underestimate the actual number of positive experiences they've had, but are better at recalling the negative ones.

So why might this be? Well, Baumeister and colleagues suggest it comes back to how we evolved. Being attuned to spot signs of danger and experiencing a strong emotional alarm when we did, helped us avoid danger and learn from mistakes. But while being hardwired to notice risks is still a good thing, we're no longer hunting or gathering out in the wilds, so thankfully far less likely to face life-threatening danger day to day. So our inbuilt propensity to pay more attention and give more weight to what's wrong and less to what's right can not only impact how we feel, but can also undermine our well-being longer term. We miss out on the benefits we've seen that positive emotions can bring. This doesn't mean we should block out things that don't feel right, it's more a question of finding a balance that's more fitting for our lives today.

We can develop our ability to notice what's already good in our lives and find ways to nurture more, helping us to feel good and deal better with what's not going so well.

The power of positive emotions
What do we mean by 'positive' emotions

Now, it's really important to be clear here. When I'm talking about 'positive' emotions, I mean those that feel good or pleasant, the ones that you've placed on the right in Pause point 2 (see page 242).

I'm not talking about positive thinking, where we are trying to convince ourselves that we feel good. Yes, looking on the bright side of life can have benefits, but trying to persuade ourselves that we feel good when we really don't isn't good for anyone.

Neither am I ignoring the fact that unpleasant or 'negative' emotions can sometimes have positive benefits (for example, anger is appropriate as a reaction to a real injustice and can help to rectify it, while guilt is appropriate when we've done something wrong, propelling us either to put it right or not do it again). Equally, I'm aware that pleasant emotions can have negative consequences (for example, partying all night can feel great but it may not be a positive thing if we have an important exam or meeting the next day).

Also we shouldn't feel bad about feeling bad; that only adds to unhappiness. In Buddhism, there's a concept for this called the 'two arrows' – the initial feeling of distress and then tormenting ourselves for feeling that way. For example, if we've lost someone we loved, it's normal and appropriate to be sad and to grieve: if someone has let us down, it's understandable if we feel hurt. Or, of course, we may have a clinical condition such as depression.

What I'm talking about here are those fleeting moments when we're experiencing pleasant emotions for real or when we're in a good mood. It turns out that these positive emotional experiences have important, and distinct, effects that enable us to flourish and better equip us psychologically, socially and physically to deal with life's difficulties. So they're more than just enjoyable moments, but actually are like tiny 'investments' in flourishing that add up over time.

Positive emotions broaden our focus

Positive emotions seem to have a different effect on what and how much we notice and how flexibly we respond than unpleasant ones. There's a good reason why. Think for a moment. You're walking down the street when suddenly a ferocious-looking dog hurtles towards you. Where would you want your attention to be? Smelling the beautiful roses you're walking past or laser-focused on the dog so you can best respond to avoid getting hurt? Of course the correct, or indeed only, answer is the latter. You'd want your eyes and ears, and even other senses, to be one hundred per cent focused on the potential danger.

Well, the good news is this is exactly what the experience of unpleasant emotions has evolved to do. Fear, anger or disgust narrow our focus to where it most needs to be, and not only that, they narrow the range of likely actions we'll take in response – whether that needs to be attacking, fleeing, repelling or expelling. In such dangerous situations we have to act fast, so we're unlikely to have the time to weigh up our choices. Therefore, we've evolved so that each unpleasant emotion propels us to respond in a limited number of specific ways, which through evolution have been found to mean we're most likely to survive.

In contrast, positive emotions have the opposite effect. They broaden our focus and facilitate a wider range of responses. When we're in a pleasant emotional state, we notice more and tend to respond more flexibly and creatively. This makes sense since these experiences don't usually occur in life-threatening situations, so it's less crucial we act in specific ways.

Experiments have shown that when we're in a positive emotional state, we're more likely to:

★ See the bigger picture rather than zooming in on a detail.
★ Seek and notice what's happening in the periphery of our vision.
★ Be more open to new information and ideas.
★ See more connections and find more novel and creative solutions.
★ Be more flexible and inclusive.
★ Recognise people from other cultures better.
★ Be more trusting.
★ See more options and opportunities.

Positive emotions build our resources

The broadening effect of positive emotions gradually builds our psychological, social, intellectual resources, literally changing our minds and lives for the better, helping to make us happier and more resilient. For example: if we're more open to, and trusting of, others we're more likely to form more and closer relationships; if we're able to see the big picture and develop flexible solutions we're likely to be better at dealing with difficulties and overcoming challenges; if we seek and are open to more information and ideas, we're likely to learn more and develop expertise, and if we develop more creative solutions we find new ways to progress.

There's an upward spiral effect too. If we have positive interactions with others, discover new ideas and find solutions to our problems we're more likely to experience positive emotions, which perpetuates the 'broaden and build' effect, so fuelling our well-being, helping us to be happier. Many studies show that those who more frequently experience and express positive emotions are more resilient, more resourceful, have higher self-acceptance and higher psychological well-being and more positive social connections. (We saw in Chapter 2 that more positive interactions between couples predict longer-lasting, higher-quality relationships.)

In this way, positive emotions, not just unpleasant ones, also contributed to our survival. The latter enabled us to survive in the short term, but pleasant experiences enable us individually and as a species to adapt, evolve, develop and grow over the longer term.

This 'broaden and build' effect of positive emotions isn't just for those who naturally have sunnier dispositions. It can help to maintain and increase happiness and well-being for most of us and, in fact, may have the greatest benefit for those who don't naturally look on the brighter side of life. The research shows too that the benefits aren't restricted to the high points in life, it's more about small, pleasant, ordinary day-to-day moments that add up.

The undo effect
As well as broadening and building, positive emotions have a third effect. They can help to undo the damage negative emotions may do to our brains and our bodies.

Certainly people who experience more positive emotions are more likely to be healthy. They tend to be less susceptible to colds and illness and they may even live longer. The relationship between positive emotions and health was famously shown in the 'Nun Study', as it's known. Psychologists Deborah Danner, David Snowdon and Wallace Friesen analysed the emotional content in the autobiographical essays young women (average age twenty-two years) had written decades earlier on entering a closed order of nuns and compared this to how long the women lived. The twenty-five per cent whose essays contained the highest positive emotional content lived on average ten years longer than those with little or negative emotional content.

So what might be behind these physical health effects? It's likely connected to the effect positive emotions have on our automatic stress response. As we cover in other chapters, when we feel fear or anger in the face of a perceived threat, the stress response kicks in (raising cortisol levels, heart rate and blood pressure), preparing us to maximise our chances in dealing with that danger. When the threat subsides, the body then returns to normal. The quicker we recover, the better it is for our health.

This response evolved to deal with occasional dangerous situations. Although the stresses we face today aren't generally as extreme, they tend to be frequent. However, our brain doesn't distinguish well between life-threatening situations and ones that are merely frustrating, so our bodies can be more or less constantly in stress mode and this can have damaging health consequences. Positive emotions have been shown to help us to recover more quickly from the stress response and deal with anxiety. Since stress is inevitable this may account for why people who experience more frequent positive emotions have better health.

Positive emotions in tough times

The effects of positive emotions are important for day-to-day life, but what about when times are really tough? While we may think that moments of enjoyment might be trivial or even signs that we're in denial, actually they have been shown to be helpful in coping with some of life's most difficult and unhappy situations. For example, studies have shown that people who were bereaved who have some moments of positive emotion in the midst of their sadness, have better psychological well-being one year later. Finding opportunity to experience positive emotions can help to alleviate some of the negative effects of the unpleasant emotions and help to broaden our mindset even in tough situations. This helps, even if just a bit, to build our resources so we might be more able to find coping strategies and see ways to move towards a better future.

Positive emotions might also be helpful in the treatment of mild or moderate depression, a condition associated with a downward spiral, where low moods lead to pessimistic thinking and lower resourcefulness, which in turn lowers the mood further. Having some pleasant emotional experiences can disrupt this spiral and even initiate an upward one, although in some cases of clinical depression or anxiety, negative emotions may need to be lowered before positive ones can have an effect.

Therapeutic approaches incorporating a number of the ideas for action we cover in this book, alongside conventional methods, are being developed and trialled. Early indications suggest potential benefits but much more research is needed into what works and for which specific conditions.

Cultivating positive emotions

Barbara Fredrickson's research has identified ten pleasant or positive emotions that people experience most frequently. This isn't by any means a complete list, but it's a great place to start. Let's look at what they are and the ways the Keys to happiness in this book can help you nurture and grow each of them in your life (see chart opposite).

Increasing joy

'The most visible joy can only reveal itself when we've transformed it within.'
Rainer Maria Rilke, *Duino Elegies 7*

How do we make the most of the positive experiences and transform them into joy? It's a question psychologists have been looking at and the answer seems to be learning how to 'savour'. Savouring is the active process of prolonging and maximising the pleasure we derive from positive experience by deliberately focusing on the details of the moment and the sensations we're experiencing, and delighting in them. (The mindfulness skills in Chapter 4 are helpful here.) It's about making the most of our enjoyment. For example, we may luxuriate in a bath or wonder at a piece of music. It's about lingering and taking the scent in, not just getting a quick whiff when smelling the roses.

We can enhance savouring by:
★ Immersing ourselves in the experience (something like our mindful chocolate-eating exercise in Chapter 4).
★ Paying attention to all our senses or specifically to one, such as shutting our eyes to really listen to a piece of beautiful music.
★ Anchoring the experience in our memory, such as asking ourself questions about it or finding a souvenir of that time.
★ Sharing the moment with others.
★ Taking moments to be pleased with ourself for having had that moment where we felt good, perhaps even some healthy pride.

Pleasant emotions			
Top 10	Feels like	We feel it when	Nurturing it
Love	Care, connection, closeness, trust.	When we experience a moment of shared connection with another person (not just romantically).	Lots of ideas in Chapters 1 and 2. Also sharing other positive emotions with people.
Joy	Glad, happy, joyful.	When we're pleased about something or when something unexpectedly good happens.	We'll look at cultivating joy in this chapter. It can also come from taking action in any of the other Keys.
Gratitude	Appreciative, grateful, thankful.	Noticing, receiving or valuing having something/ someone; receiving a gift.	We'll look at cultivating this in this chapter.
Serenity/ contentment	Calm, peaceful, content, serene.	Being at ease, safe, comfortable; cherishing current circumstances or the moment as it is.	See Chapter 4 – mindfulness practice can foster a greater sense of peace and contentment.
Interest	Curious, alert, interested, engaged.	Noticing the novel, mysterious or challenging (usually when we feel we're in a safe context).	See Chapter 5 – lots of ideas for nurturing our curiosity and interests.
Hope	Optimistic, forward-looking, encouraged.	We can see beyond current circumstances or envisage a future and believe we can find ways to get there.	Chapter 6 looks at what hope is in more detail and gives ideas for fostering it.
Pride	Proud, self-assured, self-accepting.	Taking appropriate credit for a valued positive outcome.	Chapter 6 looks at how to achieve goals and Chapter9 helps us to identify strengths.
Amusement	Fun, playful, humour.	Finding something funny; playing; not being serious.	Chapters 1, 2, 3 and 5, as well as this one, have ideas for having fun and amusement.
Inspiration	Uplifted, elevated, inspired.	When we witness human excellence.	Chapters 6, 7 and 9 look at having inspiring role models; Chapters 2 and 9 help us see the strengths of others.
Awe	Wonder, amazement.	When we encounter beauty or goodness on a grand scale.	Chapter 4 and this one have ideas to help us notice and appreciate what's around us. Chapter 10 is about connecting to something bigger than yourself.

Based on: Fredrickson, B. L. (2013). Positive emotions broaden and build. *Advances in Experimental Psychology*, 47, 1–53

KEY EIGHT: EMOTIONS

Savouring isn't limited to the present, either. We can savour past experiences or future ones. Taking time to reflect on times when we've experienced joy and happiness can have a positive benefits for well-being. In one study, participants who spent fifteen minutes a day for three days recalling and thinking about their happiest times showed increased well-being one month later. Barbara Fredrickson suggests the idea of creating a 'positive portfolio', collecting together in a file, notebook or online images, music, poetry, readings or physical souvenirs that can enable us to recall and savour times of happiness in our lives.

We can also savour in a future-focused way. Have you ever enjoyed thinking about something almost as much as the event itself? Many people say that an enjoyable aspect of having a holiday is looking forward to it. In fact, positive 'mental time travel' has been shown to increase happiness and reduce anxiety. Psychologists call this anticipatory enjoyment savouring. Try this out and take a trip into the future yourself.

Try this! Mental time-travelling

Each day for the next week or two spend fifteen minutes trying to imagine, in a detailed way, four positive events that could reasonably happen tomorrow. They could be anything simple, day-to-day pleasures or something bigger or more important. Once you've thought about them, take a minute to make a brief note about each one. Perhaps you could do this on the way to work or college.

For example, you might imagine meeting a friend for a coffee, getting some nice feedback from a customer or colleague, having a snuggle on the sofa with a loved one, having a good workout at the gym, finishing a project you've been working on, receiving a gift or even being offered a new job: whatever comes to mind that is within the realms of possibility.

After the week or two weeks is up, what did you notice?

★ Did the exercise help you feel less worried?

★ Did it make you feel happier?

Based on: Quoidbach, J., Wood, A. M., & Hansenne, M. (2009). Back to the future: The effect of daily practice of mental time travel into the future on happiness and anxiety. *The Journal of Positive Psychology*, 4(5), 349-355

Gratitude

'The test of all happiness is gratitude.' G.K. Chesterton, *Orthodoxy*

Gratitude, being thankful and appreciative, is a simple but powerful force for happiness and well-being. It helps to train our brain to notice and appreciate what's good, so balances out our natural focus on what's wrong. It's an emotion that connects us to other people and the world around us. Some researchers say that it opens the door to other positive emotional experiences.

The thoughts and interpretations that lead us to feeling grateful usually involve two parts: noticing and acknowledging what's good or has helped us, and recognising its source or sources. These often lie, fully or in part, outside of ourselves – in someone or something else. Gratitude is motivating and energising in such a way that propels us to 'pass it on' through doing something positive or helpful for others, so it connects giving and receiving. When we feel gratitude not only are we thankful for what we've received, but we're motivated to be kind as a result.

We vary in our natural tendency towards being grateful, but we can all take action to increase it in our lives with some simple practices and activities, which we'll look at below. And there are good reasons to do so.

Reasons to practise gratitude

Robert Emmons, the world's expert in the psychology of gratitude, has shown that when people consistently practise gratitude it is associated with a whole range of personal benefits including:

★ Being happier, experiencing more pleasant emotions such as joy, being more optimistic.
★ Experiencing fewer unpleasant emotions.
★ Feeling more alert and alive.
★ Feeling less affected by aches and pains.
★ Building a stronger immune system and having lower blood pressure.
★ Sleeping better.
★ Exercising and taking more care of our health.
★ Social benefits including: being more generous, compassionate, kind, forgiving; feeling less lonely and isolated; being more outgoing.

In fact, Emmons says he sees gratitude as an emotion that strengthens our relationships because it helps us realise how we're supported, which is affirming for us and in turn expressing our gratitude to others is affirming for them. He says it's essential in building and sustaining good social relationships.

Furthermore, if our contributions towards others are appreciated, it encourages us to help others more. It's thought that gratitude may have evolved as an emotion to encourage reciprocity and even moral behaviour in social groups, not only directly between people doing things for each other, but motivating us to be altruistic and help others who haven't done something for us.

Gratitude seems to help us deal with stress and fosters resilient behaviour. For example, it has been associated with resilient thinking, active coping and problem-solving, and seeking social support (see Chapter 7). It has also been shown to facilitate recovery from trauma and contribute to post-traumatic growth. It may even help us feel better about ourselves and what we have. Gratitude is associated with being less materialistic and feeling less envious or resentful of others. Such toxic emotions are strongly associated with unhappiness and low psychological well-being: it's hard to be envious and grateful at the same time! It's thought that these factors, combined with feeling affirmed by others, mean that gratitude is likely to be associated with higher self-esteem, which is an important ingredient in happiness (see Chapter 9).

Increasing gratitude

One of the most effective ways we can increase our gratitude is by simple writing activities. Spending a few moments each day or each week writing things down we've appreciated, enjoyed and were grateful for can have a powerful impact. Emmons says that there's something about the act of writing that really helps us to get the benefit from these activities. When we write, whether by hand or electronically, we engage more of our senses and focus more. This helps to organise and clarify our thoughts and better integrate them within ourselves.

It's important not to rush through these activities – like something to tick off your to-do list. View each thing you write down as a gift, noticing how you feel when you reflect on why you've appreciated each one.

Daily 'three good things' activity

In a now-classic positive psychology study by Martin Seligman and colleagues, people were asked each night for a week to reflect on their day and write down three things that went well and what caused them. Participants' happiness and any depression-type symptoms were measured before the activity started, immediately after it and then one, two and six months later. This simple activity gradually increased people's happiness and decreased depression symptoms over the six-month period. Why did this work and why did its effects build over time? While participants were only asked to write down their three good things for one week, some continued it. Those who continued it had the greatest benefits. In my view, this activity literally trains our brain to start noticing what's right, not just what's wrong. It helps to counterbalance our natural negativity bias.

This activity is not about inventing or making up good things in our lives, it's about noticing what's already there. The things we can overlook because of the 'bad is stronger than the good' effect (see page 248) and so we miss out on the psychological benefits. It's also not just about noticing 'big' good things, but the small day-to-day events, such as getting a seat on the train or getting through your to-do list quickly, chatting with a friend, sharing a smile with someone while waiting in a queue, eating your favourite food. Anything. Even on the worst days some good things happen, however tiny, and even if three feels like a stretch we can usually manage one or two. Like a colleague noticing we were overloaded and offering to lend a hand or coming home after a tough day and having five minutes to yourself to have a nice cup of tea. If you only take one action for your personal happiness, try this one. It only takes two or three minutes a day, so only fifteen to twenty minutes out of your whole week!

I've found this exercise has made a difference for me and countless others who attend my workshops say it has for them too. If you do it regularly, then looking back through your notes not only helps bring back positive memories, but you can also start to notice what makes a difference in your life – what matters most and sources of meaning (we'll look at meaning in Chapter 10). Here's what Action for Happiness member and volunteer, Natasha, says:

'Three good things can drag me out of a slump by opening my eyes to the great things in my life: the people and situations I can take for granted. It helps me focus on what I have in my life instead of always thinking "What next?" It helps me savour the good moments rather than letting them fly by without acknowledgement. It even renews the joy in things that were exciting at first but have become routine. If I don't do it for a while I notice I get grumpy more easily!'

My workshop participants have also experimented with the idea with their friends, families and at work. Here's the sort of things they say:

★ 'I encouraged my partner to try it too and now most evenings we each share our three good things. It's switched our conversation from just moaning. We still talk about things that haven't gone so well, but sharing the small, good things in each of our days has helped to bring us closer.'

★ 'It's now part of the kids' bedtime routine – sharing three things they've enjoyed during the day. It's led to some really nice moments and gives an insight into what they're noticing. Somehow asking "What did you enjoy today?" opens them up more than asking "What did you do today?"

★ 'We now start our team meetings with what's gone well and why. At first my team thought I'd gone mad (or joined a cult) and took a bit of persuading, but now they're into it. It's made the meetings more enjoyable, we're getting to know each other more and we seem to tackle problems in a different way.'

Weekly 'five good things' activity

Other experiments on gratitude have asked people, once a week for several weeks, to reflect on what they're grateful for over the past week. This also led to happiness and well-being boosts. This has the advantage in that you only do it once in a week, and so this helps to keep the activity fresh. But it may also mean you forget some of the small daily things that happened earlier in the week. Try it and see what you think.

Try this! Daily three good things

Think back over the last 24 hours or so. What were three things you enjoyed, appreciated or were grateful for? Write them down, with a note about why they had such a positive impact for you.

> **Good thing 1**
> Example: Best night's sleep for ages, so felt really refreshed. Switching my phone off an hour before bedtime really worked.

> **Good thing 2**
> Example: Bumped into Alex. It was really good to catch up and she's always interested in what's happening for me.

> **Good thing 3**
> Example: Walked through the park today, noticed the colours of the autumn leaves. Having some green space in the middle of a busy town is great.

Over the next week, try to do this each day. Many people find doing it at the end of the day helps them switch off and go to sleep. So you could try keeping a notebook and pen on your bedside table so you can note down your three good things before you turn off the light. Other people do it on their commute home after work or first thing in the morning.

Experiment in order to find a time that is best for you. Also if you forget to do the exercise, don't worry – find a way to remind yourself to do it the next day.

At the end of the week, what have you noticed?

★ How did you feel each evening when you were noting your three good things down?

★ Looking back over your notes from the week, what do you think and feel?

★ Are any themes emerging from what you've written down?

Based on: Seligman, M. E., Steen, T. A., Park, N. & Peterson, C. (2005). Positive psychology progress: empirical validation of interventions. *American Psychologist*, 60(5), 410-421

G
R
E
A
T
D
R
E
A
M

Try this! Weekly five good things

Each week over the next two months, reflect back over your week and write down five things you were grateful or thankful for. You may find it helpful to schedule a time to do this each week in your diary or set up a weekly reminder on your phone.

As you write your five things down, think about what is it that you've appreciated about these things. Notice how it makes you feel as you do so.

★ What do you notice about what you've written down?

★ What themes are there in what you're grateful and thankful for in your life? What does this make you think?

Based on: Emmons, R. A. & McCullough, M. E. (2003). Counting blessings versus burdens: an experimental investigation of gratitude and subjective well-being in daily life. *Journal of Personality and Social Psychology*, 84(2), 377-389

Life list activity

I haven't seen any scientific studies on this activity, but this is one that I found personally powerful and it helped me put things into perspective. It's very simple: reflecting on your life to date, list one hundred things you're grateful for – things that have made a difference in some way for you, whether big or small, from a long time ago or more recently. Try to be as specific as you can. For example, rather than only noting: 'I'm grateful to my parents for all the support they've given me', list some of the different ways they did this. For example: 'They really encouraged me during my GCSEs. Dad helped me understand physics when I was struggling and when I was little each week Mum took me to the local library to pick out a book that we read together every night. They were both really helpful when I moved flats recently – taking two days off to help me pack up and move my stuff.'

I found it hard to do this all in one go. I started by sitting in a café, notebook in hand, and then added to it over a period of three weeks as things came into my mind. I started out being quite general and then found I was able to remember more specifically. Have a go and see what you notice. You may also find this activity useful when we look at meaning and purpose in Chapter 10.

Gratitude letter and visit

Who has made an important difference in your life and have you ever told them so? Doing this in the form of a letter and delivering it in person has been shown to be one of the most powerful ways to boost happiness, in fact one of the largest immediate effects seen from any intervention, it still had a positive impact one month later. The power seems to come from a combination of reflecting on what another person has meant to you, thoughtfully considering how to express it in writing and then the act of sharing it with them in person. We saw in Chapter 2 that shared experiences with others are important for happiness, and this exercise combines that with gratitude. It certainly can be a deeply connecting and emotional (in a good way) experience for you both.

Try this! Make someone's day!

Who would you write a letter of gratitude to? Is there someone who has made a difference, for the better, in your life, whom you've never properly thanked? Why not write a letter to them? It doesn't need to be long, but be sure to be specific about what that person did for you and how it impacted you then and even how you are and what you're doing now. Importantly, can you deliver and read it out loud to them in person? This is not always easy, but it can have a huge impact for both you and the other person. Notice how you and the other person feel. You may even want to talk about that with them.

Based on: Seligman et al (2005), Seligman (2011)

KRAITHAWAT'S GRATITUDE LETTER

In Thailand we'd always had a 'teacher appreciation day', where the class would decorate a tray of flowers and present it to their teacher. So I was surprised there wasn't something similar in the US. I was on a year-long exchange programme from my high school in Bangkok to one in Minnesota, so I decided to do my own version. My history teacher, Mr Quinn, had been particularly kind. I decided to write him a letter to thank him. I'd always hated history, but he realised that my English wasn't so good at that point, so he spent time with me after class explaining what we'd covered in more detail. He was so patient. I really appreciated it. So when I'd written the letter I delivered it to him during my free study period. I think he was a little surprised! As I read it out loud, I could see his eyes moisten with tears. When I'd finished he said that moments like this made all the effort he put into his teaching worthwhile and certain he'd made the right career choice. And you know what? After that year I started to enjoy history more too!

To sum up

Here are five key points to take away from this chapter:

1 Good and bad emotions are part of what makes us human and they evolved long ago to help us survive. More than mere feelings, they involve changes in our body that prepare us to act in certain ways and signal to others how we're feeling through our facial expressions, tone of voice and body language.

2 Being able to name and articulate our emotions and recognise them in others is good for well-being (and our relationships).

3 Pleasant, 'positive' emotions are good for us – causing us to literally perceive more, spot opportunities and be more flexible and open to others. Over time this builds our psychological and social resources, which creates an upward spiral of well-being.

4 Humans have a natural 'negativity bias', meaning we're more likely to notice what's wrong rather than what's good and going well. We also feel unpleasant emotions more strongly than pleasant ones. While this can help us avoid dangers and learn from mistakes, it can also

undermine our well-being, so we can benefit from training our brains to notice and savour what's right in our lives.

5 Developing an 'attitude of gratitude' can have a powerful benefit for our happiness and well-being and help us squeeze more joy out of life. There are some simple actions we can take to help us do this!

Connections to other Keys

Other Keys you might like to explore in connection with Emotions:

★ **AWARENESS** (See page 108)
Mindfulness can help us tune into the emotions we are experiencing, but not get caught up in them. It can also help us to feel calmer and less anxious when we are feeling stressed.

★ **RESILIENCE** (See page 198)
Resilience skills can help us reduce and manage negative emotions.

All the other Keys
As you might expect, all the Keys in this book, including this one, provide ideas and actions to help increase and enhance your experience of positive emotions (and manage difficult ones). The chart on page 255 shows some specific pleasant emotions and lists which chapters are especially helpful in nurturing each of those.

G
R
E
A
T

265

D
R
E
A
M

ACCEPTANCE

Be comfortable with who you are

How you know and treat yourself is central to your well-being. You don't need to be perfect (none of us is), yet we can easily undermine our own well-being by being far too tough on ourselves. We can be happier if we learn to be as compassionate towards ourselves as we would be to a friend and find ways to recognise, use and nurture our strengths – what's best in us.

Acceptance:
introduction

> 'We are all meant to shine, as children do. It's not just in some of us; it's in everyone. And as we let our own light shine, we unconsciously give other people permission to do the same.'
>
> Marianne Williamson, *A Return to Love*

We generally accept and love our friends for who they are. We know their good and bad sides, what they're great, and not so great, at and their quirks... and we love them all the same. So how come many of us don't love and treat ourselves in the same way? We can be our own harshest critic, often measuring ourselves against impossibly high standards and berating ourselves when we fail to reach them. With constant criticism running in our head about not being good enough, that's a pretty good route to being unhappy. And what are the qualities we focus on when we're thinking about ourselves? Chances are we focus on our weaknesses or what's wrong with us, rather than what's best, strongest or good.

It's especially hard today, when on social media people are constantly sharing images and updates that paint an idealised view of how well their lives are going. This can make us see our friends as being happier, having more fun or being more beautiful than us. But comparing ourselves to others is one of the most toxic things we can do for our happiness and it stops us from nurturing what's unique and best about ourselves.

Psychology is showing that when we treat ourselves with more compassion, focus on what's right with us, stop comparing ourselves to others and find ways to make the most of our strengths, it makes a big difference to our happiness, fulfillment and resilience.

✎ Pause point...

Think about your best friend/someone you know well and care about.

★ What are their top strengths, the qualities in them you value, admire and like?

★ How do their weaknesses or limitations impact on how you think and feel about them?

★ What's your approach to them when they make mistakes?

★ How does that compare to how you think about and treat yourself?

Self-acceptance

A sense of self-worth and acceptance has long been regarded as central to well-being. This means knowing both our strengths and limitations and liking and treating ourselves respectfully just the same. Recognising that, just like us, no one is perfect, that everyone makes mistakes or fails sometimes.

Albert Ellis, a renowned psychologist, described two choices: accepting ourselves conditionally (i.e. only under certain conditions, for example when we succeed or are 'perfect') or unconditionally (under all circumstances). The first choice, he suggested, is 'deadly'. If we don't fulfill the conditions we set ourselves, and so fail, we think of ourselves as being a loser rather than accepting failing as a normal part of life. This doesn't mean we should ignore our weaker areas, but keep them in perspective, knowing that, however painful it is, making mistakes is part of life and something to learn and grow from rather than dwell on and beat ourselves up about. In fact, research is showing that if we accept and are kinder to ourselves, we're likely to be more open to addressing our weaknesses.

Research is also showing that knowing and making better use of our strengths can lead to greater happiness and fulfillment, yet when it comes to learning and developing, we're mostly taught to focus on weaknesses. Of course we need to address issues if these are stopping our strengths from shining through, but there's evidence that we'll develop more from getting better at what we most naturally do best.

So in this chapter we'll be looking at how we relate to, and what we nurture in, ourselves, exploring two important questions that are central to our own happiness but we seldom ask:

★ How good a friend are you to yourself?
★ How do you find and nurture the best of you?

Try this! You at your best

Before we get into the detail of this chapter, bring to mind a time when you were at your best.

★ Perhaps it was a time when you were proud of yourself or a time when you felt you were really doing what comes naturally to you, when some of your best qualities had a chance to shine. It can be recent or from a long time ago, and from any area of your life. It doesn't need to be a big thing – it can be small. It doesn't need to be a time when others recognised or rewarded you. What's most important is that it's a time when *you* were genuinely proud of *you*.

Now spend 20 or 30 minutes writing about the time in your notebook. Tell the story as it happened. What was the context? What did you do? What led you to that? Afterwards, reflect on it.

★ Was it easy or hard to think and write about a time when you were at your best?

★ How did you feel as you were thinking and writing about it?

We'll come back to your story later in the chapter.

Being a good friend to ourselves

> 'Be kind, everyone you meet is fighting a hard battle.'
>
> John Watson, *The British Weekly*

This is an often-quoted saying… and maybe you're fighting a battle with yourself inside too. Many of us expect to be perfect and feel embarrassed, or even ashamed, when we make mistakes or fail. It's a habit that can seriously impact happiness. Indeed, a rapidly growing body of research into what's called 'self-compassion' is showing that how we see and relate to ourselves has important consequences for our well-being.

What is self-compassion?

Self-compassion is simply compassion we direct towards ourselves. It's about the way we treat and relate to ourself and the dialogue that goes on inside our own head. So to understand it, let's first look at compassion. It's a concept that is commonly used in the West in connection with how we relate to the difficulties of others. It's described as being 'sensitive to or touched by the suffering of others, opening our awareness to their pain not disconnecting from it, rather turning towards it, so feelings of kindness and wanting to alleviate their suffering or prevent it emerge.'

For example, if we notice that a friend is unhappy, instead of brushing this aside and saying 'cheer up', we accept that they are sad and treat them kindly, acknowledging and not pushing away how they're feeling, and perhaps giving them a hug and a sense that we want to help. Likewise, if we pass a homeless person in the street, seeing them as a fellow human being, recognising 'there but for the grace of good fortune go I' and smiling, stopping to chat or buying them something to eat.

KEY NINE: ACCEPTANCE

A key point is that we all experience suffering and pain: that's part of the human condition. Compassion enables us to connect and help each other. Professor Paul Gilbert, an expert in compassion-focused therapy, says that compassion is essentially a social 'mentality' that can flow in different directions:

★ **From ourselves to others,** when we notice their suffering, feeling compassionate towards them.

★ **From others to ourselves,** when they notice our suffering, receiving compassion from them.

★ **Directing compassion inwards towards ourselves,** when we're experiencing suffering: in other words, being self-compassionate.

The elements of self-compassion

We can be self-compassionate if we've caused a problem or made mistakes, or if things have gone wrong for reasons beyond our control. It's also beneficial when we're simply having a hard time – perhaps pressures at work, difficulties at home or in our relationships.

Psychologist Kristin Neff, a leading researcher on self-compassion, has identified three parts to it, which combine and act together. These are: being kinder to ourselves rather than judging harshly; having a sense of common humanity rather than disconnection from others and mindfulness, which helps us recognise our thoughts and feelings without getting caught up in them. All three elements interact to give us a compassionate attitude towards ourselves.

1 Being kinder to ourselves

Most people recognise that it's important to be kind to others, but we often don't apply this to ourselves. When we mess up, make a mistake or fail at something, our inner voice might say: 'You're useless/careless/stupid' or similar, leading to greater pain and potentially feelings of embarrassment and shame. Neff points out that we can do this even if what has gone wrong is out of our control, e.g. we are made redundant. Even really compassionate people do this to themselves. We can continually berate ourselves for not being good enough, yet we wouldn't do that to a friend. If something had gone badly for them we'd want to be gentle or soothing, supportive and understanding. We'd likely assume they were doing their best. Being self-compassionate is about being more like this towards ourselves: actively soothing and comforting ourselves at times of distress. There's a good biological reason for this, as we'll see.

2 Common humanity

Can I let you into a secret? It's not just you that gets it wrong or doesn't measure up, it's everyone. The truth is no one is perfect and no one has a perfect life. No one, not you, not me, not that highly successful person you've seen on TV. We all make mistakes, we all fail. We all have disappointments, whether about ourselves, how things have turned out or our situation in life (or probably all three). This is what it means to be human and part of the human experience. It's something we all share.

Often when we feel we're not good enough or have made mistakes we think there's something wrong with us so we want to hide away and disconnect ourselves from others. But we humans are social creatures and cutting ourselves off increases feelings of isolation, leading to further feelings of unhappiness. Yet it's our flaws and imperfections that help us connect to each other. If we let others see us more as we are, it enables them to be themselves too.

Recognising that everyone has difficulties or shortcomings, not just us, helps us to be more compassionate towards ourselves. As Neff says 'We forget that falling flat on our face now and then actually is normal.' As uncomfortable as it feels, it is part of what makes us similar to others rather than different or odd. She also points out that being self-compassionate isn't self-pity, which is when we get submerged in our own problems and feel sorry for ourself. Recognising that everyone has similar problems helps to keep us connected and afloat.

3 Mindfulness

We often don't notice or acknowledge our emotional pain, whether that's caused by our inner critic, for example feelings of shame, guilt or sadness from beating ourselves up for making an error. Or what we're experiencing when we're working to tackle difficult problems or struggling to overcome challenges, recognising just how hard that can be. Mindfulness (see Chapter 4) helps because it enables us to be aware of our negative thoughts and feelings but, importantly, not getting caught up in them. To notice them with a sense of objective distance or detachment, recognising that they, like all thoughts and feelings, will come and go and aren't a permanent part of us. So knowing that although we're experiencing feelings of inadequacy at a particular moment, we, as an individual, are not inadequate.

THE HUMAN CONNECTION

I'd been invited to speak at a big conference for state primary-school head teachers. I was second on the bill and my topic was resilience and well-being. I'd prepared and rehearsed. Experience earlier in my career had led me to believe that presentations and presenters should be perfect and fully armed with facts. That's what people want from an expert. But I wasn't prepared for what happened.

The headline speaker went on first. His job was to kick off the conference and get people engaged and switched on. He gave an impassioned talk called 'Mind the Gap' on how education could change kids' lives for the better. I knew I'd been emotionally affected by what he said, only I didn't quite realise how much.

I was on straight after, so got up ready to speak. But instead of my carefully planned opening, what came out was not words, but tears. Floods came pouring out… right in front of 200 school leaders, who'd paid to hear me speak. After what seemed like ages I was able to muster a few choked words to explain. The previous speaker's message had moved me to my deepest core – giving chances to children through learning struck a personal chord as I felt passionately that what they did as teachers and leaders in helping kids lead flourishing lives couldn't be more important. Eventually, my emotions subsided and I proceeded with my talk. But from that moment I sensed a deeper connection between me and my audience. Rather than being ashamed of my unprofessional outburst, I realised that my vulnerability and emotion meant I wasn't seen as a sterile, perfect expert but as a fellow feeling human being. As applause erupted, I realised I'd learned an important lesson.

Try this! Self-compassionate rewind

Make a note of a time when you messed up/failed, which made you feel bad about yourself. What led up to it and what happened?

Now reflect on the three aspects of self-compassion in relation to this event and write these thoughts down for yourself:

★ **Kindness** Write a letter to yourself as if it was a good friend writing to you about the situation, expressing caring, understanding, kindness and concern for you. You might want to re-read the letter a few times over the next week.

★**Common humanity** List ways or situations in which other people could have experienced something similar (this doesn't have to be people you know, it could be anyone).

★ **Mindfulness** List the emotions you experienced in this situation. Do this as if you were a neutral observer, noting the facts.

Based on: Leary, M. R., Tate, E. B., Adams, C. E., Batts Allen, A. & Hancock, J. (2007). Self-compassion and reactions to unpleasant self-relevant events: the implications of treating oneself kindly. *Journal of Personality and Social Psychology*, 92(5), 887-904

275

What self-compassion isn't

Being self-compassionate is NOT about being too soft on ourselves, passive or weak. Neither is it brushing problems away or failing to take responsibility for them. It's precisely the opposite. It enables us to face what's not right or is making us feel bad and so more likely to do something about it.

When we face problems self-compassionately we are less caught up in unpleasant feelings but, as Neff says, importantly, it doesn't mean we push issues away. In fact it means we are less likely to suppress difficult feelings because we know they're important to address. Neither are we masking negative feelings with pleasant ones. We experience more positive feelings because we are able to face our difficult feelings.

Self-compassion doesn't make us complacent. Rather it helps us learn and get better. Studies have found that self-compassionate people fear failure less and if they do fail are more likely to try again. They seem to be more driven to improve and avoid repeating mistakes. Neff says this is because it creates a sense of psychological safety, in which we can recognise our weaknesses and see what we need to work on. In contrast, when we berate ourselves for failure it sets up a sense of fear, meaning we're less likely to try or if we push ourselves hard to succeed it's to avoid harsh self-judgement. However, if we're self-compassionate we can better tolerate the ups and downs of learning and we try because we care. We know that learning and challenging ourselves contribute to being happy.

Self-compassion, happiness and well-being

'A man cannot be comfortable without his own approval.'
Mark Twain, *What is Man?*

Although the scientific study of self-compassion is a young field, research is increasing and results look promising. In short, self-compassion seems to help us to be happier and more likely to thrive. Therefore, it's probably not surprising that people who are more compassionate towards themselves have more pleasant and fewer negative emotions. Self-compassion seems to help us lead more satisfying, meaningful lives. People who are more self-compassionate are much more likely to have higher 'eudemonic well-being', which is about personal growth, mastery and having purpose: in other words, achieving their potential. It's also associated with experiencing more curiosity and creativity, more wisdom and higher emotional intelligence. Conversely, being overly self-critical means we are more likely to experience depression and anxiety. Being self-compassionate reduces self-criticism and so helps to protect us from these, and it seems to go beyond this. People with more of it are less likely to ruminate on problems/limitations and they experience less anxiety when thinking about their weaknesses.

There are also benefits for our resilience. Studies show that being more self-compassionate during major life difficulties, such as divorce, predicted better psychological functioning nine months later. It generally seems to help us to put problems into perspective, since we recognise that everyone has difficulties, we're less likely to feel our problems are worse than other peoples'.

It seems to help us to feel more connected to others and benefit our close relationships too. For example, self-compassionate people are seen by their partners as being more accepting and less controlling, less detached or verbally or physically aggressive and more emotionally connected. So it's good for our partners' well-being as well as our own! It also seems to make us more forgiving and more able to face others' pain and suffering without being overwhelmed.

Self-compassion isn't self-esteem

It's easy to confuse self-compassion and self-esteem, but they are different. Self-esteem is a judgement about ourselves. Having high self-esteem means we see ourselves positively and value and like ourselves. This is important for happiness and well-being and lack of it can lead to ill-health, such as depression and anxiety. However, self-esteem can also be problematic. Often we base our own self-esteem on how well we think we compare to other people; for us to have high esteem we have to feel we're better than others. Or it's contingent on external factors such as performing well, status, looks or having money. Our desire to have self-esteem can lead us to try to find it in ways that are ultimately detrimental to our own and others' well-being, such as putting others down or inflating our self-worth to make us feel good. At extremes, this can lead to antisocial behaviour such as bullying, self-conceit and self-obsession.

Self-compassion is not about judgement or how we compare to others but how we treat ourselves. It seems to help us deal with failure and negative feedback better, accepting that we have negative as well as positive personality aspects and, in contrast to self-esteem alone, are less prone to feeling humiliated by others pointing out our mistakes.

Our old and new brain – how self-compassion works

Paul Gilbert believes that the way self-compassion works is to do with how our brains evolved. Up to about two million years ago, our brains were much like most other mammals' today (he calls this 'old brain'), and it's still responsible for our instinctive behaviours and emotional reactions. Our old brain has three main emotion-regulation systems, each associated with different emotions:

* ★ The 'seeking and achieving' system – joy and excitement.
* ★ The 'threat-focused protection system' – fear, anger, anxiety, disgust.
* ★ The 'affiliation-care system' – contentment, connection and safety.

These systems also interact to activate or inhibit each other in specific ways. For reasons of survival our threat-focused protection system is our most dominant one (see Chapter 8). It's designed to deal with short-term threats, giving us a burst of emotions like fear, anger or disgust, which provoke us to take action accordingly and then, as the danger passes and its activity subsides, so we return to a calmer state.

As we saw in earlier chapters, human beings evolved as social creatures. In part this is because the newer part of our brain, which began to evolve about two million years ago, is big, so we're born relatively early in our physical development (otherwise our heads would be too big for the birth process). As we can't look after ourselves we need to be cared for. To facilitate this we evolved a powerful drive to connect, belong, care and be cared for – the role of our affiliation-care system. Being with others feels good and it helps us recover from stressors (imagine a returning antelope who has escaped from a lion: cortisol and adrenalin pumping, heart pounding, feeling calmer and safer once back in its herd). Feeling safe and connected also enables us to explore and seek good things (our old brain's third system).

Our newer brain can also be 'tricky', as Dr Gilbert calls it. It's given humans the unique capacity to imagine, to think about what might be or what could have been. This has meant we're able to be creative and solve problems, which has helped us to advance as a species, but it can cause us problems too. It means we worry – about what might have been or what could be. Unlike the returning antelope who just goes back to grazing and resting, if we'd experienced danger it's likely we'd start replaying it in our mind, thinking about how we could have suffered further or worrying about next time. This means our newer brain activates the threat system in our old brain. Continuous worry and anxiousness mean it can be activated most of the time.

Self-criticism works in the same way and can be particularly powerful. Being social by nature, our innate drive to connect is strong, so any criticism is experienced as a threat of exclusion, disconnection or being unloved and unwanted. Our triggers for excessive self-criticism are often based in this sort of underlying threat, evoking feelings such as anger and contempt towards ourselves. These feelings may then provoke behaviours such as defensiveness, submission or withdrawal. For example, a woman may criticise herself for being fat because she sees this as a potential reason for being rejected, triggering feelings of shame that cause further anger towards herself and wanting to withdraw from social contact or 'hide' from others.

Kristin Neff points out that our inner critic can be brutal because there is no social censure. If someone had put on weight we wouldn't say: 'You're so disgusting', but we do that to ourselves. Such reactions are influenced by our social context and past experience, particularly during childhood. So, says Dr Gilbert, it's important to realise that feeling like this is not our fault. It's how our brains are designed and shaped as we grew up. However, importantly, we can use the understanding of how our brains developed to help us, which is what self-compassion does.

Self-compassion practices help to stimulate our affiliation-care system when we are experiencing difficulties and emotional pain, triggering feelings of being cared for, soothed and loved. As well as calming our stress reactions, this also has other knock-on consequences. As we've seen in earlier chapters, experiencing such positive or pleasant emotions then makes us more likely to be open to connecting and caring, creating an upward spiral for well-being. Further replacing our self-criticism with a more compassionate attitude towards ourselves reduces the pain and emotional difficulties we cause ourselves, enabling us to face and address issues it would be helpful to deal with. Compassion and our affiliation-care system are not only about relieving, calming and soothing in response to suffering, they're also about nurturing, designed to foster positive change and growth in ourselves and caring for and nurturing other humans, as well as other species. As Gilbert points out – we're one of the only species that cares for its old and sick as well as its young.

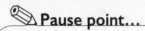

Pause point...

Touch can be a powerful way to stimulate the affiliation-care system in the old part of our brain, which then releases the hormone oxytocin, calming down our threat-protection system. What's great is that we can do this for ourselves. Even gentle touch works.

Psychologist Kristin Neff suggests giving ourselves a hug when we're having a tough time. Even if we're in public we can surreptitiously have a mini hug by crossing our arms, holding the outside of our elbows and gently stroking.

When we're practising being more self-compassionate, gestures such as lightly stroking our arm or hand can help, as can placing our hand on our heart.

See: Neff, K. (2011)

Developing self-compassion

'To be beautiful means to be yourself. You don't need to be accepted by others. You need to accept yourself.' Thich Nhat Hanh, *The Art of Power*

The good news is that self-compassion has been shown to be something we can learn and get better at. The more we practise, the better the impact seems to be – it's complementary to mindfulness (see Chapter 4) but has benefits beyond it and can also be practised without formal mindfulness training. Some structured approaches have been developed to teach it and there are also activities you can practise yourself (see page 282 onwards).

Kristin Neff and colleague Chris Germer have developed a programme called Mindful Self-Compassion (MSC) with a format similar to the Eight-Week Mindfulness-Based Stress Reduction programme we looked at in Chapter 4. Initial studies of the programme showed that, compared to a waitlist control group, participants had very significant increases in self-compassion levels, as well as increases in mindfulness, life satisfaction and compassion for others. It also decreased anxiety and depression. What's more, these benefits were still there in follow-ups six months and one year later.

Studies are also starting to find that shorter activities can have a positive impact. For example, recently a three-session programme improved participants' self-compassion, optimism, confidence in their own abilities and they were less likely to dwell on negative thoughts. Interestingly, participants' mindfulness also improved, even though formal mindfulness meditation wasn't taught. This study was specifically aimed at female students, because it has been found that they can be particularly prone to self-criticism. Another study asked participants to write about a time they'd experienced failure, humiliation or rejection. Those who were then guided to reflect on their event in a way designed to increase self-compassion experienced lower unpleasant emotions than other participants (even those whose reflection was designed to increase self-esteem). For a similar guided reflection – see the Try this! Self-compassionate rewind on page 275.

We can worry that being more kind and self-compassionate could make us weak and self-indulgent if we don't use self-criticism to address our shortcomings. But Dr Gilbert says being compassionate is not about being weak, it enables us to be courageous. This is the courage to acknowledge our pain and suffering, recognise our shortcomings and know that these are normal. They're not our fault, but they are our responsibility, and by being more caring and nurturing of ourselves we can help ourselves improve for the sake of our own well-being – and that of others.

Part of developing more compassion is being able to receive it. And at first, for some people, this may be hard, even when it's compassion that is coming from themselves. If we struggle with receiving compassion it could be because in our upbringing the people who cared for us also harmed us in some way, be that emotionally or physically, and so we learnt not to trust warmth and soothing directed our way and it became mixed up with anxiety and fear. If this is the case for you, Dr Gilbert suggests taking the process of developing self-compassion slowly. It may also be helpful to find a therapist who is trained in Compassion-Focused Therapy, a therapeutic approach he developed specifically for people suffering from clinical levels of depression and anxiety and who are severely self-critical.

KEY NINE: ACCEPTANCE

Try this! Tuning in/changing your inner critic

★ Find yourself a bracelet or wristband that you can wear all the time. Or if you typically wear trousers or some other clothing with pockets, you could find a small, smooth pebble or stone that you could keep in your pocket. Over the next week, each time you notice your inner voice being critical, swap the bracelet to the other wrist or the pebble to the other pocket.

★ As you notice yourself being critical start to recognise the things you typically say and the way in which you say them. What words do you use? What is the tone of your voice (e.g. cold, angry, stern, contemptuous)? How does it make you feel? Are there times when it's particularly active?

★ Being compassionate and warm to your inner critic, say to it something like: 'I know you're trying to keep me safe and help me be better, but the way you are doing it is causing me unnecessary pain. Please stop being so critical.'

★ Now find a different, more compassionate and positive, way to approach what your inner critic was saying. Imagine it was a good friend talking kindly to you in a warm, gentle tone. Use words that work for you, such as: 'I can tell you're feeling upset because you forgot your notes for your important meeting, but everyone forgets things sometimes and you've been really busy. What would help you to remember them next time?'

Or 'You're angry with yourself for eating that chocolate, even though you ate it to cheer yourself up. What are other, more healthy, ways you could cheer yourself up with next time? How about phoning a good friend or going for a walk around the park?'

As you are doing this, if you can, gently and kindly stroke your arm or your hand for the reasons we noted in the pause point on page 280.

Note: Some people find that writing these dialogues down in a journal helps them to think them through.

Based on: Neff, K. (2011) *Self Compassion: stop beating yourself up and leave insecurity behind.* Hodder & Stoughton; Smeets, E., Neff, K., Alberts, H. & Peters, M. (2014). Meeting Suffering With Kindness: Effects of a Brief Self-Compassion Intervention for Female College Students. *Journal of Clinical Psychology,* 70(9), 794-807

Activities to increase our self-compassion

In addition to the self-compassion rewind activity we looked at on page 275, here are two more activities to try. As we have already noted – the more practice you have, the more likely you are to experience benefits. Remember, it can take time to get the hang of them.

In preparation, you may find it helpful to do a mindful breathing exercise to get into a calm and clear state. (We looked at a one-minute and a three-minute breathing space activities in Chapter 4 on pages 117 and 136.) You might also find bringing to mind an image of a safe, warm space and your ideal caring and compassionate person (they don't need to be someone you know) and imagine that person directing compassion towards you.

Try this! Start the day with self-compassion

Before you get out of bed in the morning, spend three minutes or so cultivating self-compassion. Do this each morning over several weeks or longer.

★ Bring a compassionate expression to your face, such as one you would use towards a friend or a child, and bring to mind how you would be if you were at your compassionate best.

★ Breathing slowly and calmly, bring to mind something you have to do today that might be a challenge.

★ Using a friendly and warm inner voice, imagine how your best compassionate self would approach it. Use your own wisdom of how everyone struggles and that dealing with challenges is hard, but we can be kind to ourselves. As you do this stroke your arm/hand gently,

★ Finally, calmly and mindfully, repeat a few times some loving kindness phrases directed to yourself and others: May I be safe, may I be kind, may I be well, may I live with ease.

This is a slight variant of the loving kindness meditation we looked at in Chapter 4, page 140.

Based on: Gilbert, (2010), (2015); Smeets et al (2014)

Nurturing what's best in you

> 'We must strain every nerve to live in accordance with the best thing in us.'
>
> Aristotle, *Nichomachean Ethics*

It's likely we've not met, but I can tell you the following: you are unique and you have some great personal qualities. You really do. We all do and we're all different. You won't be perfect. No one is. And what does 'being perfect' mean for a human being anyway? This world needs a mix of personalities, passions and interests, and so the question is – are you making the most of what's best about you? Leading psychologists believe that those qualities, what they call your 'strengths', are an important source of your own well-being and your greatest potential for contributing to that of others – doing your bit, however tiny, to make the world a better place.

Many of us don't know what our strengths really are, let alone how to use and develop them. However, I bet most of us could list our flaws and weak spots. We often believe that to develop and grow we need to focus on our weaknesses. To some extent that's true – if they are holding us back from making the most of what we do best or are a stepping stone to it. Yet in investment terms, we're likely to get greatest returns from nurturing and amplifying what we're already good at. Our strengths, what's best in us, are our potential and a source of energy and vitality too. It's the path of least resistance, if you like, to doing/being the best we can.

As we've already seen in this book for good reason we're hardwired to focus on the bad over the good, and that applies to ourselves. Becoming more consciously aware of our strengths helps us to redress the balance and to be more accepting of ourselves.

What are strengths?

'Use what talents you possess; the woods would be very silent if no birds sang there except those that sang best.' Unattributed

Strengths are our core capacities for 'thinking, feeling, willing and behaving' says psychologist and strengths expert Ryan Niemiec. They're part of our core identity – what we're drawn by, motivated towards and do most naturally. When we're using our strengths it's enjoyable for us, energising rather than depleting, and it helps us be our most effective.

Yet it's not always easy for us to spot our own strengths. The thing is, they are so natural to us that we may not even realise they're strengths, something that doesn't come so easily and naturally for everyone.

This came home for me at a talk I once went to on teaching creativity. A professor from one of the top UK art schools (and an artist in his own right), Michael Craig Martin, was on the panel. He said that his job as a teacher of future artists was to help them see what they uniquely did best and help them nurture that. However, because that came so easily to them it was often what they valued least. They wanted to do what the other students were doing. In contrast, they didn't notice or value what they themselves did naturally well. They assumed it was something that everyone could do because it was so easy! He didn't mean they shouldn't work hard and put effort into developing their particular strength or talent and the skills that went along with it, but by going with the grain rather than against it they were most likely to flourish.

So what's the different between strengths, talents and skills? There is a range of different definitions out there, but what I find helpful is to think of it this way:

Strengths

These are key positive characteristics of our personality influencing how we approach the world, what we think and feel, what we're most naturally motivated towards using and doing. They also connect to our values and what we find meaningful.

Our strengths of character are a core and enduring part of who we are. Using them is energising rather than depleting, and we can learn to nurture and use them more, finding the best contexts for us to apply them, to allow them to shine.

Talents

We may have particular talents – obvious ones, for example, such as being able to sing or draw, being musical, or having athletic or sports ability. Or less obvious ones such as having an ability with electronic or mechanical things or being able to explain things simply or being organised or dealing with animals. There are many!

We can squander our talents. For example, we could be naturally athletic, but if we can't be bothered to train, then we won't make the most of that talent and it will diminish over time.

Our strengths of character help us to develop and nurture our talents. For example, if we have a strength of perseverance that will help us to stick with a training regime. If social intelligence is a strength, we may prefer to train in a team environment rather than alone.

Skills

These are the capabilities that we learn within, or across, our strengths and talents or as part of other activities such as at work. We develop our skills through intentional training and practice. Because of who we are, some skills may be easier for us than others, but within a given field certain skills are required. For example, if I have a talent for singing and I want to make the most of this professionally, I will need to learn skills to help me project and modulate my voice.

So our strengths, talents and skills work together to help us bring the best out of ourselves and enjoy the process of doing so more. However natural our strengths and talents are, nurturing and developing them takes focused effort and attention. We may see people on TV or online who appear to do something amazing so effortlessly, be that a singer on *X Factor*, a footballer in the Premier League or a leader or expert giving an inspiring and funny speech, but they will have worked hard at developing

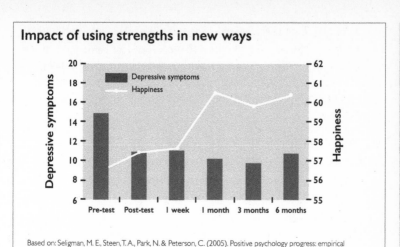

Impact of using strengths in new ways

Based on: Seligman, M. E., Steen, T. A., Park, N. & Peterson, C. (2005). Positive psychology progress: empirical validation of interventions. *American Psychologist*, 60(5), 410-421

their strengths and talents in order to do what they do. Psychologist K. Anders Ericsson famously found that top performers, regardless of their field, put in many thousand of hours of deliberate practice. Those who were considered world-class put in the most – 10,000 hours is often the quoted figure.

Understanding our strengths also helps us to better spot the opportunities for us to use them, instead of these passing us by.

Strengths and happiness

'[Happiness] is inward, and not outward; and so it does not depend on what we have, but on who we are.' Henry Van Dyke, *Joy and Power*

Knowing and using our strengths can lead to being happier, more confident, having higher levels of energy and vitality, greater resilience and less stress, and being more effective in developing ourselves. In a classic, and replicated, positive psychology experiment, people were asked to identify their top five strengths and then use one of them in a new and different way every day for one week. At the end of that week there was a small initial increase in their happiness, and as time passed those benefits grew and stayed higher up to six months later.

KEY NINE: ACCEPTANCE

Importantly, the same study (and subsequent ones) showed that putting our strengths into action made the difference, not just being more aware of our strengths. This can also be a way to boost and repair our day-to-day moods. A recent study found that using strengths on one day predicted being in a better mood the next day.

As well as increasing our well-being, using our strengths can help us achieve our goals (and of course the two are related). In a study over a three-month period, strengths use was also found to increase progress towards, and achievement of, goals that were personally meaningful. The researchers suggested that applying our strengths in pursuit of our goals could lead to an 'upward spiral' of success and well-being.

There is a growing body of evidence that being able to use our strengths at work means we are more likely to enjoy and be engaged by our jobs and perform better. Feeling that we are able to do what we do best every day means we are six times more likely to be engaged by our jobs, and if we aren't able to use our strengths we're more likely to dread going to work, have fewer positive interactions with colleagues, treat customers less well and have fewer moments of creativity. Being able to use more of our character strengths in our jobs is associated with more positive experiences at work. We can even find ways to use our strengths to overcome obstacles at work, so potentially creating a virtuous circle of strengths use. Recently it's been found that being able to use our top strengths could help maintain life satisfaction if we don't have a strong sense of meaning and purpose (see Chapter 10).

Finding and using your strengths

Strengths expert, Ryan Niemiec, recommends three steps to understanding and getting the most from our strengths:

1 **Becoming aware** There are a number of activities we can use to build our awareness of what our strengths actually are. We'll look at three.
2 **Exploring** Looking at how we're using our strengths in different parts of our lives and also how we might have used our strengths in the past. This might also include how we can over- and underplay them too.
3 **Applying and developing** Finding ways we can use our strengths more and in different ways.

As we have seen, the impact of our strengths on our happiness and well-being grows over time, as we become more aware and explore how and when to use them, what they 'look like' in different contexts and the variety of ways we can apply them. Let's look at some activities you can use to get started.

1 Becoming aware of your strengths

Looking for clues

Reflect on things you are drawn to doing, that you find help you feel energised rather than depleted. Because our strengths are core features of who we are, we may find there are clues to them from an early age. These questions will get you started:

Think of the things that:
★ You loved doing as a child – what was it about them that you loved?
★ Come very easily to you and you pick up quickly.
★ You associate with the words: 'I love to'.
★ Get done quickly on your to-do lists.
★ Your friends, colleagues and family come to you for help with.

Jot these things down. Look at what underlies them too. For example, in one workshop, two men, Andy and Mike, both said that as kids they loved playing football, but when I asked what was it about playing football that they enjoyed most, Andy said: 'I loved honing my skills with the ball', while Mike said: 'I loved being part of a co-ordinated team.' So both enjoyed the same activity, but for different underlying reasons. These reasons gave clues to their strengths. Later they took a strengths survey (see page 292). Andy found he had a 'signature', or top strength, of 'appreciation of beauty and excellence' (wanting to hone skills) while one of Mike's included leadership and teamwork.

You at your best

Part 1 At the start of this chapter you wrote about a time when you felt at your best: a time when *you* were proud of *you*. Go back to that story. What personal qualities and strengths did you use or display in that situation? Note these down.

Can you think of other situations where you felt at your best, perhaps in a different context (for example – if your story was of a leisure activity or something at home, think of a time at work, school or college, or vice versa). What strengths did you use this time – were they similar or different to the first story? Which feel most energising or most 'you'?

Part 2 Find someone you trust and are comfortable sharing your story with. Before you start, ask them to listen out for strengths you displayed and share these with you when you've finished – naming each strength they heard and what it was that you did that illustrated it.

Sharing stories of when we felt at our best isn't always a comfortable thing to do, but it is a powerful and valuable activity. It's likely that the other person will hear strengths in your story that you didn't notice or think of. Why not offer to listen to them share a story of when they felt they were at their best so you can spot strengths for them too?

Identifying your signature strengths

The research on strengths psychology usually recommends we identify and focus on our 'signature strengths': a limited number, say between three and seven, of the strengths that most feel like 'us', that we find are most energising and fulfilling to use and that we use in a wide range of situations. Having a short list of top strengths helps us focus, too, on using and developing those areas that are most likely to contribute to our happiness and effectiveness.

So what are your signature strengths? Look at the list of strengths you've identified in the activities above and, if you've taken the survey (see page 292), look at the strengths towards the top of your ranking. Ask yourself which of these are really 'you', for example:

★ You feel most ownership of them, most drawn to them and most want to use them.
★ You have a rapid learning curve when using them.
★ It's inevitable you'll use these strengths – they just pop out!
★ You feel energised and invigorated when you're using them rather than depleted.
★ Using them is fulfilling for you.

If you've taken the survey, your signature strengths are usually those that are right at the top of your ranking, usually in your top five, but sometimes we may feel that the sixth or seventh in our ranking is much more 'us' than one (or more) of the top five. That's fine (it's often because we come out as equally strong in those areas). The most important thing is that our shortlist of signature strengths is those that most fulfill the above criteria. Now you've identified your signature strengths, it's time to explore them.

2 Exploring your strengths

How are you currently using your strengths?

It takes time to get to know your strengths and how they play out at different times, in different situations and in the different parts of your life. Now you've identified your signature strengths, explore what these look like for you.

★ Start to notice when you are using them at home, at work, socially or in your community. How do you express them in these different situations?

★ Notice when and where you don't apply your strengths.

★ How do you feel when you're using these strengths and when you're not?

★ How do your strengths interact?

What do others see?

To get a different perspective on when and how you're currently using your strengths, you may want to get input from people who know you well.

When I first took the survey, I wanted to test it out. I sent a list of my top ten to some of my family, a few close friends and some close colleagues, asking them:

★ If they noticed me using each of those strengths regularly.

★ If there were any in that list of ten that they considered to be particular top strengths of mine.

Their feedback was really affirming and informative. Almost everyone could think of examples of when I'd used each of these strengths, regardless of the context in which they knew me. However, what they perceived as my top strengths varied. For example, my work colleagues

Taking a strengths survey

Psychologists have developed a variety of 'strengths inventories': sets of strengths most frequently observed when people are at their best and most effective. These give us a language for strengths, so helping us to notice and label what we observe in ourselves and others. Each inventory has been developed and validated as an online survey that takes us through multiple-choice questions. Having answered all the questions, we receive a list of our top strengths.

Values In Action (VIA) Classification of Character Strengths

One of the most widely used strengths inventories is the 'Values in Action (VIA) Classification of Character Strengths', which has been taken by millions of people in over 190 countries. You can take the survey for free at: www.viacharacter.org

Developed by a team of scientists led by Drs Martin Seligman and Christopher Peterson, their aim was to identify core positive human characteristics valued across cultures and time. They examined philosophy, psychology, major religious faiths and literature. Eventually, they narrowed the list to the twenty-four most commonly recognised character strengths. For a strength to be included it needed to fulfill a number of criteria, including being universal, distinct and measurable; people find it fulfilling and it doesn't diminish others. The survey takes about twenty minutes to do. Be sure to answer the questions as you really are, not what you want to be or think you should be! You'll receive your personal ranking of twenty-four strengths, in order of strength, from the highest (number 1) to the lowest (number 24). Just because a strength is at the bottom of your list, it doesn't mean that you can't, or don't, use it. We probably use all the strengths listed from time to time, as needed in different situations. But the ones towards the top of your list will be the ones that are likely to be the best of you, those that are most fulfilling and energising for you.

When I'm referring to specific strengths in this chapter, they're from the VIA. There's an overview of the VIA Character Strengths in the chart on pages 294–5.

clearly agreed that creativity was a top strength, but my friends and family didn't. I feel that creativity is a signature strength for me, yet I wasn't using it in some important areas of my life! So that's a current strengths goal for me.

It's important to note that this activity isn't to get other people's opinions on whether your signature strengths are right or not. We can be good at many things, but not all of those will be strengths – what we personally find energising, invigorating and fulfilling. Only you can know that.

Are you over- or underplaying your strengths?

Now because our signature strengths are so natural to us, we can easily overplay them. For example, on occasion my strength of humour has popped out at inappropriate moments. Likewise, there might be situations where we are underplaying our strengths. It can be helpful to understand this to give us greater awareness of the particular contextual conditions for us that support or undermine us in using our signature strengths.

We of course need to be sensitive to what's appropriate to the situation and 'dial up' or 'dial down' our strengths accordingly. For example, when working on projects with tight deadlines I realised that my strength of creativity can lead me to spend too long generating ideas. However, if I'm not able to do this it causes me a lot of tension. So I've learnt to moderate this by building in some brainstorming and idea development time early in the process to allow me to make best use of this strength, do the project well and complete it by the deadline (important for my appreciation of beauty and excellence strength!).

Interestingly, what might be perceived as a weakness might, in fact, be a strength overplayed. For example, my overuse of creativity could have been perceived as procrastination or time-wasting.

Building on work by psychologist Christopher Peterson, Ryan Niemiec has developed a useful guide of what the VIA strengths look like if they are over- and underplayed. Have a look at the chart on pages 294-95 and see if you're overplaying any of yours.

Overview of the 24 VIA Character Strengths

VIA character strength	At its core	Overuse	Underuse
Appreciation of beauty and excellence	Seeing the life behind things; quality or aesthetic sense	Perfectionism or snobbery	Oblivion (insensibility, sloppiness)
Bravery	Facing fears, confronting adversity	Foolhardiness	Cowardice
Creativity	Originality that is useful	Eccentricity	Conformity
Curiosity	Exploration, seeking novelty	Nosiness	Disinterest
Fairness	Equal opportunity for all	Detachment	Partisanship
Forgiveness	Letting go of hurt when wronged	Permissiveness	Mercilessness
Gratitude	Thankfulness	Ingratiation	Rugged individualism (rudeness)
Honesty	Being authentic	Righteousness	Phoniness
Hope	Positive expectations	Pollyanna-ism (very rose-tinted spectacles)	Negativity
Humility	Achievement does not elevate worth	Self-deprecation	Baseless self-esteem
Humour	Offering pleasure/laughter to others	Giddiness	Overly serious/ humourlessness
Judgement	Critical thinking and rationality	Cynicism, narrow-mindedness	Unreflectiveness
Kindness	Doing for others	Intrusiveness	Indifference
Leadership	Positively influencing others	Despotism	Compliance
Love	Genuine, reciprocal warmth	Emotional promiscuity	Emotional isolation
Love of learning	Deepening of knowledge and understanding	Know-it-all	Complacency

Overview of the 24 VIA Character Strengths continued

VIA character strength	At its core	Overuse	Underuse
Perseverance	Keeping going, overcoming obstacles	Obsessiveness	Fragility
Perspective	Taking a wider view	Overbearing	Shallowness
Prudence	Wise caution	Stuffiness	Sensation-seeking
Self-regulation	Self-management	Inhibition	Self-indulgence
Social intelligence	Tuned into others	Over-analysing	Socially clueless
Spirituality	Connecting with the sacred	Fanaticism	Anomie
Teamwork	Collaborative, participating in group efforts	Dependent	Selfishness
Zest	Enthusiasm for life	Hyperactivity	Sedentary

3 Applying and developing your strengths
Finding new ways to use your strengths

This is based on the classic positive psychology experiment we looked at on page 289). Pick one of your signature strengths. Over the next week find a new and different way of using it each day. Notice how you feel when you do so. Over time, try this for each of your other signature strengths.

Strengthening your future self

In Chapter 6, one activity I suggested was writing about your life goals (see page 185). To what extent did these stories reflect your signature strengths? How would you edit them if you could have more fully used these strengths?

KEY NINE: ACCEPTANCE

Role models and examples

Psychologist Albert Bandura's research found that one of the best ways we can build our skills and confidence is through observing expert role models. So for each of your signature strengths, who stands out as exemplars of it for you? How do they use this strength and what can you learn from this? You may find it helpful to get other people's ideas of role models to help you see this strength in action from different perspectives.

Dr Niemiec suggests that looking for examples from literature, TV and the movies can also be helpful in seeing these strengths in action. The VIA website gives some examples and more can be found in his book – *Positive Psychology at the Movies* (see Resources).

To sum up

Here are five key points to take away from this chapter:

1 We can undermine our own happiness and be at greater risk of depression by not accepting ourselves for who we are – being too harsh a critic of ourselves and focusing on what we're not good at rather than on our areas of strength.

2 Being self-compassionate is a way of relating to ourselves, it's not about being self-indulgent. And it has significant positive benefits for well-being.

3 We can become more self-compassionate by noticing and acknowledging when we're suffering emotional pain – especially when it's caused by ourselves, recognising that no one's perfect and being kinder to ourselves and even giving ourselves a hug! Treating ourselves more as we treat a valued friend.

4 Everyone has strengths. Our strengths of character are at the essence of us, influencing how we think, what we feel and what we're drawn to do. They're things we find naturally energising and easy to learn.

5 Identifying our signature strengths and finding ways to use them in new ways and in different parts of our lives can help us to make the most of other talents and live a happier, more fulfilling, life.

Connections to other Keys

Other Keys you might like to explore in connection with Acceptance:

★ **GIVING AND RELATING** (See pages 10 and 36)
Being more self-compassionate towards ourselves enables us to be more compassionate towards others.

★ **AWARENESS** (See page 108)
Mindfulness can help build compassion and character strengths, which can help us develop and sustain mindfulness practice.

★ **TRYING OUT** (See page 144)
• Being more self-compassionate means we're more open to exploring and learning new things.

• Applying our strengths in new ways helps us to learn rapidly and find what we're interested in and passionate about.

★ **DIRECTION** (See page 170)
Being self-compassionate and knowing our strengths means we're likely to reach our goals.

★ **RESILIENCE** (See page 198)
Being self-compassionate and using our strengths means we're less likely to undermine our own resilience.

★ **EMOTIONS** (See page 238)
When we're using our strengths we're much more likely to find what we're doing enjoyable and fulfilling, and being more self-compassionate means we're less likely to cause ourselves unpleasant emotional experiences.

★ **MEANING** (See page 298)
Our strengths give us clues as to what we value and find meaningful in how we live our lives.

Note: It's likely that you can find ways to use your strengths to help you put the other Keys into action.

G
R
E
A
T

D
R
E
A
M

10

MEANING

Be part of something bigger

Having a sense of purpose, understanding why
we're here and feeling that what we do matters
are what 'meaning' is all about. It's a firm foundation
for a fulfilled and happy life, and can help us get
through even the most challenging times. One of the
best ways to find meaning is through contributing
something that's for others – bigger and
beyond oneself.

Meaning: introduction

What really matters? What's the meaning of my life? Why am I here? What's my purpose? How should I live my life? How does what I do make a difference? These are BIG questions and having our own answers for them is a key ingredient for happiness and well-being for many people, though finding the answers isn't always easy as there's no single or simple formula.

We're a species that needs to find meaning, perhaps the only one that does. It helps us to feel that who we are and what we do matter. It helps us to make sense of what happens to us and how the different parts of our life fit together. A clear sense of meaning informs our sense of identity and self-worth – one way of thinking about it is as our personal story from our past to the present and how we'd like to shape our future.

Knowing where we find meaning and defining our purpose enables us to direct our life, from setting big and long-term goals through to our smaller ones – what we want to accomplish and need to do. It helps us to make choices – at the big turning points of our life through to how we spend our time day to day.

Meaning is important when we face big challenges, helping us to cope with, and rise above, our suffering and difficulties rather than being consumed by them. And clarity on what matters most to us can emerge from such challenging times.

The path to meaning isn't always straight or easy and can take time. It may change as we develop our understanding of ourselves and the world. It can come through deep reflection and through trying things out. And it usually involves knowing how we're connected and how we contribute to something bigger and beyond ourselves. In this chapter we'll look more closely at where and how we find meaning and why that matters. There are also some activities to try that can help you clarify what gives meaning to your life.

What does meaning mean?

Viktor Frankl, an Austrian psychiatrist and Holocaust survivor, wrote a powerful short book called *Man's Search for Meaning* as a result of his experience. In his view it was up to us to discover and define what meaning in our life signifies.

His book and work inspired the current psychological research into meaning. It's a relatively new but growing field and there is a range of views on what 'meaning in life' is, where it comes from and what contributes to it.

For the 'father' of positive psychology, Martin Seligman, a meaningful life is one where we are connected or contribute to something beyond, or larger than, ourselves. Studies have shown that this is most strongly related with having a sense of meaning. The term used for these types of sources is 'self-transcendent' – taking responsibility for, or contributing to, something or someone beyond immediate concerns. This could be caring for or helping others. Of these 'generative' sources, i.e. those that contribute to developing or benefiting future generations, have a strong relationship to meaning. This could be caring, guiding, nurturing children or leaving a positive legacy. And the older we get, the stronger the association between generativity and meaning is.

 Pause point...

What is it that makes your life meaningful?

★ What comes to mind most quickly?

★ If you've kept a journal of your daily three good things (see Chapter 8) are there any common themes that have emerged?

★ What are your passions and interests? (See Chapter 5)

★ Who's closest to you in your community? (See Chapter 2)

★ Who do you help and who helps you? (See Chapter 1)

We'll look at some specific activities to help you explore this in more detail later in this chapter.

Michael Steger, a leading expert on the psychology of meaning, suggests that from a psychological point of view, having a sense of meaning in our life boils down to questions about three core elements of meaning:

★ **Significance** Do we feel our life is worthwhile and significant?
★ **Comprehension** Does our life 'make sense' to us? Do the different parts fit together?
★ **Purpose** Do we feel we have purpose? Do we have one or more over-arching purposes or missions that we value?

Let's look at these in a bit more detail.

Significance can come from feeling connected to something beyond ourselves (for some, the essence of meaning) and feeling what we do and who we are makes a difference. For example, this can be through our faith, the belief that we as human beings are part of nature, through helping others or being part of a family, community or other social group, or indeed a combination of all these factors – and others too.

Comprehension is about how we make sense of life, what it and we stand for, and how the different parts of our lives connect. Steger likens it to 'our story', which weaves together 'the themes, lessons, patterns, preferences, memories, perceptions, coincidences, strengths, weaknesses and other people' we encounter in life to give us order and congruence.

Purpose is about what we're motivated and striving towards at the highest level – our aims in life. This sits above our goals (see Chapter 6), providing an overarching focus and helping different goals hang together. Steger says, unlike a goal, our purpose may be open-ended, something that we aspire towards but in reality can never achieve – or not within a fixed timeframe, e.g. 'being a good parent'. Our sense of purpose may be life-long or change as life evolves. For example, self-knowledge may be a driving purpose in early life, being a good parent in the mid-section and being of service to our community could be a focus for all adult life.

Steger says that combining these three elements provides a framework for understanding ourselves in relation to the world, making sense of what happens to us, our choices, and the goals we set and pursue.

Meaning & happiness

'We have a choice to use the gift of our lives to make a difference. It's up to us to decide what kind of difference we're going to make.'

Dr Jane Goodall

Meaning matters

It's clear that having a sense of meaning is related to a happier, healthier, flourishing life.

Psychological research is showing that people who feel they have meaning in life tend to experience more positive emotions; have a more positive outlook on the world and the future; higher life satisfaction and higher psychological well-being. The stronger their sense of meaning, the greater the benefit for well-being seems to be. It's also related to feeling better about ourselves – both in terms of self-esteem and self-acceptance.

Curiously, studies have also shown that if we're happier we're also likely to see our life as more meaningful, this might be explained by the fact that if we're happier, we're more likely to interpret our life and what happens to us more positively, be more open to other people and the world around us (see Chapter 8 for more details).

People with a strong sense of meaning have also been shown to have greater control over themselves and their lives, do better academically and be more engaged at work yet less likely to be workaholics. It's also related to better physical health and taking fewer risks, such as substance abuse.

Meaning as we age

Older adults tend to report a greater sense of meaning. Indeed, meaning and purpose seem to be particularly important as we age and may even help us to live healthily for longer. Relative to other elements of well-being, meaning has been shown to be strongly associated with lower physical and cognitive decline. For example, a study which followed older people over a number of years found that those with the highest purpose in life were 2.4 times more likely to remain free from Alzheimer's than those with the lowest levels of purpose. Post-mortem studies reveal that those with higher purpose had physically healthier brains.

Meaning doesn't always feel good

Meaning is more about fulfillment than pleasure. Viktor Frankl argued that people function best when they have a purpose. Although this can be pleasurable, pursuing it by working towards our goals takes effort and we'll often face struggles along the way, which might not feel good, in fact quite the opposite! We may even face challenges we can't overcome and have to adapt or change our goals to achieve our purpose in a different way. But this struggle is all part of having a fulfilling life. It's how we learn and grow (see Chapter 5), find and achieve meaning.

Meaning and resilience

'He who has a why to live for can bear almost any how.'
Nietzsche, cited by Viktor Frankl in *Man's Search for Meaning*

Having a sense of meaning in life has been found to be an important component in resilience (which could be why it's linked to living longer). Feeling what we're trying to do is meaningful and matters in some way helps to keep us going as we work hard and wrestle with life's challenges. Researchers suggest it may help to protect our brain against the damage from the accumulated effects of stress and challenges over our lifespan. It's associated with being less stressed and having fewer negative emotions such as fear, anger, shame and sadness. It seems to help us to cope better with stressors by having slower and lower reactions to negative triggers and being quicker to recover from them. Indeed, people with a sense of meaning report having fewer negative life events and fewer hassles in general.

Many studies have shown that having a sense of meaning means that we are less likely to experience hopelessness, depression and anxiety, and suicidal tendencies. We are also less likely to be disparaging of ourselves or experience a wide gap between who we are and who we'd like to be.

If we face extreme situations, such as natural disasters, having meaning and purpose can be protective, helping to lower the likely severity of symptoms resulting from trauma and lowering the likelihood of post-traumatic stress disorder. Why? Rather than dwelling on negative events, meaning enables us to re-focus onto higher goals and to learn from what's happened.

Searching for meaning

While having a sense of meaning is associated with higher well-being, the search for it isn't. That's not so surprising – if we're searching for meaning it's likely to be because we feel we lack it. The stronger our search, the less likely we are to be happy and the more we're likely to ruminate on what's wrong, feel less self-accepting and therefore more unhappy.

So does this mean we shouldn't look for meaning? Well, we know that finding it isn't always easy as we seek to develop a deeper understanding of our self and our contribution to the world. However, having a sense of meaning is a key component of happiness and a flourishing life, so it's likely to be worth trying to find. Psychologist Paul Wong points out that even though feeling that our lives don't have meaning is painful, it's a helpful warning signal, spurring us to find a more authentic way of living.

Rather than focusing on what's missing in life, one of the best routes to developing meaning is to find ways to help others, concentrating on something beyond ourselves (Chapter 1 has lots of ideas). This can take our mind off how we're presently feeling and give us an emotional boost to help us feel happier.

The search for meaning isn't always associated with being unhappy. We may feel that meaning isn't important to us. And people who already have it, but who are searching for more, experience higher well-being despite their search.

HELEN FINDS MEANING

'For me, this Key is the most important of the ten, but it took me a few years to realise that,' says Helen. 'I grew up in a house devoid of meaning. For my family the point of life was drinking. My parents were both alcoholics and my brother and I joined them from an early age. I was bright and did well at school, so the academic side of my life was okay, but beyond that my free time was spent at home or with friends getting drunk. I started to suffer from depression and anxiety in my late teens. What was behind that and the drinking was a crisis of meaning, which continued to mark the next decade.

I had no idea what I was living for or working towards. I've got drive, but without purpose I had nothing positive to funnel it into, so my drive got turned destructively inwards. I spent years addicted to drink and drugs. I wanted to get clean, but each time I did all I found was an aching void, so went back to my addictions. Eventually, I realised that I needed to find something more meaningful.

I joined Narcotics Anonymous (NA). Its first step is about surrender and the second/third are about trusting in something greater than yourself. This was the turning point. I'd always been independent, determined to fix my problems alone, so letting go, trusting in the greater good, was a leap, but it made me realise it wasn't me versus the world, it was me as part of the world. I could collaborate with the world to make me, and others, better. In a way it felt sort of spiritual.

I decided to do a PhD in counselling psychology with a view to working in depression and addiction. I started to volunteer in organisations like Action for Happiness. I found it refreshing to focus on happiness rather than not being depressed! I used the Ten Keys to Happier Living to take small daily steps to feel better and I focused on my family. I realised I could be a positive ingredient in the negative stew. My mum had developed Alzheimer's and my nephew had been ill. I could help them. I want to ensure that the future for the younger members of my family would be different. Finding what brings meaning to my life has made staying clean possible and life is so much better now. It hasn't been easy, but these days I find I'd rather do something difficult and fulfilling than doing something easy that is not.'

Where do we find meaning?

> 'Many persons have a wrong idea of what constitutes true happiness. It is not attained through self-gratification but through fidelity to a worthy purpose.'
>
> Joseph Addison

Where might we find meaning? What are its potential sources? Viktor Frankl believed the 'will for meaning' was universal – a primary drive for all humans and the key to living a worthy, fulfilling life, regardless of who we are and our circumstances. He didn't think meaning was something we're born with but something that must be learned, discovered or created and so different for each of us. We need to define it for ourselves.

In his view there were three main sources of meaning in life:
★ **Creative or significant work,** such as achievements or good deeds.
★ **Valued or elevating experiences** of relationships, art or beauty.
★ **Suffering** Our ability to reflect and grow from negative experiences or suffering and the attitude we take towards situations we can't change.

Since Frankl, psychologists have used different approaches to identifying the main sources of meaning in people's lives, areas in which they are personally invested and committed to in the way they live their lives. Some researchers have simply asked questions like: 'What are the things you consider most meaningful/necessary in life?' or 'If money was no object what would you really want in order to live a meaningful life?' Others have gone further, to dig beneath the surface of people's immediate answers. (A good way of doing this for ourselves is to successively ask: 'Why? Why? Why?' for each immediate thought, until we get to the ultimate reason behind each one.)

KEY TEN: MEANING

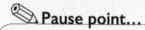

Pause point...

Psychologist Martin Seligman views our greatest potential to achieve meaning (and well-being) as coming through using our signature strengths in service of something bigger than ourselves. How could you use your strengths to do this?

★ Reflect on the signature strengths you identified in Chapter 9 (see page 290). How could you use these to make a meaningful difference to something or someone else? Think about what you could do at work and/or at home or elsewhere.

Based on: Seligman, M.E.P. (2002). Authentic Happiness: Using the new positive psychology to realize your potential for lasting fulfillment. Nicholas Brearley

Although studies show differences in what people find meaningful in their lives, there are consistent themes. Family and relationships are often at or near the top of the list. Other people matter for meaning as well as happiness in general (as we saw in Chapter 2). Other common sources of meaning include: nurturing and helping others, our work, religion or faith, nature, creativity, hobbies, interests and passions, achievement, contributing to a cause and growing as a person.

A 'broad foundation' seems to be beneficial. If we have several diverse sources of meaning in our life, the greater our sense of meaning is likely to be. It also helps us maintain a sense of meaning even if one source is threatened. Studies have shown that five to eight sources seems optimal (having more may be hard to maintain). For example, as well as caring for close relationships and/or children, we might find meaning through our work, volunteering in our local community, our hobby playing music, seeing friends and continuous learning.

We looked in detail at helping others and relationships in Chapters 1 and 2, and at hobbies, interests and passions in Chapter 5. Let's take a look at some of the other most common sources of meaning.

Meaningful work

'...the only way to do great work is love what you do. If you haven't found it yet, keep looking.' Steve Jobs, 2005 commencement speech, Stanford University

Our work can be an important potential source of meaning in our lives. Given that for many of us it's how we spend a large part of our waking hours, thinking about ways in which work could be meaningful is certainly worthwhile. Work gives us a reason to get out of bed in the morning and connect with others, and studies have shown that not having work when we want it or being unemployed is highly detrimental to our well-being over and above loss of income, because it makes us feel we're not needed.

Yet how many of us stop to reflect what we find most meaningful at work? When I ask managers I'm training what's most meaningful for each of their team members at work, often they don't know but try to guess. I ask them to go and have a conversation because what's most meaningful is different for each person and may not be the same as their performance goals. Even if people are carrying out the same role, what's meaningful for each person could be different.

In studies that ask people about what makes their work most meaningful the most frequent answer, regardless of type/level of role, is helping others or feeling we're contributing to society in some way. Feeling as though work matters in some pro-social way is a key source of meaning, over and above doing our bit to contribute to profit or performance.

Psychologist Martin Seligman suggests that some key routes towards building a meaningful life through our work include:
Increasing knowledge For example: learning, teaching, bringing up or educating children, science, literature and the media.
Increasing the 'power' of society For example: technology, engineering, construction, medicine or manufacturing.
Service For example: law, policing, health, ethics, religion, charity work or volunteering, emergency services.

Callings at work

Experiencing our work as a 'calling' – something we're strongly drawn to or even regard as our destiny and a core part of who we are – is strongly associated with increased meaning in life. Callings align with our life's purpose, fit our strengths and talents, and clearly connect to how we make a positive difference to others and/or the world. This has benefits for well-being, including increased job and life satisfaction and better health; being less likely to suffer from stress and depression; and being less likely to have conflict between work and non-work parts of our lives.

Importantly, callings are not restricted to high status or highly paid jobs, but can be any role, at any level. There's a famous story of a cleaner at the NASA Space Center, who when asked what he was doing replied 'I'm helping to put man on the moon'. Of course many people don't experience work as a calling. Some see it as a 'job' – a means to an end. Others consider their work as a 'career' – a pathway to challenge, achievement, status, prestige and personal identity.

So how do we find our calling? We may think it's something that just happens, a message from a higher source, but that's not the case for most people who find one. It's actually something that unfolds through long periods of exploration to find a role that was a perfect fit for talents, passions, values and interests. A good route is to find ways to use more of our strengths. A recent study suggested that if we can use four or more of these strengths at work we are more likely to consider it a calling. Like the search for meaning, the search for a calling can be associated with indecision and confusion about our identity. However, since for many of us work is a big part of our lives, it might be worth the discomfort!

Crafting our work for more meaning

'Job-crafting' is a way to help people shape their roles to fit their strengths and what's meaningful to them. It's been shown to help in a wide range of types and levels of role. Roles can be crafted in three ways:

1 **Crafting our tasks** Adding, changing, emphasising or even swapping the tasks so we do more of what we love, find meaningful or most fully use our strengths. For example, we could volunteer for an extra task that we're drawn to doing; think of a new way to do something

we dislike, for example swapping parts of our role with colleagues with different signature strengths to us, so we do something they dislike, but which we like – and vice versa.

2 **Crafting our relationships at work** This could mean building or changing social interactions at work, even doing this in small ways can make a difference. For example, we could invite a colleague for a coffee or spend time getting to know someone from a different department.

3 **Crafting our perceptions** This could include stepping back to see the bigger picture, zooming in to see the detail, finding connections between things that matter to us or others or reframing our work. Another story of cleaners, this time in a hospital, illustrates this. One saw the work as demeaning and menial while her colleagues saw it as essential in 'fighting the spread of infection'.

Faith, religion, spirituality as a source of meaning

A source of meaning important for many people is spirituality – typically religion, faith and relationship with God. Or for people who aren't religious – a connection with nature. Spirituality is a source of self-transcendence, connecting us to something 'higher' and larger than our self. For some it is the ultimate source of meaning in psychological terms. Spirituality is a more general term taken to be the 'pursuit of significance in what is sacred'. Religion is the search for what's sacred in life within a structured or formal context.

People who feel they have religious or spiritual satisfaction tend to have higher meaning in life and for people who have devoted their lives to their religious beliefs it's even higher. It's important to note that these studies primarily look at religious behaviours rather than just belief. In fact, actively participating in one's religion is a predictor of well-being. As well as helping to answer some of the big questions about meaning in life and providing a firm belief system including that we matter to a higher power (e.g. 'God'), participation in a religion typically involves other factors known to be associated with well-being. These include being part of a community, social support, time for quiet and reflection (such as meditation or prayer), influencing healthier lifestyles, promoting altruism and helping us cope effectively with our problems and put them in perspective.

Religious or spiritual practices can be a source of positive emotional experiences such as joy, and foster hope, optimism and compassion. They can also encourage greater self-control and reduce unpleasant emotional experiences and thoughts such as fear, anxiety, sadness and anger. Religious faith seems to be especially beneficial as we get older. Some studies suggest that being religious was one of the strongest predictors of well-being in old age. One study even found that a belief in an afterlife among older adults was correlated with feeling that their life on this earth was exciting!

ALEX AND THE ANSWER WITHIN

'We often expect meaning to be 'out there' and are upset not to find it. When meaning is a capacity within, it comes out when you invest yourself in the well-being of others. I was a troubled adolescent and I got to the point where everything felt meaningless. I was all but dropping out of school, struggling towards a future that didn't make sense. Eventually, I got on a course to play electric guitar and I spent the next two years hanging out, but found I wasn't any happier.

The turning point came when I was twenty-one. I got in touch with my estranged dad. I had to go to Ukraine, where I discovered he'd started a social project to fight corruption. I got involved and gradually got to know him, and myself, better. I found that I was good at communication, strategic thinking and problem-solving. Instead of focusing on my own problems it felt good to be applying my strengths to helping others.

I decided to live a life with more purpose. I've noticed three ways in which I invest meaning into my life: by putting my strengths to work for social good, by living mindfully and by actively cultivating compassion for others. The foundation for all this is connection. I'm supported by friends in my mindfulness group, and the practice has also helped me find something I could respect and love in my dad. Having spent time with him, I can see the bravery, creativity and care he puts into his projects, and the difference that he makes to other people's lives. So that's what I choose to focus on about him... and what I'm learning to recognise in me.'

Finding meaning in tough times

Life inevitably has ups and downs. There will be times we have to deal with illness, pain, getting older and death. As we've seen, meaning can help us come to terms with, and make sense of, these experiences and pull through them. Tough times can also be an important source of meaning. As Frankl highlighted (as do many religions) – meaning may be found as a result of negative experiences in life or through suffering. Psychologist Paul Wong has built on Frankl's work and points out that often positives and negatives in our life co-exist (in fact that's usually the case) – even if we're successful beyond our wildest dreams we won't be free of pain and psychological suffering. Dr Wong believes that having meaning in life depends on discovering meaning in our difficulties and suffering. He has identified five principles we need to apply to do this:

★ **Face reality** Accept and confront the reality of the situation.
★ **Have faith** Believe that life is worth living.
★ **Take action** Commit to goals and action.
★ **Find your Aha!** Discover the meaning and significance of the situation and of yourself.
★ **Reflect** Learn from the processes above.

Psychologists Tedeschi and Calhoun, who have researched how people can be transformed after experiencing trauma, suggest that suffering can be an avenue for creating and changing our meaning in life along with the possibility of increased self-confidence and enhanced relationships.

Activities for finding meaning

> 'The least of things with a meaning is worth more in life than the greatest of things without it.'
>
> Carl Jung, *Modern Man in Search of Soul*

Getting started

As we've seen, meaning has three different elements: feeling that we, and what we do, matter in some way; our life story and understanding of how the different parts of our life fit together; and having purpose – our over-arching mission and aims for our life, from which we can develop goals. We've also covered how finding meaning in our lives is personal and is different for each of us. Our strengths, talents, interests, circumstances, experiences and dreams are all individual. Of course, there are some common areas of life that many of us say are important, but how we each interpret these and how they manifest in our lives will vary.

What is the same for all of us is that our time and energy are limited. Being clear on our main sources of meaning helps us to allocate limited time and other resources appropriately, making sure we're giving attention to our most important life priorities among all the other day-to-day demands. Knowing what really matters for us in our lives in the long term helps us to prioritise and make choices in the short term and it can help to keep things in perspective.

Finding meaning usually takes both reflection and action. You can use a logical, analytical approach or simply what feels right for you. Often a mix of the two works the best. Some forms of therapy include a specific focus on this. Life-coaching can help too, and there's a lot that you can do for yourself.

As yet, psychological research hasn't thrown up many activities that help us find meaning. That's because as an area of study it's relatively new.

So the activities below are based on ideas from science, but they have not been specifically scientifically tested. You may not need to do all of them, but each one could offer you different insights and help you to identify cross-cutting themes. They'll help you reflect on your past and present and think about the future, so that you can become clearer on what meaning means for you and craft your purpose in life. Over the next few days, weeks or months, why not set aside some time when you can find a quiet space to work through a few (or all) of these activities, capturing your thoughts in your notebook as you do.

1 Points of meaning in your life

At the start of Chapter 9 (see page 270), I asked you to write about a time when you genuinely felt at your best. As you reflect over your life, other times and stories will stand out as having been important in shaping who you are and what you value – perhaps times, experiences or people that really helped you gain insight into yourself and positive growth. These may be:

High points When you've felt really fulfilled, at your best or when you successfully met a big challenge.

Low points Times of struggle, pain or suffering.

Turning points Where you've faced an important dilemma/had to make major choices.

Influence points Time(s) when someone had a great influence on you.

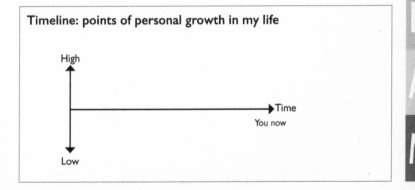

Timeline: points of personal growth in my life

How to do it

Put all the points of meaning you can think of on a timeline (see page 315). Plot times that stand out, whether these are as an adult or as a child. Then pick three – what did you learn? What impact did they each have on your life from that point? How do they influence you now? How will they help you grow in the future?

2 Writing your own obituary

Reading obituaries can be inspirational as they are usually interesting accounts of lives lived fully and time used well. Often there's a clear story of the person's strengths and talents, what mattered to them and how they used those to shape their lives and make the most of opportunities, and finally what legacy they left.

Writing an obituary may seem morbid, but it is a great way of focusing on what's important to you, how you want to make a difference and what you really want to achieve. The one certainty we all share in life is that one day it will end, yet many of us live as though time is infinite and put off deciding what really matters most.

How to do it

Imagine you've reached a ripe old age and lived a rich, fulfilling life. Think about what you would like to be written in your obituary. What positive legacy would you like to leave? Spend time writing, without censuring yourself. For example:

★ How would you like those closest to you to remember you?
  • What would they know and value about you, what strengths would they have seen you display?
  • What would they say about your passions and interests?
  • How have you impacted your loved ones' lives?
★ How have you impacted your community?
★ How would you have made a difference through your work?
★ How have you influenced or inspired those around you?

Spend as much time as you want to. Then put the obituary away for a day or two before reviewing it. Having reflected consciously or subconsciously, think about whether there's anything you'd add or change.

Having thought about how you'd like to be remembered and the legacy you'd leave, how might this influence your current and future priorities/goals? Keep your obituary somewhere safe and review it yearly. How have you made progress towards your legacy? Is there anything you'd add/change as your life unfolds?

3 Discover your real priorities

This activity will help you identify what your life aims are in different areas of your life. Prioritise which of those are the most important and then compare that to what's actually taking priority for you currently. If you have completed the 'Write your obituary' activity before doing this one, you will find this will help you develop more detailed life aims.

How to do it

There are five steps to this activity. They need to be done in order.

A Your meaning ranking

Which are the most important sources of meaning in your life? The list below is of typical things that people identify as priorities/sources of meaning. Reflect on the list. You can interpret the areas in any way that makes sense to you. Write down a ranking of these items in order of importance in terms of your priorities for meaning and fulfillment. Rank the most important as number 1, the next-most important as number 2, etc. Put each one in order of importance.

★ Which are your top seven priority areas? These are what most matters to you – your essentials for meaning.

★ Which are your bottom seven? These are the things you'd be most willing to forgo in order to focus on your priorities.

Life priority areas		
Achievement	How I feel about myself	Personal growth
Children	Influence	Play and leisure
Community	Interests and hobbies	Professional growth
Creativity	Learning	Relatives and friends
Health and fitness	Making a social difference	Romantic partner/spouse
Helping others	Money	Spirituality/religion/faith
Home/where I live	Nature/natural environment	Work

Informed by: Frisch (2005), Schnell (2011), Burton & Wedemeyer (2002), Shin & Steger (2014)

★ The middle seven are the 'nice-to-haves' in terms of meaning. They may be important for maintaining life (such as earning money). It's important that these don't take all your energy and attention away from your top seven.

B 'Private Detective' ranking

Imagine you've hired a private detective to observe you in your daily life for a month. You've asked him/her to find out how you spend your time and rank the priority areas based on this, ranking the area receiving most attention and focus = 1, next-highest = 2, etc.

C Priorities in action check

Now compare your ranking in step A to that in step B – how do they compare? Are your most important priority areas receiving sufficient focus? Are you spending too much time on areas that aren't meaningful? There are things we have to do that take up more time than we might like – usually work or running a home. But being clearer about what matters most means we can start to plan for them. We may also find ways to craft what we 'have' to do to make that more meaningful.

D Your top long-term aims

For each of your top seven areas, write down your long-term aim for that area. A simple sentence is enough. Examples of long-term aims could be:

★ **Romantic partner** *To keep my relationship fresh and alive by spending time with each other doing things we both care about.*

★ **Work** *To have a job that uses my strengths, where it makes a clear difference.*

★ **How I feel about myself** *I want to be less shy and develop confidence in sharing ideas and be more assertive about things that matter for me.*

★ **Money** *I don't want earning money to dominate my life, but it is important. I'd like to earn enough to be able to live near decent schools, not have to worry about paying the bills and have enough to have fun with my kids.*

E Meaningful goals

What ideas for goals do you now have? How and when will you give more time and attention to your top priority areas? For example, if physical health is important, are you exercising as much as you'd like? What goal could you set to do this?

MARK FINDS HIS REAL PRIORITIES

'I first did the "discover your real priorities" activity ten years ago and found it difficult to choose between many of the items. I spent a long time trying to think through what mattered most and I kept revising my list. I decided my 'non-negotiables' were personal growth, my partner, relatives and friends, making a social difference and health. I was pleased with my list. But then I did the detective ranking and had to admit that the way I was living was out of balance with my priorities. I was working long hours as a stressed-out consultant and the detective would have probably concluded my priorities were work, money, influence and professional growth!

Being forced to see this inconsistency so clearly shook me and was a big factor in deciding to make a career change and focus on finding a job that made a positive contribution. With hindsight, doing this exercise helped me make some of the best and most important decisions I have ever made. I've also repeated the exercise every few years, which has been really helpful.'

4 A picture says a thousand words

This activity is based on an approach to identifying and clarifying our sources of meaning, recently piloted by Dr Michael Steger. It's using photography, thinking visually about what pictures to take and what these images represent for you. It may help you access different, richer thoughts and feelings than writing alone.

How to do it

A Over the next week take a maximum of twelve pictures that visually show what makes your life meaningful. These could be pictures of actual things, or people themselves, or of something that represents them – perhaps an object, souvenir or work of art: anything that is an important source of meaning for you.

B At the end of the week download/print your twelve photos and either:

- Write a short description for each one of what it represents for you and how it adds meaning in your life. Or:
- Find a trusted friend or partner who'll listen as you explain why you chose each picture and how it adds meaning to your life. Their role

is to listen, not to judge, comment or add their opinion! How they
interpret the picture doesn't matter – it's about what it means to you.

C When you've reflected on each picture, put them in order of
importance. Make a note of your ranking.

D What does this make you think about your purpose, priorities and goals?

5 Your one sentence

I love this activity from Dan Pink in his book *Drive*. He tells a story about
some advice apparently offered to US President John F. Kennedy by Claire
Booth Luce. Concerned that Kennedy's focus was spread too thinly, she
told him that a great person can be summed up in one sentence, giving
the examples of previous US Presidents, such as Franklin Roosevelt:
'He lifted us out of a great depression and helped us win the war.'

Our priorities may be different, but this is a great activity to get us to
really focus. It can help us avoid the risk that our lives are more of a
'muddled paragraph' than a crisp, clear single sentence!

How to do it

Doing some of the other activities above is best, but it's not essential.
Here are two examples: *'He brought up two kids to be caring adults and made
his neighbourhood a friendlier place.'*/*'Her artwork made people stop and think.'*

What's your one sentence?

★ Reflect on the activities and pause points in this chapter (and even
those from elsewhere in this book) and write your sentence in your
notebook or journal. You may want to keep it somewhere you'll see it
regularly – to help keep you focused on what's most important for you.

To sum up

Here are five key points to take away from this chapter:

1 Having a sense of meaning in our lives is an important foundation for
happiness and a fulfilling life and helps us to be resilient.

2 According to psychology, a sense of meaning is made up of three parts:
feeling that we and what we do matter in some way; understanding
how the different parts of our life fit together; and having a purpose in
life from which we can develop our goals.

3 What we feel is meaningful in our lives is very individual and we have to find it for ourselves. Sources might include our relationships with others, especially those close to us; a religious faith; our work; creativity; our hobbies or nature. Finding meaning in difficult times can be an important source too.

4 The richest sources of meaning tend to be bigger than or beyond ourselves, where we make a difference to something or someone else, e.g. helping others or working for a good cause or doing something that benefits future generations.

5 Feeling that our life lacks meaning is associated with lower well-being. But meaning isn't something that comes to us – we have to actively seek it. Through a process of reflection and activity, there is a range of different actions to take to help us understand what's most meaningful to us and clarify our purpose in life. This helps us shape our goals and make choices about what we do and how we use our time.

Connections to other Keys

Other Keys you might like to explore in connection with Meaning:

★ **GIVING** (See page 10)
Doing something for other people or contributing to a cause can be a rich source of meaning.

★ **RELATING** (See page 36)
Our relationships with other people, especially those close to us, is one of the most important sources of meaning.

★ **TRYING OUT** (See page 144)
Trying things out is a good way to explore what's meaningful for us. Learning and developing our interests, passions and creativity are all potential sources of meaning too.

★ **DIRECTION** (See page 170)
Knowing what's meaningful to us and getting clear on our purpose in life is the foundation from which we can set fulfilling goals.

★ **ACCEPTANCE** (See page 266)
Using our strengths in our work and to help others can make these more meaningful and it can help us to find a calling too.

Further reading and resources

I hope this book has inspired you to take action to increase your own and others' happiness. If it's sparked curiosity to find out more here are suggested evidence-based books, along with other resources.

Action for Happiness
Please visit Action for Happiness – www. actionforhappiness.org. It's packed with more ideas and resources. You can become a member of the Action for Happiness movement (it's free), take part in one of our courses, join our active social media community and lots more.

Chapter 1 GIVING
Altruism: The Power of Compassion to Change Yourself and the World, Matthieu Ricard
Give and Take: A Revolutionary Aapproach to Success, Adam Grant
Happy Money: The Science of Smarter Spending, Elizabeth Dunn & Michael Norton

Chapter 2 RELATING
Connected: The Surprising Power of Our Social Networks, Nicholas Christakis & James Fowler.
The Relationship Cure: A 5-Step Guide to Strengthening Your Marriage, Family and Friendships, John Gottman & Joan DeClaire
The Seven Principles for Making Marriages Work, John Gottman & Nan Silver
Love 2.0: How Our Supreme Emotion Affects Everything we Think, Do, Feel and Become, Barbara Fredrickson
Non-Violent Communication: A Language of Life, Marshall Rosenburg

Chapter 3 EXERCISING
Spark! How Exercise Will Improve the Performance of Your Brain, John Ratey & Eric Hagerman
Go Wild: Free Your Body and Mind from the Afflictions of Civilization, John Ratey & Richard Manning
Eat, Move, Sleep, Tom Rath
The Blue Zones: 9 Lessons for Living Long, Dan Buettner

Chapter 4 AWARENESS
Mindfulness: A Practical Guide to Find Peace in a Frantic World, Mark Williams & Danny Penman
Real Happiness: The Power of Meditation, Sharon Salzberg
Full Catastrophe Living (revised edition): How to Cope with Stress, Pain and Illness Using Mindfulness Meditation, Jon Kabat-Zinn
Mindfulness in Eight Weeks, Michael Chaskalson
Online mindfulness-based resources: bemindful.co.uk – the UK's Mental Health Foundation's mindfulness website. It has a four-week online course, which you can trial for free. For people in the UK there's also an interactive map to help you find a local qualified mindfulness teacher

www.headspace.com – a popular app including animated guides.
www.oxfordmindfulness.org – a leading centre for mindfulness teacher training and research. Includes a good practice guide to finding a teacher, many links to mindfulness-related resources and a free, guided 3-minute breathing space video by Dr Mark Williams, the UK's leading Mindfulness expert.

Chapter 5 TRYING OUT
Curious? Discover the Missing Ingredient to a Fulfilling Life, Todd Kashdan
Flow: The Psychology of Optimal Experience (published in UK as *Flow: The Classic Work on how to Achieve Happiness*), Mihalyi Csikszentmihalyi
Mindset: The New Psychology of Success, Carol Dweck
Mindfulness, Ellen Langer
Flex: Do Something Different, Ben C. Fletcher & Karen Pine
Wired to Create: Discover the 10 Things Great Artists, Writers and Innovators do Differently, Scott Barry Kaufman & Carolyn Gregoire

Chapter 6 DIRECTION
Making Hope Happen: Create the Future You Want for Yourself and Others, Shane Lopez
Succeed: How we can Reach Our Goals, Heidi Grant Halvorson
Rethinking Positive Thinking: Inside the New Science of Motivation, Gabriele Oettingen

Chapter 7 RESILIENCE
Resilience: the Science of Mastering Life's Greatest Challenges, Steven Southwick & Dennis Charney
The Resilience Factor: Seven Keys to Finding Your Inner Strength and Overcoming Life's Hurdles, Karen Reivich & Andrew Shatté
The Upside of Stress: Why Stress is Good for You (and how to get good at it), Kelly McGonigal
What Abi Taught Us, Lucy Hone

Chapter 8 EMOTIONS
Emotions Revealed: Understanding Faces and Feelings, Paul Ekman
Emotional Intelligence: Why it can matter More Than IQ, Daniel Goleman
Positivity: Groundbreaking Research Reveals how to Embrace the Hidden Strength of Positive Emotions, Overcome Negativity, and Thrive, Barbara Fredrickson
The Emotional Life of your Brain: How its Unique Patterns Affect the Way You Think, Feel and Live – and How You Can Change Them, Richard Davidson & Sharon Begley
The Power of Negative Emotion: How Anger, Guilt and Self-doubt are Essential to Success and Fulfillment, Todd Kashdan & Robert Biswas-Diener
Gratitude Works! A 21-Day Program for Creating Emotional Prosperity, Robert Emmons

Chapter 9 ACCEPTANCE
The Compassionate Mind, Paul Gilbert
Self Compassion: Stop Beating Yourself Up and Leave Insecurity Behind, Kristen Neff
Mindfulness and Character Strengths: A Practical Guide to Flourishing, Ryan Niemiec
Positive Psychology at the Movies 2: Using Films to Build Character Strengths and Well-being, Ryan Niemiec and Danny Wedding
Average to A+: Realising Strengths in Yourself and Others, Alex Linley
StrengthsFinder 2.0, Tom Rath
VIA Character Strengths survey available at www.viacharacter.org

Chapter 10 MEANING
Man's Search for Meaning, Viktor Frankl
Drive: The surprising truth about what motivates us, Daniel Pink
Force for Good: The Dalai Lama's vision for our world, Daniel Goleman
The Job Crafting™ Exercise from the Centre for Positive Organisations: www.jobcrafting.org -

General
Happiness: Lessons from a new science, Action for Happiness founder, Richard Layard
Flourish: A visionary new understanding of happiness and well-being, Martin Seligman

Need More Help and Support?
Any of us could experience times when we feel stuck. At those times we can seek help and support from:
Medical or Health Services: your doctor or local health practitioner – they should be able to refer you to other support as required. You can also search online. For example in the UK www.nhs. uk has lots of guidance and advice and you can find your local Improving Access to Psychological Therapies (IAPT) service.
Mental Health charities: in many countries there are not-for-profit organisations that provide dedicated support and advice for people dealing with mental health challenges through their websites and phone lines. For example in the UK – organisations like MIND, Rethink, the Mental Health Foundation and Sane.
Helplines: if you are experiencing very dark times then call a confidential helpline where you'll find someone friendly who can listen to your problems and help you. For example, in the UK and elsewhere – organisations like the Samaritans and Nightline. The Samaritans 24-hour helpline in the UK is: 116 123 (UK) / 116 123 (Republic of Ireland).

The Action for Happiness website has more information on how and where you can get support if you're struggling: www.actionforhappiness.org/unhappy

References: The evidence

This book is based on over 420 scientific research articles, papers, reviews and books (listed below). A full, specific citation listing is available at: www.actionforhappiness.org/10-keys-references

INTRODUCTION

Aked, J., Marks, N., Cordon, C. & Thompson, S. (2008). Five Ways to Wellbeing: A report presented to the Foresight Project on communicating the evidence base for improving people's well-being. Centre for Well-being, nef (new economics foundation). www.fivewaystowellbeing.org

Aknin, L. B., Dunn, E. W. & Norton, M. I. (2011). Happiness Runs in a Circular Motion: Evidence for a positive feedback loop between prosocial spending and happiness. Journal of Happiness Studies, 13(2), 347-355

De Neve, J. E., Diener, E., Tay, L. & Xuereb, C. (2013). The Objective Benefits of Subjective Well-being. World Happiness Report.

Dodge, R., Daly, A. P., Huyton, J. & Sanders, L. D. (2012). The Challenge of Defining Wellbeing. International Journal of Wellbeing, 2(3).

Foresight Mental Capital and Wellbeing Project (2008). Final Report. The UK Government Office for Science, London

Fowler, J. H. & Christakis, N. A. (2008). Dynamic Spread of Happiness in a Large Social Network: Longitudinal analysis over 20 years in the Framingham Heart Study. British Medical Journal, 337, a2338.

Hone, L. C., Jarden, A., Schofield, G. M. & Duncan, S. (2014). Measuring Flourishing: The impact of operational definitions on the prevalence of high levels of well-being. International Journal of Wellbeing, 4(1).

Ryff, C. D. (2014). Psychological Well-being Revisited: Advances in the Science and Practice of Eudaimonia. Psychotherapy and Psychosomatics, 83(1), 10-28.

Seligman, M. E. (2007). Authentic Happiness: Using the new positive psychology to realize your potential for lasting fulfillment. Nicholas Brearley

Seligman, M.E.P. (2011). Flourish: A visionary new understanding of happiness and well-being. Free Press

Chapter 1 GIVING

Aknin, L. B., Dunn, E. W. & Norton, M. I. (2011). Happiness Runs in a Circular Motion: Evidence for a positive feedback loop between pro-social spending and happiness. Journal of Happiness Studies, 13(2), 347-355

Aknin, L. B., Dunn, E. W., Whillans, A., Grant, A. M. & Norton, M. I. (2013). Making a Difference Matters: Impact unlocks the emotional benefits of charitable giving. Journal of Economic Behavior and Organization, 88, 90-95

Aknin, L. B., Sandstrom, G. M., Dunn, E. W. & Norton, M. I. (2011). It's the Recipient that Counts: Spending money on strong social ties leads to greater happiness than spending on weak social ties. PLoS ONE, 6(2), e17018

Aknin, L.B., Barrington-Leigh, C.P., Dunn, E.W., Helliwell, J.F., Burns, J. Biswas-Diener, R., Kemeza,I., Nyende, P., Ashton-James, C. & Norton M.I. (2013). Pro-social Spending and Well-Being: Cross-Cultural Evidence for a Psychological Universal. Journal of Personality and Social Psychology 104, 4 635-652

Algoe, S. B. & Haidt, J. (2009). Witnessing Excellence in Action: the 'other-praising' emotions of elevation, gratitude, and admiration. Journal of Positive Psychology, 4(2), 105-127

Anik, L,. Aknin, L. B., Norton, M. I., Dunn, E. W. (2009). Feeling Good about Giving: The Benefits (and Costs) of Self-Interested Charitable Behavior. Harvard Business School Working Paper, 10-012

Borgonovi, F. (2008). Doing Well by Doing Good. The Relationship Between Formal Volunteering and Self-Reported Health and Happiness. Social Science & Medicine, 66(11), 2321-2334

Brown, S. L., Nesse, R. M., Vinokur, A. D. & Smith, D. M. (2003). Providing Social Support May be More Beneficial than Receiving it: results from a prospective study of mortality. Psychological Science (Wiley-Blackwell), 14(4), 320-327

Brown, S. L., Smith, D. M., Schulz, R., Kabeto, M. U., Ubel, P. A., Poulin, M., Yi, J., Kim, C. & Langa, K. M. (2009). Caregiving Behavior is Associated With Decreased Mortality Risk. Psychological Science; Apr2009, 20(4), 488-494

Brown, W.M., Consedine, N.S., Magai, C. (2005). Altruism Relates to Health in an Ethnically Diverse Sample of Older Adults. Journal of Gerontology: Psychological Sciences, 60B, 143-152

Darley, J. M. & Batson, C. D. (1973). From Jerusalem to Jericho: A study of situational and dispositional variables in helping behavior. Journal of Personality and Social Psychology, 27, 100-108

Dunn, E. W., Aknin, L. B. & Norton, M. I. (2014). Pro-social Spending and Happiness Using Money to Benefit Others Pays Off. Current Directions in Psychological Science, 23(1), 41-47

Dunn, E. W., Gilbert, D. T. & Wilson, T. D. (2011). If Money Doesn't Make You Happy, Then You Probably Aren't Spending It Right. Journal of Consumer Psychology, 21(2), 115-125

Dunn, E.W., Aknin, L.B. & Norton, M.I. (2008). Spending Money on Others Promotes Happiness. Science, 319, 1687-1688

Fehr, E. & Camerer, C. F. (2007). Social Neuro-economics: The Neural Circuitry of Social Preferences. Trends in Cognitive Sciences, 11(10), 419-427

Fowler, J.H. & Christakis, N.A. (2010) Cooperative Behavior Cascades in Human Social Networks. Proceedings of the National Academy of Sciences of the United States of America. 107(12), 5334-5338

Frimer, J. A., Walker, L. J., Dunlop, W. L., Lee, B. & Riches, A. (2011). The Integration of Agency and Communion in Moral Personality: Evidence of enlightened self-interest. Journal of Personality and Social Psychology, 101, 149-163

Grant, A. (2013). Give and Take: A revolutionary approach to success. Hachette UK

Greenfield, E. A. & Marks, N. F. (2004). Formal Volunteering as a Protective Factor for Older Adults' Psychological Well-being. The Journals of Gerontology Series B: Psychological Sciences and Social Sciences, 59(5), S258-S264

Harbaugh, W. T., Mayr, U. & Burghart, D. R. (2007). Neural Responses to Taxation and Voluntary Giving Reveal Motives for Charitable Donations. Science, 316(5831), 1622-1625

Harlow R.E., Cantor N. (1996). Still Participating After All These Years: A study of life task participation in later life. Journal of Personality and Social Psychology 71: 1235-1249

Luks, A. (1988). Helper's High: Volunteering makes people feel good, physically and emotionally. And like 'runner's calm,' it's probably good for your health. Psychology Today, 22(10), 34-42

Lyubomirsky, S, Sheldon, K M, & Schkade, D. (2005). Pursuing Happiness: The Architecture of Sustainable Change. Review of General Psychology, 9(2), 111-131

Lyubomirsky, S. (2008). The How of Happiness: A New Approach to Getting the Life You Want. Penguin

Lyubomirsky, S., King, L. & Diener, E. (2005). The Benefits of Frequent Positive Affect: Does Happiness Lead to Success? Psychological Bulletin, 131, 803-855

Midlarsky, E. (1991). Helping as Coping. Pro-social Behavior: Review of Personality and Social Psychology, 12, 238-264

Mogilner,C., Chance, Z. & Norton, M.I. (2012). Giving Time Gives You Time. Psychological Science, 23(10), 1233-1238

Moll, J., Krueger, F., Zahn, R., Pardini, M., de Oliveira-Souza, R. & Grafman, J. (2006). Human Fronto-Mesolimbic Networks Guide Decisions About Charitable Donation. Proceedings of the National Academy of Sciences of the United States of America, 103(42), 15623-15628

Pay-it-Forward http://www. catherineryanhyde.com/pay-it-forward

Piliavin, J. (2003). Doing Well by Doing Good: Benefits for the benefactor. In C. M. Keyes, J. Haidt, C. M. Keyes, J. Haidt (Eds.) , Flourishing: Positive psychology and the life well-lived (pp.

227-247). Washington, DC US: American Psychological Association

Piliavin, J. & Siegl, E. (2007). Health Benefits of Volunteering in the Wisconsin Longitudinal Study. Journal of Health & Social Behavior, 48(4), 450-464

Post, S. G. (2005). Altruism, Happiness and Health: It's good to be good. International Journal of Behavioral Medicine, 12(2), 66-77

Ricard, M. (2015). Altruism: The power of compassion to change yourself and the world. Atlantic Books, London. pp77-81

Rudd, M., Aaker, J. & Norton, M. I. (2014). Getting the Most Out of Giving: Concretely framing a pro-social goal maximizes happiness. Journal of Experimental Social Psychology, 54, 11-24

Ryan, R. M. & Deci, E. L. (2000). Self-determination Theory and the Facilitation Of Intrinsic Motivation, Social Development, and Well-being. American Psychologist, 55, 68-78

Transport for London. www.tfl.gov.uk/corporate/about-tfl/what-we-do/london-underground/facts-and-figures Accessed 3 June 2015

Vaillant, G.E. (2008). Spiritual Evolution: How we are Wired for Faith, Hope and Love. Broadway Books

Warburton, J. (2006). Volunteering in Later Life: is it good for your health? Journal for the Institute of Volunteering Research, 8, 3-15

Weinstein, N and Ryan, R.M. (2010). When Helping Helps: Autonomous Motivation for Pro-social Behavior and its Influence on Well-Being for the Helper and Recipient. Journal of Personality and Social Psychology, 98, No. 2, 222–244

Wilson, J. (2000). Volunteering. Annual Review of Sociology, 26, 215

Yaffe, K. (2009) Predictors of maintaining cognitive function in older adults: The Health ABC Study, Neurology, 72, 2029-2035

Chapter 2 RELATING

Aked, J., Marks, N., Cordon, C. & Thompson, S. (2008). Five Ways to Wellbeing: A report presented to the Foresight Project on communicating the evidence base for improving people's well-being. Centre for Well-being, nef (the new economics foundation)

Allen J. (2008). Older People and Wellbeing. Institute for Public Policy Research. London

Bacon,N., Brophy, M., Nguni, N., Mulgan, G. & Shandro, A. (2010). The State of Happiness: Can Public Policy Shape People's Wellbeing and Resilience? London: Young Foundation

Baumeister, R.F. & Leary, M. (1995). The Need to Belong: Desire for Interpersonal Attachments as a Fundamental Human Motivation. Psychological Bulletin, 117, 497-529

Berkman, L.F. and Syme, S.F. (1979) Social Networks, Host Resistance, and Mortality: a nine-year follow-up study of Alameda county residents, American Journal of Epidemiology, 109, 186-204

Brugha, T. S., Weich, S., Singleton, N., Lewis, G., Bebbington, P. E., Jenkins, R. & Meltzer, H. (2005). Primary Group Size, Social Support, Gender and Future Mental Health Status: A prospective study of people living in private households throughout Great Britain. Psychological Medicine, 35(05), 705-714

Buonfino, A. & Thomson, L. (2007). Belonging in Contemporary Britain. The Commission on Integration and Cohesion, Department of Communities and Local Government, Government of Great Britain

Cacioppo, J. T & Cacioppo, S. (2014). Social Relationships and Health: The Toxic Effects of Perceived Social Isolation. Social and Personality Psychology Compass, 8(2), 58-72

Cacioppo J. T., Hughes M. E., Waite L. J., Hawkley L. C., Thisted R. A. (2008), Loneliness as a Specific Risk Factor for Depressive Symptoms: cross-sectional and longitudinal analyses, Psychology and Aging 2006 Mar; 21(1):140-51

Chartered Institute of Personnel and Development (2014). Absence Management Report. London

Cohen S. (2004). Social Relationships and Health. American Psychologist 59 (8):676-684

Compton, W.C. & Hoffman, E. (2013) Positive Psychology: The Science of Happiness and Flourishing. Wadsworth CENGAGE Learning

De Neve, J. E., Diener, E., Tay, L. & Xuereb, C. (2013). The Objective Benefits of Subjective Well-being. World Happiness Report

De Silva, M. J., McKenzie, K., Harpham, T. & Huttly, S. R. (2005). Social Capital and Mental Illness: a systematic review. Journal of Epidemiology and Community Health, 59. 619-627

Deci, E. D. (1995) Why We Do What We Do. Penguin

Diener, E. & Biswas-Diener, R. (2008) Happiness: Unlocking the Mysteries of Psychological Wealth. Blackwell

Driver and Gottman (2004) cited in Meunier, V. & Baker, W. Positive Couple Relationships: The Evidence for Long Lasting Relationship Satisfaction and Happiness in In Roffey, S. (Ed.), (2012) Positive Relationships: Evidence-based practice from across the world, Springer

Dutton, J. E. (2003). Energize Your Workplace: How to create and sustain high-quality connections at work. John Wiley & Sons

Flückiger, C. & Grosse Holtforth, M. (2008). Focusing the Therapist's Attention on the Patient's Strengths: A Preliminary Study to Foster a Mechanism of Change in Outpatient Psychotherapy. Journal Of Clinical Psychology, 64, 876-890

Fowler, J. H. & Christakis, N. A. (2008). Dynamic Spread of Happiness in a Large Social Network: longitudinal analysis over 20 years in the Framingham Heart Study. British Medical Journal, 337, a2338

Fredrickson, B.L. (2013). Love 2.0 – How our supreme emotion affects everything we think, do, feel and become. Hudson Street

Gable, S. L. & Gosnell, C. L. (2013). Approach and avoidance behavior in interpersonal relationships. Emotion Review, 5(3), 269-274; Umberson, D. & Montez, J. K. (2010). Social Relationships and Health A Flashpoint for Health Policy. Journal Of Health and Social Behavior, 51(1 suppl), S54-S66.

Gable, S. L., Gonzaga, G. & Strachman, A. (2006). Will you be there for me when things go right? Supportive responses to positive event disclosures. Journal of Personality and Social Psychology, 91, 904-917.

Gable, S. L., Gosnell, C. L., Maisel, N. C. & Strachman, A. (2012). Safely Testing the Alarm: Close others' responses to personal positive events. Journal of Personality and Social Psychology, 103(6), 963

Gottman, J. & DeClaire, J. (2001). The Relationship Cure: a 5 step guide to strengthening your marriage, family and friendships. Three Rivers Press

Gottman, J.M. & Silver, N (2000). The Seven Principles for Making Marriages Work. Orion

Hasson, U. (2010) I Can Make Your Brain Look Like Mine. Harvard Business Review

Hasson, U., Ghazanfar, A. A., Galantucci, B., Garrod, S. & Keysers, C. (2012). Brain-to-Brain Coupling: A mechanism for creating and sharing a social world. Trends in Cognitive Science, 16(2): 114-121

Holt-Lunstad, J, Smith, T. B., Baker, M., Harris, T. & Stephenson, D (2015). Loneliness and Social Isolation as Risk Factors for Mortality: A Meta-Analytic Review. Perspectives on Psychological Science, 10: 227-237

Holt-Lunstad, J., Smith, T. B. & Layton, J. B. (2010). Social Relationships and Mortality Risk: a meta-analytic review. PLoS medicine, 7(7), e1000316

Huppert, F.A. (2008). Psychological Wellbeing: Evidence regarding its causes and consequences. State of the Science Review: SR-X2, UK Government Foresight Project, Mental Capital and Wellbeing

Kitchen, S., Michaelson, J., Wood, N., and John, P. (2006a) 2005. Citizenship Survey Cross Cutting Themes Report. London: Department for Communities and Local Government

Kok, B. E., Coffey, K. A., Cohn, M. A., Catalino, L. I., Vacharkulksemsuk, T., Algoe, S. B., Brantley, M. & Fredrickson, B. L. (2013). How Positive Emotions Build Physical Health: Perceived positive social connections account for the upward spiral between positive emotions and vagal tone. Psychological

Science, 24, 1123-1132

Layard, R. (2005). Happiness: Lessons from a New Science. London: Penguin

Majors, K, Friendships: The Power of the Positive Alliance. In Roffey, S. (Ed), (2013). Positive Relationships: Evidence Based Practice from across the World

McCarty & McCarthy (2009) cited in Meunier, V. & Baker, W. Positive Couple Relationships: The evidence for long lasting relationship satisfaction and happiness in Roffey, S. (Ed), (2013). Positive Relationships: Evidence Based Practice from across the World, Springer

Pahl, R. & Spencer, L. (2010). Family, Friends, and Personal Communities: Changing Models-in-the-Mind. Journal of Family Theory & Review, 2(3), 197-210

Peterson, C. (2006). A Primer in Positive Psychology. OUP

Peterson, C. (2013). Pursuing the Good Life. OUP

Putnam, R. (2000). Bowling Alone: The collapse and decline of American community. Simon & Schuster

Rath, T. & Harter, J, (2010). Wellbeing – The Five Essential Elements. Gallup Press

Rosenburg, M.B. (2003). Non-Violent Communication – A Language of Life: A detailed guide to developing and using this essential skill. Puddle Dance Press

Ryan, R. M. & Deci, E. D. (2001). On Happiness and Human Potentials: A review of research on hedonic and eudaimonic well-being. Annual Review of Psychology, 52, 141-66

Ryan, R. M. & Deci, E. L. (2000). Self-Determination Theory and the Facilitation of Intrinsic Motivation, Social Development and Well-being. American Psychologist, 55(1), 68

Ryff, C. (1989). Happiness is Everything, or Is It? Explorations on the meaning of psychological well-being. Journal of Personality and Social Psychology, 6. 1069-81

Scott, S. (2015). Why We Laugh. TED. www.ted.com/talks/sophie_scott_why_we_laugh?

Seligman, M.E.P. (2011). Flourish: A visionary new understanding of happiness and well-being. Free Press

Stafford, M., McMunn, A., Zaninotto, P. & Nazroo, J. (2011). Positive and Negative Exchanges in Social Relationships as Predictors of Depression: evidence from the English Longitudinal Study of Aging. Journal of Aging and Health, 23(4), 607-628

Stephens, G. J, Silbert, L. J. & Hasson, U. (2010). Speaker–Listener Neural Coupling Underlies Successful Communication. Proceedings of the National Academy of Sciences, 107(32), 14425-14430

Umberson, D. & Montez, J. K. (2010). Social Relationships and Health a Flashpoint for Health Policy. Journal of Health and Social Behavior, 51(1 suppl), S54-S66

Wild, B., Erb, M., Eyb, M., Bartels, M. & Grodd, W. (2003). Why are smiles contagious? An fMRI study of the interaction between perception of facial affect and facial movements. Psychiatry Research: Neuroimaging, 123(1), 17-36

Chapter 3 EXERCISING

Ahlskog, J. E., Geda, Y. E., Graff-Radford, N. R. & Petersen, R. C. (2011, September). Physical Exercise as a Preventive or Disease-Modifying Treatment of Dementia and Brain Aging. In Mayo Clinic Proceedings (Vol. 86, No. 9, pp. 876-884). Elsevier

Biddle, S. J. & Asare, M. (2011). Physical Activity and Mental Health in Children and Adolescents: a review of reviews. British Journal of Sports Medicine, 45, 886-895

Biddle, S. J. H. & Mutrie, N. (2007). Psychology of Physical Activity: Determinants, well-being and interventions. 2nd edition. Routledge

Blumenthal, J. et al (1999) cited in Ratey, J. & Hagerman, E. (2008). Spark! – How exercise will improve the performance of your brain. Quercus

Booth, F. W., Roberts, C. K. & Laye, M. J. (2012). Lack of Exercise is a Major Cause of Chronic Diseases. Comprehensive Physiology. 2(2): 1143-1211

Bramble D. M., Lieberman D. E. Endurance Running and the Evolution of Homo. Nature 2004; 432: 345-52

Buckworth, J, Dishman, R. O'Connor, P. & Tomporowski, P. (2007). Exercise Psychology Second Edition. Human Kinetics

Carek, P. J., Laibstain, S. E. & Carek, S. M. (2011). Exercise for the Treatment of Depression and Anxiety. The International Journal of Psychiatry in Medicine, 41: 15-28

Colcombe, S. & Kramer, A. F. (2003). Fitness Effects on the Cognitive Function of Older Adults a Meta-Analytic Study. Psychological science, 14(2), 125-130

Costa, G. (2003). Shift Work and Occupational Medicine: an overview. Occupational medicine, 53(2), 83-88

Crowley, C. & Lodge, H.S. (2007). Younger Next Year. Workman

Diamond, A. & Lee, K. (2011). Interventions Shown to Aid Executive Function Development in Children 4–12 Years Old . Science (New York, N.Y.),333(6045), 959-964. doi:10.1126/science.1204529

Drake, C. L., Roehrs, T., Richardson, G., Walsh, J. K. & Roth, T. (2004). Shift Work Sleep Disorder: prevalence and consequences beyond that of symptomatic day workers. Sleep, 27(8), 1453-1462

Dunstan, D. W., Howard, B., Healy, G. N. & Owen, N. (2012). Too Much Sitting: a health hazard. Diabetes Research and Clinical Practice, 97(3), 368-376

Ericsson, K. A., Krampe, R. T. & Tesch-Römer, C. (1993). The Role of Deliberate Practice in the Acquisition of Expert Performance. Psychological

Review, 100(3), 363. Cited in Rath, T. (2013) Eat, Move, Sleep: How Small Changes Lead to Big Changes. Missonday

Faulkner, Hefferon & Mutrie (2015). Putting Positive Psychology Into Motion Through Physical Activity. In Positive Psychology in Practice. Linley P.A. & Joseph, S. (Eds), second edition

Fowler, R. (2009). Lecture. University of Pennsylvania, Masters of Applied Positive Psychology programme

Germano, S. (2015) American Inactivity Level Is Highest Since 2007, Survey Finds. Wall Street Journal. www.wsj.com/articles/american-inactivity-level-is-highest-since-2007-survey-finds-1429796821

Griffiths, A., Kouvonen, A., Pentti, J., Oksanen, T., Virtanen, M., Salo, P., Vahtera, J. (2014). Association of Physical Activity With Future Mental Health in Older, Mid-Life and Younger Women. The European Journal of Public Health,24(5), 813-818

Hallgren, M., Kraepelien, M., Öjehagen, A., Lindefors, N., Zeebari, Z., Kaldo, V. & Forsell, Y. (2015). Physical Exercise and Internet-Based Cognitive Behavioural Therapy in the Treatment of Depression: Randomised controlled trial. The British Journal of Psychiatry, 207(3), 227-234

Harrington, J. M. (2001). Health effects of shift work and extended hours of work. Occupational and Environmental medicine, 58(1), 68-72

Harvard Health Publications. Harvard Medical School (2009). Newsletter - Sleep and Mental Health www.health.harvard.edu/newsletter_article/Sleep-and-mental-health

Hefferon, K. (2013). Positive Psychology and the Body: The Somatopsychic Side to Flourishing. McGraw Hill

Hillman, C. H., Erickson, K. I. & Kramer. A. F. (2008). Be Smart, Exercise your Heart: exercise effects on the brain and cognition. Nature Reviews Neuroscience, 9(1), 58-65

Hogan, C. L., Catalino, L. I., Mata, J. & Fredrickson, B. L. (2015). Beyond Emotional Benefits: Physical activity and sedentary behavior affect psychosocial resources through emotions. Psychology & Health, 30, 3, 354-369

Homan, K. J., & Tylka, T. L. (2014). Appearance-Based Exercise Motivation Moderates the Relationship Between Exercise Frequency and Positive Body Image. Body Image, 11(2), 101-108

Hopkins M. E., Davis F. C., Vantieghem M. R., Whalen, P. J. & Bucci D. J. (2012). Differential Effects of Acute And Regular Physical Exercise On Cognition And Affect Neuroscience 215 59-68

Howie, E. K. & Pate, R. R. (2012). Physical Activity and Academic Achievement in Children: A historical perspective. Journal of Sport and Health Science 1 160-169

Kelly, M. E., Loughrey, D., Lawlor, B. A.,

Robertson, I. H., Walsh, C. & Brennan, S. (2014). The Impact of Exercise on the Cognitive Functioning Of Healthy Older Adults: A systematic review and meta-analysis. Ageing research reviews, 16, 12-31

King,G.F. (2015). The Meaning of Light. Kinfolk Magazine

Mammen, G. & Faulkner, G. (2013). Physical Activity and the Prevention of Depression: a systematic review of prospective studies. American Journal of Preventive Medicine, 45(5), 649-657

Maurer, R. (2004). One Small Step Can Change Your Life: The Kaizen Way. New York, Workman Publishing Group

Mental Health Foundation (2006). Feeding Minds – The impact of food on mental health. www.mentalhealth.org.uk/publications/feeding-minds

Owen, N., Healy, G. N., Matthews, C. E. & Dunstan, D. W. (2010). Too Much Sitting: the population-health science of sedentary behavior. Exercise and sport sciences reviews, 38(3), 105

Petruzzello, S.J. (2012). The Ultimate Tranquilizer? Exercise and its influence on anxiety. In E.O Acevedo (Ed.) The Oxford Handbook of Exercise Psychology

Privitera, G. J., Antonelli, D. E. & Szal, A. L. (2014). An Enjoyable Distraction During Exercise Augments the Positive Effects of Exercise on Mood. Journal of sports science and medicine, 13(2), 266

Puig-Ribera, A., Martínez-Lemos, I., Giné-Garriga, M., González-Suárez, Á. M., Bort-Roig, J., Fortuño, J. & Gilson, N. D. (2015). Self-Reported Sitting Time and Physical Activity: interactive associations with mental well-being and productivity in office employees BMC Public Health, 15(1), 72

Raichlen, D. A. & Polk, J. D. (2013). Linking Brains and Brawn: exercise and the evolution of human neurobiology. Proceedings of the Royal Society of London B: Biological Sciences, 280 (1750)

Ratey, J. (2013). Lecture. MAPP Summit, University of Pennsylvania

Ratey, J. & Hagerman, E. (2008). Spark! – How exercise will improve the performance of your brain. Quercus

Ratey, J. & Manning, R. (2014). Go Wild: Free your body and mind from the afflictions of civilization. Little, Brown

Rath, T. & Hartner, J. (2010), Wellbeing: The Five Essential Elements. Gallup Press, New York

Rath, T. (2013). Eat, Move, Sleep: How Small Changes Lead to Big Changes. Missonday

Ruby, M. B., Dunn, E. W., Perrino, A., Gillis, R. & Viel, S. (2011). The invisible benefits of exercise. Health Psychology, 30(1), 67

Seaman, A. M (2012). Sleepy, Drunken Drivers Equally Dangerous: study www.reuters.com/article/2012/05/30/us-drunken-drivers-idUSBRE84T14W20120530

Segar, M. L. & Richardson, C. R. (2014). Prescribing Pleasure and Meaning:

cultivating walking motivation and maintenance. American journal of preventive medicine, 47(6), 838-841

Sibbold, J. S. & Berg, K.M. (2010). Mood Enhancement Persists for Up to 12 Hours Following Aerobic Exercise: A Pilot Study. Perceptual and Motor Skills, 111, pp333-342

Smith, P. J., Blumenthal, J. A., Hoffman, B. M., Cooper, H., Strauman, T. A., Welsh-Bohmer, K., Browndyke, J. N., Sherwood, A. (2010). Aerobic exercise and neurocognitive performance: a meta-analytic review of randomized controlled trials. Psychosomatic Medicine 72, 239–252

Spedding, S. (2015). Exercise for Depression: Cochrane systematic reviews are rigorous, but how subjective are the assessment of bias and the practice implications? Advances in Integrative Medicine, 2, 1, pp 63-65

Start Active, Stay Active (2011). A report on physical activity for health from the four home counties. Chief Medical Officers, UK Government

Steptoe, A., O'Donnell, K., Marmot, M. & Wardle, J. (2008). Positive Effect, Psychological Well-being, and Good Sleep. Journal of Psychosomatic Research, 64(4), 409-415

Teychenne M., Ball K., Salmon J., Physical Activity, Sedentary Behavior and Depression Among Disadvantaged Women. Health Education Research. 2010;25(4):632-44

UK Active (2014). Turning the Tide of Inactivity Report

UK Government Food Standards Agency & Department of Health (2007). Update on Vitamin D: Position statement by the Scientific Advisory Committee on Nutrition

UK NHS www.nhs.uk/Livewell/fitness/Pages/whybeactive.aspx

UK NHS www.nhs.uk/Conditions/Depression/Pages/Treatment.aspx

UK Physical Activity Guidelines (2011). www.gov.uk/government/publications/uk-physical-activity-guidelines

UK Sleep Council Press Release (2013) – The Great British Bedtime Report www.sleepcouncil.org.uk/2013/03/first-ever-great-british-bedtime-report-launched

US Centers for Disease Control and Prevention www.cdc.gov physicalactivity/data/facts.htm

US National Sleep Foundation drowsydriving.org/about/facts-and-stats

US National Sleep Foundation: sleepfoundation.org/media-center/press-release/annual-sleep-america-poll-exploring-connections-communications-technology-use

Wood, A. M., Joseph, S., Lloyd, J. & Atkins, S. (2009). Gratitude Influences Sleep Through the Mechanism of Pre-Sleep Cognitions. Journal of Psychosomatic Research, 66(1), 43-48

World Health Organsation (2010). Global Recommendations on Physical

Activity for Health

Zadeh, R. S., Shepley, M. M., Williams, G. & Chung, S. S. E. (2014). The Impact of Windows and Daylight on Acute-Care Nurses' Physiological, Psychological, And Behavioral Health. HERD: Health Environments Research & Design Journal, 7(4), 35-61

Chapter 4 AWARENESS

Atkinson, B. J. (2013). Mindfulness training and the cultivation of secure, satisfying couple relationships. Couple and Family Psychology: Research and Practice, 2(2), 73

Baer, R. A., Lykins, E. L. & Peters, J. R. (2012). Mindfulness and Self-Compassion as Predictors of Psychological Wellbeing in Long-Term Meditators and Matched Non-Meditators. The Journal of Positive Psychology, 7(3), 230-238

BBC Magazine Monitor (2014). Who, What, Why: What is mindfulness? Retrieved from www.bbc.co.uk/news/blogs-magazine-monitor-27299696

Boroson, M. (2011). One-Moment Meditation: How to Meditate in a Moment. Retrieved from: www.youtube.com/watch?v=F6eFFCi12v8

Brown, K. W. & Kasser, T. (2005). Are Psychological and Ecological Well-Being Compatible? The role of values, mindfulness, and lifestyle. Social Indicators Research, 74(2), 349-368

Brown, K. W., Ryan, R. M. & Creswell, J. D. (2007). Mindfulness: Theoretical foundations and evidence for its salutary effects. Psychological Inquiry, 18(4), 211-237

Brown, K. W., Kasser,T., Ryan, R. M., Linley,P. A. & Orzech, K. (2009). When What One Has is Enough: Mindfulness, financial desire discrepancy and subjective well-being. Journal of Research in Personality, 43, 727-736

Carson, J. W., Carson, K. M., Gil, K. M. & Baucom, D. H. (2004). Mindfulness-Based Relationship Enhancement. Behavior Therapy, 35(3), 471-494

Cavanagh, K., Strauss, C., Forder, L. & Jones, F. (2014). Can Mindfulness and Acceptance be Learnt by Self-help? A systematic review and meta-analysis of mindfulness and acceptance-based self-help interventions. Clinical Psychology Review, 34(2), 118-129

Center for Mindfulness, University of Massachusetts Medical School. MBSR 8-Week: How it works. Retrieved from: www.umassmed.edu/cfm/stress-reduction/mbsr-8-week

Condon, P., Desbordes, G., Miller, W. B. & DeSteno, D. (2013). Meditation Increases Compassionate Responses to Suffering. Psychological Science, 24(10), 2125-2127

Davidson, R. J. & Begley, S. (2012). The Emotional Life of Your Brain: How its unique patterns affects the way you think, feel and live – and how you can change them. Hodder & Stoughton

Fredrickson, B. L. (2013). Love 2.0

– How our supreme emotion affects everything we think, do, feel and become. Hudson Street

Garland, E., Gaylord, S. & Fredrickson, B. (2011). Positive Reappraisal Mediates the Stress-Reductive Effects of Mindfulness: An Upward Spiral Process. Mindfulness, 2(1), 59–67

Garland, E. L., Farb, N. A., Goldin, P. R. & Fredrickson, B. L. (2015). Mindfulness Broadens Awareness and Builds Eudaimonic Meaning: A Process Model of Mindful Positive Emotion Regulation, Psychological Inquiry, 26:4, 293-314

Greeson, J. M. (2009). Mindfulness research update: 2008. Complementary Health Practice Review, 14(1), 10-18

Hölzel, B. K., Carmody, J., Vangel, M., Congleton, C., Yerramsetti, S. M., Gard, T. & Lazar,S. W. (2011). Mindfulness Practice Leads to Increases in Regional Brain Gray Matter Density. Psychiatry Research: Neuroimaging, 191(1), 36-43

Howell, A. J., Digdon, N. L., Buro, K. & Sheptykcki, A. R. (2008). Relations among mindfulness, well-being and sleep. Personality and Individual Differences, 45, 773-777

INSEAD Business School (2007). Understanding and Responding to Societal Demands on Corporate Responsibility. Report published in relation to the final conference of the RESPONSE project

Ivtzan, I. & Lomas, T. (Eds). (2016). Introduction. Mindfulness in Positive Psychology: The science of meditation and wellbeing. Routledge

Kabat-Zinn, J. (1994). Wherever You Go, There You Are: Mindfulness meditation in everyday life. Hyperion. Cited in in Hart, R., Ivtzan, I. & Hart, D. (2013). Mind the gap in mindfulness research: a comparative account of the leading schools of thought. Review of General Psychology, 17(4), 453

Kabat-Zinn, J. (2003). Mindfulness-Based Interventions in Context: past, present, and future. Clinical psychology: Science and Practice, 10(2), 144-156

Kang, Y., Gray, J. R. & Dovidio, J. F. (2014). The Non-Discriminating Heart: Loving kindness meditation training decreases implicit intergroup bias. Journal of Experimental Psychology: General, 143(3), 1306

Khaddouma, A., Gordon, K. C. & Bolden, J. (2015). Zen and the Art of Sex: examining associations among mindfulness, sexual satisfaction, and relationship satisfaction in dating relationships. Sexual and Relationship Therapy, 30(2), 268-285

Killingsworth M. A., Gilbert D. T. (2010). A Wandering Mind is An Unhappy Mind. Science, 330, 932-932 10.1126/science.1192439 [PubMed]

Kuyken, W., Watkins, E., Holden, E., White, K., Taylor, R. S., Byford, S.,

Evans, A., Radford, S., Teasdale,J. D. & Dalgleish, T. (2010). How does mindfulness-based cognitive therapy work? Behaviour Research and Therapy, 48(11), 1105-1112

Langer, E. (2009). Mindfulness Versus Positive Evaluation. In Eds: S. J. Lopez & C. R. Snyder, Oxford Handbook of Positive Psychology. OUP

Lomas, T. & Jnanavaca (2015). Types of Mindfulness, Orders of Conditionality, and Stages of the Spiritual Path. In Shonin, E., van Gordon, W. & Singh, N. N. (Eds) Buddhist Foundations of Mindfulness (pp 287-310). Springer

Malinowski, P. (2013). Flourishing through meditation and mindfulness. In David, S. A., Boniwell, I. & Conley Ayers, A. (Eds), The Oxford Handbook of Happiness, 384-396. OUP

Mindful Nation UK (2015). A Report by the Mindfulness All-Party Parliamentary Group (MAPPG)

Neff, K. (2003) cited in: Baer, R. A., Lykins, E. L. & Peters, J. R. (2012). Mindfulness and Self-Compassion as Predictors of Psychological Wellbeing in Long-Term Meditators and Matched Non-Meditators. The Journal of Positive Psychology, 7(3), 230-238

Neimiec, R. (2015). 24 Ways Make Mindfulness Stickier. Psychology Today. Retrieved from www.psychologytoday.com/blog/what-matters-most/201503/24-ways-make-mindfulness-stickier

Neimiec, R. M. (2013). Mindfulness and Character Strengths: A Practical Guide to Flourishing. Hogrefe

Neimiec, R. M. (2012). Mindful living: Character strengths interventions as pathways for the five mindfulness trainings. International Journal of Wellbeing, 2(1)

Ricard, M. (2015). Altruism: The Power of Compassion to Change Yourself and the World. Atlantic Books

Salzberg, S. (2011). Real Happiness: The Power of Mediation A 28 Day Programme. Workman

Sears, S. & Kraus, S. (2009). I Think Therefore I Om: Cognitive distortions and coping style as mediators for the effects of mindfulness meditation on anxiety, positive and negative effect, and hope. Journal of Clinical Psychology, 65(6), 561-573

Segal, Z. V., Williams, M. & Teasdale, J. D. (2002). Mindfulness-Based Cognitive Therapy for Depression: A new approach to relapse prevention. New York: Guilford Press. Cited in Williams, M. & Penman, D. (2011). Mindfulness a Practical Guide to Find Peace in a Frantic World. Piatkus

Shapiro, S. L. (2009). The Integration of Mindfulness and Psychology. Journal of Clinical Psychology, 65(6), 555-560

Shapiro, S. L., Jazaieri, H. & Goldin, P. R. (2012). Mindfulness-based stress reduction effects on moral reasoning and decision making. The Journal of Positive Psychology, 7(6), 504-515

Shapiro, S. L. (2009). Meditation and

Positive Psychology. In Eds: S. J. Lopez & C. R. Snyder, Oxford Handbook of Positive Psychology, 601-610

Smith, W. P., Compton, W. C. & West, W. B. (1995). Meditation as an Adjunct to a Happiness Enhancement Program. Journal of Clinical Psychology, 51, 269-273

Weinstein, N, Brown, K. W. & Ryan, R. M. (2009). A Multi-Method Examination of the Effects of Mindfulness on Stress Attribution, Coping and Emotional Well-being. Journal of Research in Personality, 43, 374-385

Williams, M. & Penman, D. (2011). Mindfulness a Practical Guide to Find Peace in a Frantic World. Piatkus

Williams, M., Teasdale, J. D., Segal, Z. V. & Kabat-Zinn, J. (2007). The Mindful Way Through Depression: Freeing Yourself from Chronic Unhappiness. Guilford Press. Cited in Williams, M. & Penman, D. (2011). Mindfulness a Practical Guide to Find Peace in a Frantic World. Piatkus

Chapter 5 TRYING OUT

Barry Kaufman. S. & Gregoire. C. (2015). Wired to Create: Unraveling the Mysteries of the Creative Mind. Vermillion

Cara, O. & Duckworth, K. (2012). The Relationship Between Adult Learning and Wellbeing: evidence from the 1958 National Child Development Study. Department for Business Innovation and Skill (BIS)

Compton, W. C & Hoffman, E. (2013). Positive Psychology: The Science of Happiness and Flourishing. Wadsworth CENGAGE Learning

Czikszentmihalyi, M. (1996). Creativity: Flow and the Psychology of Discovery and Invention. Harper Perennial

Czikszentmihalyi, M. (1997). Finding flow: The psychology of engagement with everyday life. Basic Books

Czikszentmihalyi, M. (1990). Flow: The psychology of optimal experience. Harper & Row (published UK as Flow: The classic work on how to achieve happiness. Rider)

Deci, E. (2015). Lecture. University of Pennsylvania MAPP Summit

Doidge, N. (2007). The Brain That Changes Itself: Stories of personal triumph from the frontiers of brain science. Penguin

Dweck, C. (2006). Mindset: The New Psychology of Success. Ballantine Books

Dweck, C. (2015). Carol Dweck revisits the Growth Mindset. Education Week. Retrieved from: www.edweek.org/ew/articles/2015/09/23/carol-dweck-revisits-the-growth-mindset.html

Feinberg, C. (2010). The Mindfulness Chronicles: On the psychology of possibility. Harvard Magazine. Retrieved from: harvardmagazine.com/2010/09/the-mindfulness-chronicles

Feinstein, L, Vorhaus, J, & Sabates, R, (2008). Mental Capital and Wellbeing: Making the most of ourselves in the

21st Century, Learning through life: Future challenges, Foresight, Government Office for Science

Feinstein, L. and Hammond, C. (2004). The Contribution of Adult Learning to Health and Social Capital, Oxford Review of Education, 30, 2, 199-221

Field, J., Adult Learning and Mental Wellbeing, Centre for Lifelong Learning, University of Stirling. Paper written for the NIACE inquiry

Frisch, M. B. (2006). Quality of Life Therapy: Applying a Life Satisfaction Approach to Positive Psychology and Cognitive Therapy. Wiley

Great British Bake-off Final 2015 Viewing Figures. Retrieved from: www. barb.co.uk/whats-new/weekly-top-30?

Hart, R., Ivtzan, I. & Hart, D. (2013). Mind the gap in mindfulness research: a comparative account of the leading schools of thought. Review of General Psychology, 17(4), 453

Jenkins, A. & Mostafa, T. (2013). Learning and Wellbeing Trajectories Among Older Adults in England. Working Paper. Institute of Education, University of London, London, UK

Jobs, S. (2005). Commencement Speech Stanford University. Retrieved from: http://news.stanford.edu/news/2005/june15/jobs-061505.html

Kaninchen und Ente (Rabbit and Duck) from the 23 October 1892 issue of Fliegende Blätter. Source: Wikipedia

Kasdan, T. B. & Silvia, P. J. (2009). Curiosity and Interest: The Benefits of Thriving on Novelty and Challenge. The Oxford Handbook of Positive Psychology. 367-374

Kashdan, T. B. (2009). Curious? Discover the Missing Ingredient to a Fulfilling Life. William Morrow/Harper Collins

King, V. (2010). Creative Hope for Non-Creatives. Capstone Dissertation, University of Pennsylvania

Langer, E. J. (2000). Mindful Learning, Current Directions in Psychological Science, 9(6), 220-223

Langer, E., Russell, T. & Eisenkraft, N. (2008). Orchestral Performance and the Footprint of Mindfulness. Psychology of Music, 37(2), 125-136

Langer, E. J. (2014). Mindfulness: 25th Anniversary Edition. Da Capo Press Lifelong Books

Little, B. R. (2014). Well-doing: Personal projects and the quality of lives. Theory and Research in Education, 12(3), 329-346

Manninen, J., et al. (2014). Benefits of Lifelong Learning in Europe: Main Results of the BeLL – Project Research Report, University of Eastern Finland

Mental Health Foundation (2011). Learning for Life: Adult learning, mental health and wellbeing. London: Mental Health Foundation

Nakamura, J. & Csíkszentmihályi, M. (2009). Flow Theory and Research. Oxford Handbook of Positive Psychology, 195-206

Perkins, R. & Williamon, A. (2014). Learning to Make Music in Older Adulthood: A mixed-methods exploration of impacts on wellbeing. Psychology of Music, 42(4), 550-567

Peterson, C. & Seligman, M. E. P. (2004). Character Strengths and Virtues: A handbook and classification. Washington, DC, American Psychological Association

Pine, K. & Fletcher, B. C. (2014). Time to Shift Brain Channels to Bring About Effective Changes in Health Behaviour. Perspectives in Public Health, 134(1), 16-17

Richards, R. (2007). Everyday Creativity and New Views of Human Nature: Psychological, social, and spiritual perspectives. Washington, DC, US: American Psychological Association

Ryan, R. M. & Deci, E. L. (2000). Self-Determination Theory and the Facilitation of Intrinsic Motivation, Social Development, and Well-being. American Psychologist, 55(1), 68-78

Ryan, R. M., Bernstein, J. H. & Brown, K. W. (2010). Weekends, Work, and Well-being: Psychological need satisfactions and day of the week effects on mood, vitality, and physical symptoms. Journal of Social and Clinical Psychology, 29(1), 95-122

Ryan, R. M., Huta, V. & Deci, E. L. (2008). Living Well: A self-determination theory perspective on eudaimonia. Journal of Happiness Studies, 9(1), 139-170

Ryff, C. D. (2014). Psychological Well-being Revisited: Advances in the science and practice of eudaimonia. Psychotherapy and Psychosomatics, 83(1), 10-28

Sabates, R., Hammond, C. (2008). The Impact of Lifelong Learning on Happiness and Wellbeing, NIACE and Institute of Education

Scott, G. M., Leritz, L. E., Mumford, M. D. (2004). The Effectiveness of Creativity Training: a quantitative review. Creativity Research Journal, 16, 361-88

Seligman, M. E. P. (2007). Authentic Happiness: Using the new positive psychology to realize your potential for lasting fulfillment. Nicholas Brearley

Thuret, S. (2015). You Can Grow New Brain Cells. Here's how. TED@BCG

Vallerand, R. J. (2012). The Role of Passion in Sustainable Psychological Well-being. Psychology of Well-being, 2(1), 1-21

Vorhaus, J., Duckworth, K., Budge, D. & Feinstein, L. (2008). The Social and Personal Benefits of Learning: A summary of key research findings. London: Centre for Research on the Wider Benefits of Learning, Institute of Education, University of London

Williams, M. & Penman, D. (2011). Mindfulness, a Practical Guide to Find Peace in a Frantic World. Piatkus

Chapter 6 DIRECTION

Aarts, H., Dijksterhuis, A. & Dik, G. (2008). Goal Contagion: Inferring goals from others' actions – and what it leads to. In Shah, J. Y. & Gardner, W. (Eds), Handbook of Motivation Science. New York: Guilford. 265-280

Adams Miller, C. & Frisch, M. (2009). Creating Your Best Life: The ultimate life list guide. Sterling

Alarcon, G. M., Bowling, N. A. & Khazon, S. (2013). Great Expectations: A meta-analytic examination of optimism and hope. Personality and Individual Differences, 54(7), 821-827

Amabile, T. M. & Kramer, S. J. (2011). The Power of Small Wins. Harvard Business Review, 89(5), 70-80

Brunstein, J. C. (1993). Personal Goals and Subjective Well-Being: A longitudinal study. Journal of Personality And Social Psychology, 65(5), 1061. Cited in Lyubomirsky, S. (2007). The How of Happiness. Penguin

Carver, C. S. & Scheier, M. F. (2014). Dispositional Optimism. Trends in Cognitive Sciences, 18(6), 293-299

Carver, C. S., Scheier, M. F., & Segerstrom, S. C. (2010). Optimism. Clinical Psychology Review, 30(7), 879-889

Cohen, P. & Cohen, J. (2001). Life Values And Mental Health In Adolescence. Life goals and well-being: Towards a positive psychology of human striving, 167-181. Cited in Massey, E. K., Gebhardt, W. A. & Garnefski, N. (2008). Adolescent Goal Content And Pursuit: A review of the literature from the past 16 years. Developmental Review, 28(4), 421-460

Deci, E. L. (2105). Lecture. University of Pennsylvania. October MAPP Summit

Emmons, R. A. Personal Goals, Life Meanings and Virtue: Wellsprings of a Positive Life, p.123. In Keyes, C.L.M. & Haidt, J. (Eds) (2003). Flourishing. Positive Psychology and the Life Well-Lived. American Psychological Association

Gagné, M. & Deci, E. L. (2005) Self-Determination Theory And Work Motivation. Journal of Organizational Behavior, 26(4), 331-362

Gallagher, M. W., Lopez, S. J. & Pressman, S. D. (2013). Optimism is Universal: Exploring the presence and benefits of optimism in a representative sample of the world. Journal of Personality, 81(5), 429-440

Gollwitzer, P. M. (1999). Implementation Intentions: strong effects of simple plans. American Psychologist, 54(7), 493

Grant Halvorson, H. (2010). Succeed: How we can reach our goals. Plume

Greenberg, M. & Maymin, S. (2013). Profit from the Positive: Proven Leadership Strategies to Boost Productivity and Transform your Business. McGraw Hill

Harris, A. J. & Hahn, U. (2011) Unrealistic Optimism About Future Life Events: a cautionary note. Psychological Review, 118(1), 135

King, L. A. (2001). The Health Benefits of Writing About Life Goals. Personality and Social Psychology Bulletin, 27(7), 798-807

Linley, P. A., Nielsen, K. M., Gillett, R. & Biswas-Diener, R. (2010). Using Signature Strengths in Pursuit of Goals: Effects on goal progress, need satisfaction, and well-being, and implications for coaching psychologists. International Coaching Psychology Review, 5(1), 6-15

Locke, E. A. (2002). Setting Goals for Life and Happiness. Oxford Handbook of Positive Psychology, 522, 299-312. OUP

Lopez, S. J. (2013). Making Hope Happen: Create the Future You Want for Yourself and Others. Atria Books

Lyubomirsky, S. (2007). The How of Happiness. A new approach to getting the life you want. Penguin

MacLeod, A., Goals and Plans: Their relationship to well-being. In Efklides, A. and Moraitou, D. (Eds). Quality of Life: A Positive Psychology Perspective. Springer

MacLeod, A. Coates, A. & Hetherton, J. (2008). Increasing Well-Being Through Teaching Goal-Setting and Planning Skills: results of a brief intervention. Journal of Happiness Studies 9.2 185-196

Martin-Krumm, C., Delas, Y., Lafrenière, M. A., Fenouillet, F. & Lopez, S. J. (2015). The Structure of the State Hope Scale. The Journal of Positive Psychology, 10(3), 272-281

Norcross, J. C. & Mrykalo, M. S. (2002). Auld Lang Syne: Success Predictors, Change Processes and Self-Reported Outcomes of New Year's Resolvers and Nonresolvers. Journal of Clinical Psychology

Norem, J. K. & Chang, E. C. (2002). The Positive Psychology of Negative Thinking. Journal of Clinical Psychology, 58(9), 993-1001

Oettingen, G. (2012). Future Thought and Behaviour Change. European Review of Social Psychology, 23(1), 1-63

Rand, K. L. & Cheavens, J. S. (2009). Hope Theory. In S. J. Lopez & C. R. Snyder (Eds) Oxford Handbook of Positive Psychology (2nd Edition). OUP

Ryff, C. D. (2014). Psychological Well-being Revisited: Advances in the science and practice of eudaimonia. Psychotherapy and psychosomatics, 83(1), 10-28

Seligman, M. E. P. (2015). Lecture, University of Pennsylvania, MAPP Summit

Sheldon, K. M. (2002). The Self-Concordance Model of Healthy Goal-Striving: When personal goals correctly represent the person. Handbook of Self-Determination Research, 65-86

Sheldon, K. M., Abad, N., Ferguson, Y., Gunz, A., Houser-Marko, L., Nichols, C. P. & Lyubomirsky, S. (2010). Persistent Pursuit of Need-Satisfying Goals Leads To Increased Happiness: A 6-month experimental longitudinal study. Motivation and Emotion, 34(1), 39-48

Sheldon, K. M., & Houser-Marko, L. (2001). Self-Concordance, Goal Attainment, and the Pursuit of Happiness: Can there be an upward spiral? Journal of Personality and Social Psychology, 80(1), 152-165

Shepperd, J. A., Klein, W. M., Waters, E. A. & Weinstein, N. D. (2013). Taking Stock of Unrealistic Optimism. Perspectives on Psychological Science, 8(4), 395-411

Snyder, C. R. (2002). Hope theory: Rainbows in the mind. Psychological Inquiry, 13, 249-275

Snyder, C. R. (1994). The Psychology of Hope: You can get there from here. Free Press

Snyder, C. R. Rand, K. L. & Sigmon, D. R. (2002). Hope Theory: a member of the positive psychology family. In S. J. Lopez & C. R. Snyder (Eds). Oxford Handbook of Positive Psychology. OUP

Thimm, J. C., Holte, A., Brennen, T. & Wang, C. E. (2013). Hope and Expectancies for Future Events in Depression. Frontiers in Psychology, 4, 470, 1-6

Chapter 7 RESILIENCE

Aldwin, C. M., Sutton, K. J. & Lachman, M. (1996). The Development of Coping Resources in Adulthood. Journal of Personality, 64(4), 837-871

Briers, S. (2009). Brilliant Cognitive Behavioural Therapy. Pearson Education

Burns, D. B. (2009). Feeling Good: The new mood therapy. Harper Health

Charney, D. S. (2004). Psychobiological Mechanisms of Resilience and Vulnerability: Implications for Successful Adaptation to Extreme Stress. American Journal of Psychiatry, 161(2), 195-216

Chesney, M. A., Neilands, T. B., Chambers, D. B., Taylor, J. M. & Folkman, S. (2006). A Validity and Reliability Study of the Coping Self-Efficacy Scale. British Journal of Health Psychology, 11(3), 421-437

Connor, K. M., & Davidson, J. R. (2003). Development of a New Resilience Scale: The Connor-Davidson resilience scale (CD-RISC). Depression and Anxiety, 18(2), 76-82

Crum, A. J., Salovey, P. & Achor, S. (2013). Rethinking Stress: The role of mindsets in determining the stress response. Journal of Personality and Social Psychology, 104(4), 716

Ellis, A. (2008). How to Make Yourself Happy and Remarkably Less Disturbable. Impact

Fletcher, D. & Sarkar, M. (2013). Psychological Resilience. European Psychologist, 18(1), 12-23

Frankl, V. E. (2004). Man's Search for Meaning. Rider

Haglund, M. E., Nestadt, P. S., Cooper, N. S., Southwick, S. M. & Charney, D. S. (2007). Psychobiological Mechanisms of Resilience: Relevance to prevention and treatment of stress-related psychopathology. Development and psychopathology, 19(03), 889-920

Keller, A., Litzelman, K., Wisk, L. E., Maddox, T., Cheng, E. R., Creswell, P. D. & Witt, W. P. (2012). Does the Perception that Stress Affects Health Matter? Health Psychology, 31(5), 677–684

Lowe, R. & Ziemke, T. (2011). The feeling of action tendencies: on the emotional regulation of goal-directed behavior. Frontiers in psychology, 2, 346 1-24

Macedo, T., Wilheim, L., Gonçalves, R., Coutinho, E. S., Vilete, L., Figueira, I. & Ventura, P. (2014). Building Resilience for Future Adversity: a systematic review of interventions in non-clinical samples of adults. BMC Psychiatry, 14(1), 227, 1-8

Masten, A. S, & Wright, M. O. (2010). Resilience Over the Lifespan: Developmental perspectives on resistance, recovery and transformation. Handbook of Adult Resilience, 213-237

Masten, A. S. (2001). Ordinary Magic: Resilience processes in development. American Psychologist, 56, 227-238

Masten, A. S., Cutuli, J. J., Herbers, J. E. & Reed, M. J. (2009). Resilience in Development. In Eds: S.J. Lopez & C.R. Snyder, Oxford Handbook of Positive Psychology. OUP

McGonigal, K. (2015). The Upside of Stress: Why stress is good for you (and how to get good at it). Vermilion

McGonigal, K. (2015). Lecture, University of Pennsylvania Masters of Positive Psychology Program

Oaklander, M. (2015). The Science of Bouncing Back. Time Magazine, 1 June

Ratey, J. & Hagerman, E. (2008). Spark! – How exercise will improve the performance of your brain. Quercus

Reivich, K. & Shatté, A. (2003). The Resilience Factor: Seven keys to finding your inner strength and overcoming life's hurdles. Broadway Books

Reivich, K. (2010). 708 Lectures, MAPP Program, University of Pennsylvania

Seligman, M. E. P. (2006). Learned Optimism: How to change you mind and you life. Vintage

Southwick, S. M. & Charney, D. S. (2012). The Science of Resilience: Implications for the Prevention and Treatment of Depression. Science, 338(6103), 79-82

Steunebrink, B. R., Dastani, M., & Meyer, J. J. C. (2009). A formal model of emotion-based action tendency for intelligent agents. Progress in Artificial Intelligence, 174-186, Springer

Tedeschi, R. G. & Calhoun, L. G.(2004). Post-traumatic Growth: Conceptual Foundations and Empirical Evidence, Psychological Inquiry, 15,1-18

Wu, G., Feder, A., Cohen, H., Kim, J. J., Calderon, S., Charney, D. S. & Mathé, A. A. (2013). Understanding Resilience. Frontiers in Behavioral Neuroscience, 7, 10, 1-15

Chapter 8 EMOTIONS

Ashby, F. G. & Isen, A. M. (1999). A Neuro-psychological Theory of Positive Effect and its Influence on Cognition. Psychological Review, 106(3), 529-550

Baumeister, R. F., Bratslavsky, E.,

Finkenauer, C. & Vohs, K. D. (2001). Bad is Stronger than Good. Review of General Psychology, 5(4), 323-370

Cohn, M. A., Fredrickson, B. L., Brown, S. L., Mikels, J. A. & Conway, A. M. (2009). Happiness Unpacked: positive emotions increase life satisfaction by building resilience. Emotion, 9(3), 361-368

Compton, W. C. & Hoffman, E. (2013). Positive Psychology: The Science of Happiness and Flourishing. Wadsworth CENGAGE Learning

Danner, D. D., Snowdon, D. A. & Friesen, W. V. (2001). Positive Emotions in Early Childhood and Longevity: findings from the nun study. Journal of Personality and Social Psychology, 80(5), 804-813

Ekman P. (2003). Emotions Revealed: Understanding Faces and Feelings. Phoenix

Emmons, R. (2010). Why Gratitude is Good. Greater Good Science Center. Retrieved from http://greatergood. berkeley.edu/article/item/why_ gratitude_is_good

Emmons, R. A. & McCullough, M. E. (2003). Counting Blessings Versus Burdens: an experimental investigation of gratitude and subjective well-being in daily life. Journal of Personality and Social Psychology, 84(2), 377

Emmons, R. A. & Mishra, A. (2011). Why Gratitude Enhances Well-being: What we know, what we need to know. Designing Positive Psychology: Taking stock and moving forward, 248-262, OUP

Fredrickson, B. L. (2013). Positive Emotions Broaden and Build. Advances in Experimental Social Psychology, 47, 1-53

Fredrickson, B. L. & Cohn, M. A. (2008). Positive Emotions. In M. Lewis, J. Haviland, & L. F. Barrett (Eds), Handbook of Emotions (3rd ed, pp. 777-796). Guilford Press

Fredrickson, B. L. (2009). Positivity: Groundbreaking research reveals how to embrace the hidden strength of positive emotions, overcome negativity and thrive. Crown

Gross, J. J. & Barrett, L. F. (2011). Emotion Generation and Emotion Regulation: One or two depends on your point of view. Emotion Review, 3(1), 8-16

Hefferon, K. & Boniwell, I. (2011). Positive Psychology: Theory, research and applications. McGraw Hill

Isen, A. M. (2001). An Influence of Positive Effect on Decision Making in Complex Situations: Theoretical issues with practical implications. Journal of Consumer Psychology, 11(2), 75-85

Isen, A. M., Daubman, K. A. & Nowicki, G. P. (1987). Positive Effect Facilitates Creative Problem Solving. Journal of Personality and Social Psychology, 52(6), 1122-1131

Kashdan, T. & Biswas-Diener, R. (2014). The Power of Negative Emotion: How Anger, Guilt, and Self Doubt are Essential to Success and Fulfillment

One World

Kashdan, T. B., Barrett, L. F. & McKnight, P. E. (2015). Unpacking Emotion Differentiation Transforming Unpleasant Experience by Perceiving Distinctions in Negativity. Current Directions in Psychological Science, 24(1), 10-16

Lomas, T. (2015). The Dialectics of Emotion in Lomas, T., Hefferon, K., Ivtzan, I. & Worth, P. (2015). Second Wave Positive Psychology: Embracing the Dark Side of Life. Routledge

Lomas, T., Froh, J. J., Emmons, R. A., Mishra, A. & Bono, G. (2014). Gratitude Interventions: A Review and Future Agenda. In Parks A.C. & Schueller, S.M (Eds) The Wiley Blackwell Handbook of Positive Psychological Interventions, 1-19

Lyubomirsky, S., Sousa, L. & Dickerhoof, R. (2006). The Costs and Benefits of Writing, Talking, and Thinking About Life's Triumphs and Defeats. Journal of Personality and Social Psychology, 90(4), 692-708

Magyar-moe, J. L. (2014). Applications of Positive Psychology to Individual Therapy. In Parks A. C. & Schueller, S. M (Eds) The Wiley Blackwell Handbook of Positive Psychological Interventions, 1-19

Marsh, J. (2011). Tips for Keeping a Gratitude Journal. Greater Good Science Center. Retrieved from: http:// greatergood.berkeley.edu/article/item/ tips_for_keeping_a_gratitude_journal

Nesse, R. M. & Ellsworth, P. C. (2009). Evolution, Emotions, and Emotional Disorders. American Psychologist, 64(2), 129

Norrish, J., Robinson, J. & Williams, P. (2011). Positive Emotions Literature Review. Institute of Education, Geelong Grammar School

Oswald, A. J., Proto, E. & Sgroi, D. (2014). Happiness and Productivity. Working Paper retrieved from www2. warwick.ac.uk/fac/soc/economics/ staff/eproto/workingpapers/ happinessproductivity.pdf

Quoidbach, J., Wood, A. M. & Hansenne, M. (2009). Back to the Future: The effect of daily practice of mental time travel into the future on happiness and anxiety. The Journal of Positive Psychology, 4(5), 349-355

Russell, J. A. (2009). Emotion, core effect, and psychological construction. Cognition and Emotion, 23(7), 1259-1283

Salovey, P., Caruso, D. & Mayer, J.D, (2004). Emotional Intelligence in Practice. In Linely, P.A. & Joseph (Eds) Positive Psychology in Practice. Wiley

Seligman, M. E., Steen, T. A., Park, N. & Peterson, C. (2005). Positive Psychology Progress: empirical validation of interventions. American Psychologist, 60(5), 410-421

Seligman, M. E. P. (2011). Flourish: A visionary new understanding of happiness and well-being. Free Press

Smith, J. L., Harrison, P. R., Kurtz, J. L. &

Bryant, F. B. (2014). Nurturing the Capacity to Savor: Interventions to enhance the enjoyment of positive experiences. In Parks A. C. & Schueller, S. M (Eds) The Wiley Blackwell Handbook of Positive Psychological Interventions, 42-65

Chapter 9 ACCEPTANCE

Allan, B. A. & Duffy, R. D. (2013). Examining Moderators of Signature Strengths Use and Well-being: Calling and signature strengths level. Journal of Happiness Studies.

Bandura, A. (1997). Self-Efficacy: The exercise of control. Macmillan

Ellis, A. (2007). How to Make Yourself Happy and Remarkably Less Disturbable. CA: Impact Publishers

Elston, F. & Boniwell, I. (2011). A Grounded Theory Study of the Value Derived by Women In Financial Services Through a Coaching Intervention to Help Them Identify Their Strengths and Practice Using Them in the Workplace. International Coaching Psychology Review, 6 (1), 16-32

Ericsson, K. A., Krampe, R. T. & Tesch-Römer, C. (1993). The Role of Deliberate Practice in the Acquisition of Expert Performance. Psychological Review, 100(3), 363

Gander, F., Proyer, R. T., Ruch, W. & Wyss, T. (2013). Strength-based Positive Interventions: further evidence for their potential in enhancing well-being and alleviating depression. Journal of Happiness Studies, 14(4), 1241-1259

Gilbert, P. (2010). Training Our Minds in, with and for Compassion. An Introduction to Concepts and Compassion Focused Exercises

Gilbert, P. (2014). The Origins and Nature of Compassion Focused Therapy. British Journal of Clinical Psychology, 53(1), 6-41

Gilbert, P. (2015). Compassion Universally Misunderstood. Huffington Post. www.huffingtonpost.co.uk

Harzer, C. & Ruch, W. (2012). When the Job is a Calling: The role of applying one's signature strengths at work. The Journal of Positive Psychology, 7(5), 362-371

Hefferon, K. & Mutrie, N. (2012). Physical activity as a "stellar" positive psychology intervention. The Oxford Handbook of Exercise Psychology, 117-130

Lavy, S., Littman-Ovadia, H. & Bareli, Y. (2014). Strengths Deployment as a Mood-Repair Mechanism: Evidence from a diary study with a relationship exercise group. The Journal of Positive Psychology, 9(6), 547-558

Leary, M. R., Tate, E. B., Adams, C. E., Batts Allen, A. & Hancock, J. (2007). Self-Compassion and Reactions to Unpleasant Self-Relevant Events: the implications of treating oneself kindly. Journal of Personality and Social Psychology, 92(5), 887

Linely, P. A, Willars, J., Biswas-Diener, R. (2010). The Strengths Book. CAPP. www.cappeu.com/Portals/3/Files/Why_Strengths_The_Evidence.pdf

Linely, P. A. (2008). Average to A+: Realising strengths in yourself and others. CAPP Press

Linely, P. A., Nielsen, K. M., Gillett, R. & Biswas-Diener, R. (2010). Using Signature Strengths in Pursuit of Goals: Effects on goal progress, need satisfaction, and well-being, and implications for coaching psychologists. International Coaching Psychology Review, 5(1), 6-15

Mongrain, M. & Anselmo-Matthews, T. (2012). Do Positive Psychology Exercises Work? A replication of Seligman et al. Journal of Clinical Psychology, 68 (4), 382-389

Neff, K. (2011). Self Compassion: stop beating yourself up and leave insecurity behind. Hodder & Stoughton

Neff, K. D. & Costigan, A. P. (2014). Self-compassion, wellbeing, and happiness. Psychologie in Österreich, 2(3), 114-119

Neff, K. D. & Dahm, K. A. (2015) Self-Compassion: What it is, what it does, and how it relates to mindfulness. In M. Robinson, B. Meier & B. Ostafin (Eds) Mindfulness and Self-Regulation. 121-137. Springer

Neff, K. D. & Vonk, R. (2009). Self-Compassion Versus Global Self-esteem: Two different ways of relating to oneself. Journal of Personality, 77(1), 23-50

Niemiec, R. M. (2013). VIA Character Strengths: Research and practice (The first 10 years). In Well-Being and Cultures (pp. 11-29). Springer Netherlands

Niemiec, R. M., Rashid, T., Linkins, M., Green, S. & Mayerson, N. H. (2013). Character Strengths: Practices for business, education, coaching, psychotherapy, and mindfulness. IPPA Newsletter, 5(4)

Niemiec, R.M. (2014). Mindfulness and Character Strengths: A Practical Guide to Flourishing. Hogrefe

Peterson, C. & Seligman, M. E. (2004). Character Strengths and Virtues: A handbook and classification. OUP

Quinlan, D., Swain, N. & Vella-Brodrick, D. A. (2012). Character Strengths Interventions: Building on what we know for improved outcomes. Journal of Happiness Studies, 13(6), 1145-1163

Rath, T. (2007). StrengthsFinder 2.0. Gallup Press

Ryff, C. D. & Singer, B. H. (2008). Know Thyself and Become What You Are: A eudaimonic approach to psychological well-being. Journal of happiness studies,9(1), 13-39

Seligman, M. E., Steen, T. A., Park, N. & Peterson, C. (2005). Positive Psychology Progress: empirical validation of interventions. American Psychologist, 60(5), 410

Smeets, E., Neff, K., Alberts, H. & Peters, M. (2014). Meeting Suffering With Kindness: Effects of a Brief Self-Compassion Intervention for Female College Students. Journal of Clinical Psychology, 70(9), 794-807

VIA Institute www.viacharacter.org

Wood, A. M., Linley, P. A., Maltby, J., Kashdan, T. B. & Hurling, R. (2011). Using Personal and Psychological Strengths Leads to Increases in Well-Being Over Time: A longitudinal study and the development of the strengths use questionnaire. Personality and Individual Differences, 50(1), 15-19

Zessin, U., Dickhäuser, O. & Garbade, S. (2015). The Relationship Between Self-Compassion and Well-being: A Meta-Analysis. Applied Psychology: Health and Well-Being, 7(3), 340-364

Chapter 10 MEANING

Berg, J. M., Dutton, J. E. & Wrzesniewski, A. (2013) Job Crafting and Meaningful Work. In B. J. Dik, Z. S. Byrne & M. F. Steger (Eds), Purpose and Meaning in the Workplace (pp 81-104). Washington, DC: American Psychological Association

Berg, J. M., Grant, A. M. & Johnson, V. (2010). When Callings Are Calling: Crafting work and leisure in pursuit of unanswered occupational callings. Organization Science, 21(5), 973-994

Burton, M. L. & Wedemeyer, R. A. (1992). In Transition: From the Harvard Business School Club of New York's Career Management Seminar. Harper Collins

Compton, W. C. & Hoffman, E. (2013). Positive Psychology: The Science of Happiness and Flourishing. Wadsworth CENGAGE Learning

Delle Fave, A., Wissing, M., Brdar, I., Vella-Brodrick, D. & Freire, T. (2013). Cross-Cultural Perceptions of Meaning and Goals in Adulthood: Their roots and relations with happiness

Diener, E. & Biswas-Diener, R. (2008). Happiness: Unlocking the Mysteries of Psychological Wealth. Blackwell

Dik, B. J., Duffy, R. D., Allan, B. A., O'Donnell, M. B., Shim, Y. & Steger, M. F. (2014). Purpose and Meaning in Career Development Applications. The Counseling Psychologist, 0011000014546872

Frankl, V. E. (2004). Man's Search for Meaning. Rider

Frisch, M. B. (2005). Quality of Life Therapy: Applying a life satisfaction approach to positive psychology and cognitive therapy. John Wiley & Sons.

Huppert, F. A. & So, T. T. (2013). Flourishing across Europe: Application of a new conceptual framework for defining well-being. Social Indicators Research, 110(3), 837-861

Layard, R. (2005). Happiness: Lessons from a new science. Penguin UK

Nemo, J. (2014). What a NASA Janitor Can Teach Us About Living a Bigger Life. The Business Journals. Retrieved from www.bizjournals.com/bizjournals/how-to/growth-strategies/2014/12/what-a-nasa-janitor-can-teach-us.html?page=all

Pargament, K. I. & Mahoney, A. (2009). Spirituality: The Search for the Sacred. In Lopez, S. J. & Snyder, C. R., Oxford Handbook of Positive Psychology. 611-619

Park, N., Park, M. & Peterson, C. (2010). When is the Search for Meaning Related to Life Satisfaction? Applied Psychology: Health and Well-Being, 2(1), 1-13

Peterson, C (2006). A Primer in Positive Psychology. OUP

Pink, D. H. (2009). Drive: the surprising truth about what motivates us. Riverhead Books

Ryff, C. D. (2014). Psychological Well-Being Revisited: Advances in the science and practice of eudaimonia. Psychotherapy and Psychosomatics, 83(1), 10-28

Schaefer, S. M., Morozink Boylan, J., Van Reekum, C., Lapate, R. C., Norris, C. J., Ryff, C. D. & Davidson, R. J. (2013). Purpose in Life Predicts Better Emotional Recovery From Negative Stimuli. PLoS ONE, 8(11)

Schnell, T. (2011). Individual Differences in Meaning-Making: Considering the variety of sources of meaning, their density and diversity. Personality and Individual Differences, 51(5), 667-673

Seligman, M.E.P. (2002) Authentic Happiness: Using the new positive psychology to realize your potential for lasting fulfillment. Nicholas Brearley

Seligman, M.E.P. (2011). Flourish: A visionary new understanding of happiness and well-being. NY: Free Press

Shin, J. Y. & Steger, M. F. (2014). Promoting Meaning and Purpose in Life. The Wiley Blackwell Handbook of Positive Psychological Interventions, 90-110

Steger, M. F. (2012). Experiencing Meaning in Life: Optimal functioning at the nexus of spirituality, psychopathology and well-being. In P. T. Wong (Ed), The Human Quest for Meaning (2nd Ed) 165-184. Routledge

Steger, M. F., Oishi, S. & Kashdan, T. B. (2009). Meaning in Life Across the Life Span: Levels and correlates of meaning in life from emerging adulthood to older adulthood. The Journal of Positive Psychology, 4(1), 43-52

Steger, M. F., Shim, Y., Rush, B. R., Brueske, L. A., Shin, J. Y. & Merriman, L. A. (2013). The Mind's Eye: A photographic method for understanding meaning in people's lives. The Journal of Positive Psychology, 8(6), 530-542

Steger, M. F., Shin, J. Y., Shim, Y. & Fitch-Martin, A. (2013). Is Meaning in Life a Flagship Indicator of Well-being. In Alan S. (Ed), (2013). The Best Within Us: Positive psychology perspectives on eudaimonia, pp. 159-182. Washington, DC, US: American Psychological Association, xv, 303 pp

Steger, M.F. (2009). Meaning in Life. In

Lopez, S.J. & Snyder, C.R., Oxford Handbook of Positive Psychology pp 679-687

Steger, M. F. (forthcoming) Meaning in Life. In Oxford Handbook of Positive Psychology, 3rd Edition

Tedeshi & Calhoun (1995). Cited in Compton, W. C. & Hoffman, E. (2013). Positive Psychology: The Science of

Happiness and Flourishing. Wadsworth CENGAGE Learning

Wong, P. T. (2012). Toward a Dual-Systems Model of What Makes Life Worth Living. In P. T. Wong. (Ed) The Human Quest For Meaning: Theories, research, and applications (2nd Ed), 3-22. Routledge

Wrzesniewski, A. (2010). Callings. In K.

S. Cameron & G. Spreitzer (Eds). In Handbook of Positive Organizational Scholarship. OUP

Wrzesniewski, A. & Tosti, J. (2005). Career as a Calling. In J. H. Greenhaus & G. A. Callanan (Eds), Encyclopedia of Career Development. Sage Publications

Index

333

Proofreaders: Corinne Masciocchi & Josh Ireland   **Indexer:** Marie Lorimer

336

With gratitude

I've learned that the research and writing of a book is only part of what brings it to fruition and I'm grateful to so many people who have helped along the way. Firstly to my publisher, Muna Reyal, for giving me the opportunity, to Jo Godfrey Wood and Peggy Sadler at Bookworx, who worked tirelessly on the editing, layout and design. And to Frances Gough, Abbie Salter and Claudia Young, who for their help in getting this book out there so many people can benefit from the scientific findings on which the book is based.

Thanks to Richard Layard and Martin Seligman, visionary thinkers whose work means happiness is taken more seriously from scientific, health and policy perspectives. And to Anthony Seldon and Geoff Mulgan, who alongside Richard, founded Action for Happiness and continue to be active members of the Board. To Mark Williamson – the amazing driving force behind the movement, for his support of this book; fellow Board members, Nic Marks and Jimmy Mulville, for their ideas and energy; and the core team of volunteers who have contributed to the movement or development of the 10 Keys along the way including: Alex, Aman, Anna, Hannah, Harriet, Izzy, Lucy, Nina, Paul A., Paul S. and Rob. With particular thanks to Natasha Warne and Tracy Ampah who, having just finished their Masters, helped me with research on a number of the chapters.

I am very grateful to my professors on the Masters of Positive Psychology Program, University of Pennsylvania, without whom I wouldn't have been in a position to write this book. These include: Marty Seligman, James Pawelski, Angela Duckworth, Chris Peterson, Ed Diener, Barbara Fredrickson, Karen Reivich, Ray Fowler, George Vaillant, Roy Baumeister and David Cooperrider.

A special big thank you to: my Masters adviser, Adam Grant of Wharton Business School, for reading the draft Chapter 1 Giving; to Mark Williams of Oxford University for his comments on Chapter 4 Awareness; and Scott Barry Kauffman of the Positive Psychology Center at the University of Pennsylvania for reviewing Chapter 5 Trying Out. I'm grateful too to the many other leading researchers who were willing to answer my questions or share with me their latest 'hot off the press' studies, including: Kate Hefferon, Felicia Huppert, Itai Ivtzan, Tim Lomas, Andrew MacLeod, Ryan Niemiec, John Ratey and Michael Steger. And to all those who allowed me to share their stories within the book.

I'm very appreciative of what good friends I have. In particular Jane Gaukroger and Suzy Greaves for wise counsel and no-nonsense advice when I needed it and Julia Lampshire for taking time to review the final draft of the book. Most importantly, I'd like to thank my partner, John, for reading each chapter as it was written and his unfaltering support, delicious meals and patience over the last few months when I pretty much withdrew from normal life to research and write.